Standing Eight

Standing Eight

THE INSPIRING STORY OF JESUS "EL MATADOR" CHAVEZ, WHO BECAME LIGHTWEIGHT CHAMPION OF THE WORLD

Adam Pitluk

DA CAPO PRESS
A Member of the Perseus Books Group

Set in 11/14.5 point Janson Text by the Interactive Composition Corporation

Library of Congress Cataloging-in-Publication Data

Pitluk, Adam.
    Standing eight : the inspiring story of Jesus "El Matador" Chavez / Adam Pitluk.
        p. cm.
    Includes bibliographical references and index.
    ISBN-13: 978–0–306–81454–9 (hardcover)
    ISBN-10: 0–306–81454–4 (hardcover)
    1. Chavez, Jesus, 1972- 2. Boxers (Sports)—Mexico—Biography. I. Title.
    GV1132.C43P58 2006
    796.83092—dc22

                                                                              2006000273

First Da Capo Press edition 2006
ISBN-10 0–306–81454–4
ISBN-13 978–0–306–81454–9

Published by Da Capo Press
A Member of the Perseus Books Group
www.dacapopress.com

Da Capo Press books are available at special discounts for bulk purchases in the U.S. by corporations, institutions, and other organizations. For more information, please contact the Special Markets Department at the Perseus Books Group, 11 Cambridge Center, Cambridge, MA 02142, or call (800) 255-1514 or (617) 252-5298, or e-mail special.markets@perseusbooks.com.

1 2 3 4 5 6 7 8 9—09 08 07 06

In loving memory of Donna Ferrante and
A. Marshall Selznick, two tough individuals
who battled cancer into the later rounds.
Your courage was inspiring.

Contents

Prologue

With five minutes until fight time, the boxer moved restlessly in the tunnel of the Arena Theater in Houston. He wore a white gym towel like a poncho, with the middle cut out for his head to fit through, and his closely cropped black hair was soaked. Boxers are supposed to sweat before they fight, but his pores were working overtime. The twenty-one-year-old pugilist had perspired through his towel, and the wet terry cloth clung to his torso as though he had worn it through a carwash.

He threw punches into the air and moved his head from side to side to loosen his neck muscles while the saltwater dripped from the seams of his towel and collected in a pool around his feet. He stood 5 feet 6 and had wide brown eyes, a pudgy nose, and thick eyebrows and eyelashes. His muscles expanded and contracted as he bounced in place, which made the tattoo of a skull wearing a top hat on his right shoulder appear to be dancing. As his body pulsed with each undulating step, his face remained stoic.

Richard Lord, his trainer, stood behind the boxer and kneaded his charge's shoulders with both hands. "Come on, champ," Lord said to the boxer from behind. "This is the moment you've been waiting for. This will make those 100-degree days in the gym worth the work. You feel good?"

"I feel real good," he replied, keeping his eyes fixed on the blue boxing ring fifteen yards down the walkway. "I'm ready for this guy. I'm ready."

"Okay, champ. You know what to do in there. He's gonna come out strong and try to push you around. I don't want you to let him do that. I want you to control the momentum. You set the tone. Remember your technique and fight the kind of fight you want to. Make a strong impression. Take control."

"Take control," the boxer repeated. "Take control." As he muttered the words, his eyes began to well up with tears. His bottom lip trembled as he tried to fight back surging emotion, but the harder he tried to keep a stone face, the more his face cramped up. And the more his face cramped, the harder he blinked.

Lord sensed his fighter's heavy heart. He knew that the boxer's parents were in the audience and realized how much this fight meant to his family. The trainer, however, had a job to do. He had to keep his fighter's head in the game. Although he sympathized with his charge's emotional state, Lord decided he'd have to take control and turn those tears of concern into tears of rage.

Lord grabbed his fighter's arm and turned him around brusquely. "Look at me. Forget about all those people. You hear me? Forget they're there. You have a job to do. You're a professional now, you got that? A professional. This is business."

The boxer turned back around and faced his destiny fifteen yards away as three more tense minutes passed. Lord resumed his rubdown. "Come on, Jesus. Get loose."

Strange. He still wasn't used to people calling him Jesus. But this was a new beginning: new professional status, new hometown, new name. With that, the announcer entered the ring and a microphone lowered from the rafters.

"Ladies and gentlemen, our first bout is scheduled for four rounds. Introducing first, the challenger, making his professional debut here tonight. From Austin, Texas, let's hear it for Jesus 'El Matador' Chavez!" Boos thundered in the boxer's ears. A smattering of fans cheered, but the boos came from everywhere.

Sitting in the middle of the arena—among the hostile fans and the reverberating hisses—were Jesus and Rosario Sandoval, the boxer's parents, and the boxer's kid brother, twelve-year-old Jimmy Sandoval. Mom and dad had pooled their savings and bought the $750 plane tickets—the cost for three to fly to Houston from Chicago at the last minute—to watch their oldest child make his entrance. They ignored the unruly spectators around them and clapped fanatically as their boy made his way to the ring.

The boxer tried to choke back the sobs as he trotted toward the squared circle, but seeing his mother, father, and younger brother in the audience and knowing how much they sacrificed to make the trip was too much for him to handle. Tears started streaming down his face, which caused his mother to start crying as well. The boxer's heavy breathing, coupled with his guttural moans, caused him to slightly as-phyxiate. He was overwhelmed with emotion as he made his way to-ward the ring for his first professional fight. This was his crowning moment: he had made it through an obstacle course laden with hope, despair, and despondency in order to showcase his pugilistic talents in front of a capacity crowd.

Then there was his family, and the young boxer wanted nothing more than to make them proud—to show them that he'd become someone. And Jimmy, his younger sibling, was there. The kid idolized his big brother. The boxer needed to make a statement on that night; successful professional pugilists don't have many losses on their record. If he was to become any kind of contender later down the road, he needed to make a memorable first impression in his professional debut. And that prospect daunted him.

Jesus Sandoval Jr., the boxer's father, knew it was up to him to hold the family together and keep them from making a public spectacle of themselves. He looked at his son firmly, clenched his fist, and nodded. His son took the cue and wiped the tears from his face with his red boxing glove.

The boxer entered the ring and raised both hands, touching off another wave of boos. Houstonians did not come out that August night in 1994 to see Jesus Chavez, but to see the professional debut of their native son, Lewis Wood. A hard-hitting southpaw and veteran of the Houston Fire Department, Lewis was a man's man. A violent fighter in the ring, he was the type of guy the Houston working class could relate to. He was grounded, dedicated, a family man after the bell and outside the ring. This was Wood's first professional fight too, and the firefighter was already looking beyond his opponent to his first major bout and big payday.

Two years earlier, Wood lost a tough amateur fight to would-be gold medalist Oscar De La Hoya in the last round of the U.S. Olympic tryouts. He hadn't lost another fight since. Because he performed so well as an amateur, Wood's professional unveiling was highly anticipated by boxing pundits. Local fight fans, who prided themselves on their resilient hometown amateur, attended this fight in droves to witness the beginning of a new era for Houston boxing, where the lightweight would be king.

"And his opponent," the announcer resumed, "fighting out of the blue corner and wearing red, white, and blue trunks, also making his professional debut here tonight, let's hear it for our own Lewis, the 'Fighting Houston Fireman' Wood!"

The two boxers approached each other in the center of the ring and the referee gave instructions. Lord continued to rub his fighter's shoulders, kneading harder as his fighter blinked repeatedly.

Wood took his opponent's eye twitching to be a sign of fear. Neither Wood nor his trainers connected the boxer Jesus Chavez with an ex-convict named Gabriel Sandoval who had the tic since he was a child. They didn't know that by twitching, the boxer was pumping up his muscles. His biceps, triceps, and forearms pulsed with each hard blink. They didn't figure their opponent picked up a vicious temperament to accompany his involuntary motions while he was in prison. And since the Lewis Wood camp didn't know the opposing fighter's identity, they had no way of knowing that although this was Jesus Chavez's first fight, in his former life he had an amateur record of 95-5 and three Golden

Glove championships. Jesus Chavez and Gabriel Sandoval were the same person: an undocumented Mexican immigrant.

When the boxer started blinking, it wasn't out of fear but rather white-hot anger. Lord sensed the confidence growing in his fighter. The harder he kneaded the boxer's shoulders, the tauter they became. Chavez's mind transported him back to the yard at Stateville maximum security prison in Joliet, Illinois. Lewis Wood was no longer his professional opponent, but a rival gang member who had just called him out and wanted him dead. And in prison, when someone calls you out, you strike first and beat him until his eyes bleed.

Lord gave his fighter some last words of instruction: use that jab, set up a left hook to the body, and follow it with a right upstairs. He pulled the wet towel off over Chavez's head and slapped him on the ass. The bell rang and both boxers, wanting to make a strong first impression, charged to the center of the ring and began throwing measuring jabs. Wood caught Chavez with a hard left cross midway through the first round, which sent the crowd into a frenzy and clouded El Matador's head for the remaining opening minute. But that did not stop the challenger from swinging away.

His opponent's lefts seemed to come from all directions. Chavez realized in the first round that he was fighting a southpaw. Since this fight was booked at the last minute and because Lord was following a course he'd plotted early in their training to only put his boxer in the ring with the toughest opponents available, neither of them had a chance to scout Wood. They prepared to fight, yes, but the measures they took were training for training's sake. Midway through the first round—before Lord even had a chance to report to Chavez that Wood was left-handed—Chavez recognized that fact and responded accordingly. Chavez withstood a bombardment of strong lefts by Wood. But before the bell sounded to end round one, Chavez adjusted his stance and began trading left-handed bombs with the stronger boxer. When he returned to his corner after round one, Lord gruffly barked out orders of encouragement.

"You look good out there," he said, taking Chavez's mouthpiece out and rubbing his bicep. "He caught you, but you took it. That's the best he's got. And you already took it! Watch those lefts and try to slip a right in there, and we'll walk outta this joint with a win."

The bell rang to signal round two, and Chavez sprinted to the center with renewed confidence. Lord did his job: he reassured his fighter, even though the trainer's face told another story. Lord was confident that his boxer had the tools to beat Lewis Wood, but he continued to grit his teeth and furrow his brow when Chavez was out of eyesight. Wood had caught El Matador, and Lord knew that there was more where that came from. In fact, Wood had a barrage of combination punches in his arsenal that Chavez hadn't sampled yet. Lord knew that his boxer would never give up, though. El Matador had an iron will, and the only way he would go down was if Wood were to knock him unconscious. That's what Lord feared the most; his professionally inexperienced fighter wouldn't know if he'd been licked and if he should take a knee. But that's not how Lord trains his boxers. And that's not how Chavez approaches a fight.

As Lord watched his prodigal son, he saw a Jesus Chavez he had not seen before. Gym training is one thing; live competition is another. Chavez, a right-handed fighter, entered a left-handed slugfest with the natural southpaw, Wood. The hometown favorite was being matched blow for blow in the center of the ring. Wood landed a powerful shot to Chavez's forehead halfway through the second round, and the fireman winced more than the punch's recipient. Wood had thumped Chavez's skull so hard that he broke his hand on his opponent's head, snapping El Matador's neck back violently. Yet this unknown from Austin shook off the blow and pressed forward. Wood threw a hard left, and Chavez returned with an even harder shot. Come round four, the hometown crowd of white and Hispanic boxing fans started cheering for Chavez: He was fighting with such pure passion that his energy became contagious. And the Mexican Americans, previously rooting for their hometown favorite, Wood, began to cheer for one of their own.

El Matador was an underdog—an opponent scheduled as an automatic mark in Wood's "win" column. Yet the fighter who showed up on that night was no pushover. Chavez came to throw leather, and if he won, his countrymen would likely rally to his corner. To beat the favorite would require pulling for the underdog, and many Mexican American fight fans in attendance clearly identified with the underdog.

Wood managed to string together a hard one-two-three series in the waning moments of the fourth and final round, and while more experienced fighters have buckled and crumbled from such ferocious punches, Chavez's taut upper body was like rubber as the blows bounced off. Lord learned something about his boxer that night: the one hundred amateur matches Jesus fought, the three-plus years of prison brawls, and Lord's own demanding training regimen so thoroughly conditioned the boxer that a rival 126-pound fighter could not deliver a punch that would put El Matador on his back.

The fight went to the judges' scorecards as both pugilists mugged for the crowd. Pandemonium engulfed the arena as the fight fans—and fighters—anxiously awaited the decision. The announcer reentered the ring, and the spectators fell silent for the first time all night.

"Ladies and gentlemen, after four rounds of boxing, we go to the scorecards. Judge McCowan scores the bout 37-39. Judges McCullough and Martin score the bout 39-37 for your winner, by split decision, Jesus 'El Matador' Chavez!"

The audience clapped and hooted with delight: they got their money's worth. Richard Lord lifted a jubilant boxer into the air. Chavez's parents and brother climbed into the ring and Lord released his charge, who ran to his younger brother and hoisted Jimmy above his head. Jesus Chavez had won his first professional fight. El Matador blew kisses to Wood's hometown crowd. He had managed to overcome incredible odds and had beaten an up-and-coming contender in a strange city.

Lewis Wood and fellow fighters on the professional boxing circuit were one challenge. But the U.S. Immigration and Naturalization Service proved to be a much tougher opponent.

Shining City upon a Hill

Gabriel Sandoval was born in 1972 in the Mexican town of Hidalgo del Parral, where the revolutionary Pancho Villa had been tracked, killed, and buried. When Gabriel was a baby, his father, Jesus Sandoval Jr., began to think seriously about migrating north to the fabled lands of the United States. But the family moved to the impoverished town of Delicias, Mexico, where they shared a humble flat with Gabriel's grandparents, Hermila and Jesus Sandoval Sr. It was an aging structure with crumbling stucco walls that hosted swarms of insects, though Hermila went to great lengths to keep her humble house clean.

A proud Mexican family, the Sandovals toiled in various impoverished towns deep in the heart of the Mexican state of Chihuahua. Most men worked in the mines. Jesus Sr. had spent the better part of forty years in the mines, and while the work fed his family, it was also destroying his health. He labored in the fetid lead, zinc, silver, and copper mines in San Francisco del Oro, where workers' lungs became coated with soot. Although Jesus Jr. had great respect for his father, he longed for a better life.

But for the mines, the region was devoid of industry. Jesus Jr. knew of other Mexicans who'd trekked north and made good lives for themselves. He made his first border crossing with a cousin and an uncle in 1964, when he was only fifteen. Their destination was Hobbs, New Mexico, where in the past some fellow Chihuahuans had found work. Jesus Sr. at first pleaded with his son not to make the journey: stay here and work in the mines with me and your uncles, he said. But Junior was spirited and told his father he had to go: a brighter future lay ahead. Jesus Sr. gave his son two hundred pesos, wished him luck, and asked him to call home when he made it to New Mexico.

The three men took a 350-mile bus trip from San Francisco del Oro to Juarez, Mexico, and then prepared to swim across the section of the Rio Grande that separated Juarez from El Paso, Texas. They waited on the banks of the river until nightfall to avoid U.S. border patrol agents making late-night sweeps. Jesus took off his cowboy boots and stuck them in his knapsack, which held sardines and a gallon jug of water.

The temperature in the Chihuahuan desert plummeted after dark, but they had a full moon, stars, and the faint lights of El Paso to navigate by. Jesus Jr. shivered beneath his flannel shirt and blue jeans. The water would surely be colder than the air. He rocked back and forth to keep his blood running. When all was quiet and the desert was still, his uncle spoke in a loud whisper. ¿Listo? Ready? Jesus Jr. nodded, and the three men eased into the icy Rio Grande as silently as they could and began to forge the river.

The cold rushing waters reached Jesus's chin. He flailed with his arms and legs to stay afloat, as the strong night current could easily knock him off his feet and send him to a certain drowning. He was not a strong swimmer, but a determined young man desperate for a brighter future than the San Francisco del Oro mines could provide. After spending an hour in the frigid river, the three men made landfall. Jesus Jr. put on his cowboy boots and followed his uncle and cousin up a mountain in the darkness. For the next seven days, the men traversed the desert, living on sardines and meager rations of water. Jesus's feet swelled inside his cowboy boots, but he refused to take them off for fear he wouldn't get them back on.

At night, when the rocky surface cooled and the desert wildlife awakened, the three men would climb to a mountaintop. It was colder at the higher altitude, but the desert overgrowth was thinner and less bothersome. They could watch the lights of border patrol vehicles from a safe distance. After walking seven days, they arrived in Hobbs, New Mexico, on the New Mexico–Texas border.

They joined a community of Mexicans and found jobs under the table. Jesus Jr. split his time between cooking and maintenance work but barely made a living and couldn't even call his father. He was toiling fourteen hours a day in sweltering kitchens and in dirty barns cleaning up after animals. After three months, sixteen-year-old Jesus Jr. decided to go home to Mexico. Alone.

He hitched a ride to Jal, New Mexico, in the southeastern corner of the state. From there, he figured he could follow the highway back into his native land, but it led deeper into the desert between New Mexico and Texas. Jesus Jr. stumbled on a farm and spent his first night away from his uncle and cousin in a stranger's chicken coop. The following morning, he went to the owner and pleaded with the lady who answered the door to give him a ride to the main highway into Mexico. He didn't speak English, but the lady could understand what the sixteen-year-old Mexican was trying to say and read the desperation on his face. Jesus did some work around the farm for a few days, spending each night in the coop with the chickens. The lady honored her promise and took him to El Paso, where he walked through a port of entry back in to Juarez, Mexico.

He had no money but found a job picking chili peppers for a few days until he could scrape together enough pesos for the bus fare back to San Francisco del Oro. At night, he slept in the orchards. Jesus Jr. eventually made it back to his father's house but felt ashamed. Jesus Sr. warmly embraced his son, hugging him while thanking God for his return.

Jesus Jr. began working in the San Francisco del Oro mines and in a plywood factory, hanging out with the men and drinking *cervezas* at night. One year after returning to Mexico he met his future wife, Rosario. Eventually they were married and moved into a tiny one-bedroom tenement in the mining town. Jesus Jr. now worked full-time in the mines, spending most days nearly 3,100 feet below ground. Dust particles saturated his lungs and the absence of natural light dampened his spirit. He'd start work at 5:30 A.M., go underground for ten to twelve hours, and emerge from the earth's bowels as the sun was going down.

In 1978, after a rainstorm damaged the Sandoval home, Jesus Jr. had enough. He had a six-year-old son and a four-year-old daughter, and their future was bleak. If they stayed in San Francisco del Oro or in neighboring Delicias, his son Gabriel would go from high school to the mines. Jesus Jr. decided to move his family to the United States, no matter what the risk.

With some money from relatives, Jesus and his family moved to an impoverished settlement in Juarez. It was a decrepit adobe structure with busted windows and crumbling ceiling and walls. The heavy wooden door, splintering and weathering, often fell off its hinges and exposed the hut's interior to the desert elements. There was a stove, a sink, a tub, and a water tank. That was it. Jesus needed to return to the United States to make enough money to move his family into a better home.

Later that year, Jesus Jr. again swam the Rio Grande—this time alone—and hitchhiked all the way to Oxnard, California. Rosario had family in Juarez who helped out with the children and provided some groceries. Jesus Jr. hired himself out as a repairman and stayed in Oxnard for about six months, making less than minimum wage. He sent his wife and children $35 each week—the bulk of his earnings. While he was in California, his sister died suddenly and Jesus Jr. hitched back to San Francisco del Oro to attend her funeral.

The whole family returned to Juarez after the burial, which is when Jesus Jr.'s youngest brother, Javier, had a proposition for him. "Jesus, I have some money saved up. There's a huge Mexican community up in the American north. Want to go to Chicago?"

"No, *hermano*. I'm either going back to California or I'm staying here in Juarez," Jesus replied.

"There's money in Chicago," Javier coaxed. "I know someone up there who will give us work. We can make real money! You can put some aside and save for your family, then you can send for them."

"Chicago is far away," he said. "And it's cold."

Javier persisted for several days and Jesus finally agreed. The brothers would swim across the Rio Grande and then fly from El Paso to Chicago. The night before his departure, Jesus and Rosario sat in the corner of their adobe and talked by candlelight. He would be gone for a few months but would send money. In due time, he would send for her and the children. Rosario agreed. She put her faith in her husband and trusted his judgment. Jesus spent the rest of the evening playing with Gabriel and his younger sister, Lidia. "I'm going on an errand," he told them. "It may take a little while, but we'll be together again soon. And we'll stay that way forever."

———

Entering the United States illegally was easier in 1979. Today, Mexicans must go to great lengths to avoid border patrol officers. Many try to enter the United States in unventilated tractor trailers only to be dumped like so much lumber in remote parts of the country or large cities. Nevertheless, these Mexicans spiritedly cling to the hope of finding gainful employment once they get into the United States.

Undocumented Mexican workers, then as now, work as hotel maids and farmhands, auto mechanics and construction laborers, meat packers and slaughterhouse butchers, always fearing discovery and deportation, constantly struggling to maintain their anonymity and stay beneath the radar of government officials who are trying to deport them. It's hard on a Mexican's psyche to live in abject poverty while up north lies a country that Ronald Reagan described as "the shining city upon a hill."

———

Jesus and Javier Sandoval made five unsuccessful attempts to cross the Rio Grande into the United States in as many days. They were turned back by border patrol agents at gunpoint, detained, and driven to the border. On their sixth attempt, the brothers Sandoval made it across the border. Using fake papers they had forged in Juarez, Jesus and Javier bought one-way tickets to O'Hare International Airport with what was left of their money. The Windy City was home to 140,000 documented Mexican immigrants, and presumably tens of thousands of undocumented ones. The living conditions would be cold and harsh, but Jesus Sandoval was a man of resolve. He would make a life for himself and his family on the shores of Lake Michigan. He had to.

Jesus Jr. landed at O'Hare on a freezing November day in 1979 with $20 in his wallet and no English-language skills. It was the first time he'd seen snow other than on distant mountaintops. Javier decided to take a train to Waukegan, a far-north Chicago suburb, where they had distant relatives. Jesus Jr. went in search of an uncle he had never met in downtown Chicago.

He had an address on a scrap of paper, and that was it. The streets were confusing to Jesus. Sure, he'd been in a big city before—Juarez was huge and sprawling. But the Windy City skyscrapers were enormous, and giant steel elevated cars zoomed by in a huff. Jesus was lost. He studied passing faces, hoping to find a fellow Mexican among the racing pedestrians.

He zeroed in on a woman who looked Hispanic, and luckily she spoke Spanish. Jesus showed her the scrap of paper with the address: it was for a tiny Mexican restaurant on State Street. She pointed him in the right direction and he walked to the address, which was several miles away. The cold air bit his ears and made them feel hot. He fought through the chill and found his uncle.

Jesus Jr. was put to work painting the restaurant for $2 an hour. Then a local businessman hired Jesus to help move furniture between warehouses. He made little money working sixty hours per week. Jesus Jr. checked into a halfway house that was already filled to capacity, but was permitted to sleep in the bathroom as long as he kept quiet. Jesus slept on the bathroom floor, with his head next to the commode and his legs jutting out into the hallway.

Jesus called his wife in October 1980 and told her he was thinking about coming back to Mexico: this was no life. He was making only

$40 a week and sending most of it to Juarez. He put the decision to her: should he save up money and bring her to Chicago, although he did not know when that would be, or should he return and take the family back to Delicias or the mines of San Francisco del Oro? Rosario said she needed time to think.

Jesus returned to his job doing heavy lifting at the warehouse. A week after his conversation with Rosario, his boss flagged him down at the loading docks. His wife was on the phone.

"My wife?" he asked questioningly. "Are you sure?"

"That's what she said in Spanish. She don't speak English."

Jesus ran back to the office. It was Rosario. And Gabriel and Lidia. The whole family was at O'Hare.

Rosario had become distraught after their last phone conversation. Life for her husband in Chicago was rough, she recognized, but life in Juarez was unbearable. She couldn't always find food and the house was falling apart around her. Family members offered to buy her and the children plane tickets from El Paso to Chicago, which she gratefully accepted, and she crossed the Rio Grande without incident. Rosario's brother escorted her, five-year-old Lidia, and seven-year-old Gabriel across the same river that caused Jesus Jr. so many headaches. Her brother carried Gabriel on his shoulders and pulled Rosario and Lidia on an old black inner tube. Once in El Paso, Rosario bought plane tickets to Chicago.

Jesus took the CTA train to O'Hare and scoured the airport for his family. And then he saw the three of them. Lidia wore a pink dress, the only hint of color against that gray Chicago backdrop, and when she saw him, she sprinted into her father's open arms. It was a loving re-union. The Sandoval family was together again and Jesus brought them back to the boardinghouse, where they all lived in a bathroom for a couple of days. Luckily for them, a cousin was moving back to Mexico, and he had already paid two months' rent on an apartment. The family moved in and Jesus went looking for a better-paying job. He answered an ad for a delivery truck driver in the *Chicago Tribune*, but when he showed up for the interview, they shoved a broom in his hand. Apparently Mexicans were only qualified to sweep floors.

Pressured by his dire circumstances, Jesus swallowed his pride and accepted the job.

Two months later, the boss's brother slipped Jesus a scrap of paper with a name and an address on it. "You go to this address tomorrow, Jesus, and you're gonna start working right away." It was the business address of Bob Powell, an administrator with the Chicago Housing Department.

"What kind of a job is it?" Jesus asked.

"I don't know," the boss's brother replied. "What difference does it make? You'll have work and a paycheck right quick."

Jesus arrived at the address and slipped the secretary the piece of paper with Bob Powell's name on it. She then handed Jesus an application for a position with the Chicago Housing Authority. The application, much to his surprise, was already filled out. "Just sign your name," she directed. It did not matter that Jesus was an undocumented immigrant and did not speak fluent English. He was issued a jumpsuit and put to work that day cleaning vacant city lots. For a while, CHA kept Jesus working outside, so as to show off to any passersby (and meddling city administrators) that there was a Hispanic on the all-black cleaning crew. Jesus became the Housing Authority's example of diversity in the workplace.

Equipped with a fake social security number, Jesus was put on the rolls of a city voucher program, which let him move his family into a government-subsidized housing project. The job paid well—more than minimum wage—but Jesus was apprehensive about using his real name and a fake social security number. But time passed and his concern faded. A week went by, then a month, then a year. Jesus eased into a routine.

He labored as an undocumented though on-the-books mainte-nance hand in West Side housing projects. Much like Jurgis in Upton Sinclair's *The Jungle*, Sandoval rose at dawn, donned his grimy blues, and trekked across Chicago Avenue to clean the day's soot. He returned to his own housing project twelve hours later, when the sun was sink-ing behind Chicago's towering skyscrapers and the streets were coated with another day's litter. Jesus became a regimented worker. Each morning he made a point to see his children before he left for the day, peeking into the small room they shared and taking a long look at their sleeping bodies, sometimes leaving a gentle kiss on each forehead. Then he went into the kitchen to bid a brief *adiós* to Rosario. He'd often remind her to make sure the kids went to school and paid attention. But Gabriel and Lidia didn't need reminding. They were dutiful children, respectful and mindful of their father and mother. Such is the custom with Mexican families: the father is the lord of the manor, even when the manor is nothing more than a stale apartment in a building with chipping lead paint and leaky pipes. Father's words had the force of law.

Jesus Jr.'s English improved on the job. In 1982, Jesus and Rosario had a third child, Jimmy, who became the first of the Sandoval clan born in America. Over time, Jesus Jr. managed to move his family out of the projects and into a modest two-bedroom house on West Rice Street. The impoverished Sandoval family felt they were living the American Dream. Jesus Jr., though, knew that West Rice Street and the surrounding areas were home to some tough *vatos*.

Their eldest child, Gabriel, was mild-mannered and polite. His English was coming along, albeit slowly. He and Lidia were each other's practice partners. They'd sit in a corner and attempt to converse in English, which for a while was more Spanglish than anything. Outside the cozy house, though, lay a fierce neighborhood, in any language.

Only ten years old, Gabriel was aware of West Side violence and wanted to learn martial arts as a means of self-defense. He watched *Kung Fu* reruns on television and asked his parents if he could take karate lessons.

Jesus was in favor of his son's request. Karate could teach young Gabriel a useful skill, but more importantly, it could keep him off the streets and away from the crowd of *vatos* who hung out on Harrison and South Cicero. Those thugs spent their time in front of Belmont Cut Rate Liquors and routinely knocked off the Vienna hotdog stand. They harassed the poor and homeless congregating in front of Precious Grove Missionary Baptist Church and robbed pedestrians at gun and knifepoint as they cut through the vacant lots.

Jesus and Rosario scouted out some local dojos, but even the cheapest ones were too expensive. Swimming lessons, however, were free for local kids at Eckhart Park, so the Sandovals signed up Gabriel and Lidia.

On the first day of lessons in 1982, Rosario dropped her children off at the Eckhart Park recreational complex an hour early, as she was being extra careful they weren't late. That one hour ended up changing her son's life.

Gabriel and Lidia sat on the concrete steps of the complex and waited for the pool to open and the lessons to start. Over the sound of chirping birds, Gabriel heard a bell ding every few minutes. He also heard muffled grunts and groans, tennis shoes screeching on wood floors, and what he would soon find out was the pounding of leather.

The Matador Gym was one of many boxing gyms in Chicago at the time. In the late 1970s and early 1980s, *Rocky* fever still had a grip on the country, and city kids wanted to learn how to box. Youngsters like Gabriel believed they could punch their way to fame and fortune.

He was a short, wiry boy with a thin frame and a nervous eye twitch. He had just returned home after spending a year with his grandparents in their humble flat in Delicias, Mexico. Rosario developed heart problems when Gabriel was nine, and she couldn't look after her children because of her unstable physical condition. She sent Gabriel and Lidia to Mexico for the year while she recuperated. When the children returned after a year, Jesus and Rosario Sandoval decided to look for an activity to better occupy Gabriel's time.

Chicago in the 1970s and 1980s had a split personality. Some neighborhoods such as Hyde Park, Lincoln Park, and Wrigleyville were being gentrified while other neighborhoods, like the area west of the Loop, fell into decay and became a refuge for illegal immigrants and a breeding ground for gangs.

On Chicago's West Side, where Chicago and Damen Avenues inter-
sect among aging bungalows and brownstones, things got sketchy at
night. The empty buildings were ideal spots for squatters and drug
dealers. Most storefronts had been tagged with graffiti, most windows
were boarded up, and English was a second language in almost every
household. Families of Mexican, Polish, and Ukrainian immigrants
lived amid persistent violence and pervasive fear: broken homes were
as common as broken glass. Hardworking immigrant families who
came to this country in search of the Jeffersonian entitlements of life,
liberty, and happiness wanted a safe, sheltered existence for their children. But they had to work too many hours to keep a constant eye on
their children's coming and goings, and gangs assumed a central position among youth culture in this brutish section of the city.

Gabriel descended a narrow concrete staircase to a basement gym. As
he opened the creaky steel door, the muffled clatter he'd heard was
amplified. The activity in the gym seemed to center around a crotch-
ety Irishman. He was only 5 feet 7, but he commanded attention.
With thick black eyebrows and dark hair on his pale athletic body, the
Irishman looked like the quintessential boxing trainer in his gray
sweatpants and sweatshirt. He wiped perspiration from his pudgy
nose and red, fleshy cheeks and onto his soaked sweatshirt sleeve.

Tom O'Shea barked orders through a nasal rasp. His face was a trove
of frowns and furrows and his gruff words of instruction outnumbered
his words of encouragement. O'Shea was the lone white face in a throng
of black and Hispanic youth, but he obviously had their respect. Gabriel
watched these neighborhood toughs—the same ones he saw walking
around Damen Avenue—taking orders from this forty-year-old white
guy. Sitting in a corner of the basement, he timidly observed them box
until it was time to check in for swimming lessons.

That night, when Jesus Sandoval returned from work, his son sat
impatiently, anxious to tell his father about the day's discovery. Jesus

listened to Gabriel's ramblings about the Matador Gym and the Irishman he saw teaching kids how to box. The father was intrigued: perhaps boxing could satisfy his son's desire to learn martial arts while keeping him away from the gangs. Also, if the gangs approached his boy looking for trouble, boxing skills might come in handy.

On his next day off, Jesus walked with his son to Eckhart Park and the Matador Gym. Right away, Jesus liked the scene. It was just as Gabriel had described it: throngs of neighborhood kids punching away at focus mitts and at their own shadows. There were other young kids there, but none as young as Gabriel.

O'Shea saw the two walk in, the father holding his eager son's hand. A seasoned boxing veteran, O'Shea knew what was coming: a parent was going to ask if his boy should learn to fight. He'd seen it a hundred times. The Irishman's first impression of Jesus was that of a loving father and an athlete in his own right. Jesus Sandoval Jr. was a tall Mexican—about 5 feet 11—with broad shoulders, a strong back, and muscular forearms. He clearly paid attention to his physical appearance: Jesus's beard was well maintained and cropped close to his angular face. O'Shea liked that: athletic fathers with a sense of self-pride instilled a certain discipline in their sons, which boded well in the ring. He also liked fathers who looked out for their kids, as not many in that neighborhood did. Truth be told, not many fathers in that neighborhood stuck around.

O'Shea sympathized with these strong-minded Mexican families. He admired their courage and spirit, their willingness to work long hours for lousy pay while still finding time to love their children. The trainer also knew what lay ahead for young Gabriel if he didn't find a way to fill his days. That too he'd seen a hundred times, like with the Hernandez boy.

Willie Hernandez had boxed since he was six years old. By fourteen, he was a successful amateur, one who used the sport as a means of avoiding gangs. Willie mouthed off to a gang member in his first year at Wells High School. The gangster knew better than to fight Willie and took the cowardly route. Willie was sitting on his stoop when a carload of thugs drove by. Willie sized up the situation, saw trouble coming, and took off around a building. But a bullet fired from the car hit a concrete wall and a piece of debris lodged in Willie's eye. He lost the eye and with it, his boxing future.

O'Shea made a point of helping kids so they didn't succumb to the same fate. Deep down, he wanted to save every one of them. He knew how to earn their respect and how to unlock each one's potential. Boxing was a way to do that. The discipline it required could keep kids on track, foster self-esteem, physical fitness, and an appreciation for combat skills, but it couldn't solve all their problems. Daedalus built wings for son Icarus, fastened them with wax, and even taught him to fly, but senior couldn't keep junior from flying too close to the sun. O'Shea could teach his kids how to live the right way in this world, but he couldn't live for them.

Jesus told his son to go sit on the lone gym bench while he talked to O'Shea. Theirs was a cordial conversation. Jesus explained that he worked hard and wasn't always around. He had brought his family to the United States for a better life—a concept that O'Shea, a son of Irish immigrants, could relate to—but the Chicago street gangs made life rougher than the streets of impoverished Delicias, Mexico. Could boxing keep Gabriel out of the gangs?

O'Shea explained that boxing was a discipline and not a lifestyle. Yes, he would keep Gabriel and his other students out of gangs and off the streets, but the kid had to commit to the regimen. And if young Gabriel was reluctant to learn, then he was out; O'Shea wasn't running a damn daycare.

On the walk home, Jesus told Gabriel that he'd let him learn to box, but he had to be committed. "It won't be easy for you, *mijo*. Those boys are bigger than you. But you're a tough *hombre*. You show them what you're made of: You show them where you're from." And father gave son one standing order, an order that he intended for Gabriel to follow in the gym as well as on the streets: "*Mijo*, you obey me, and you listen to your coach."

———————

To understand boxing and its allure for Mexicans is to comprehend their plight south of the border as well as the quandaries of immigrants who make it into the United States. Most immigrants experience some degree of desperation, even though Americans downplay their predicament. A Mexican migrant's struggle for a better life also includes an inner struggle between will and circumstance. For some Mexican immigrants, this struggle is ameliorated by boxing.

Many of the greatest boxers in the world—past and present—are Mexican, *hombres* who make a living with their fists. In fact, 37 percent of the world's top-ranked fighters are Mexican. Struggle is something the average Mexican can understand. It is, after all, what many Mexicans encounter on a daily basis.

Boxing was invented in eighteenth-century England to distinguish between fights with rules and ordinary brawls. Aristocratic English gentlemen and nobility promoted the idea of boxing as a "humane" alternative to dueling. In time boxers were designated as either amateur or professional. Amateur boxing was scored on punches rather than physical damage to an opponent. That concept was taken further at the 1904 Olympic Games in St. Louis, Missouri, when boxing made its international debut as a sport.

Professional boxing began with the Queensbury rules set by John Chambers in 1867. Instead of ending because of a knockout or sheer exhaustion, fights could then be measured by a scoring system. In 1891 the National Sporting Club of London created nine additional rules and began promoting professional boxing. The first world title fight was held a year after these rules were set: Gentleman Jim Corbett knocked out John L. Sullivan in the twenty-first round at the Pelican Athletic Club in New Orleans.

In the late nineteenth century, amateur boxing spread among universities and the U.S. military. The most successful boxers, however, came from poor city streets. This gentleman's game became the grand leveler: a way for poor folk to take it to the wealthy in a legally sanctioned contest. And the distinction resonated even louder for the underprivileged Mexicans south of the border, where more than half lived in poverty at the turn of the century. The chance for a better economic situation, for most, then as now, came with migrating to the United States.

Simply moving to the United States is not enough to create a better life. Many immigrants have people waiting back home who need money to survive. Mexican boxers fight a two-front battle for survival: against their opponents and against destitution. When Mexican boxing fans cheer for the Mexican boxer, they are cheering a countryman who shares their struggle and understands their labor. For a Mexican to beat an opponent in hand-to-hand combat—the most primitive contest of guts and will—is for a Mexican to demonstrate superiority through his own resolve. No outlying variables like poverty or circumstance can disturb the natural order of a fight. Two men enter and one man leaves a winner. When a Mexican boxer fights, every Mexican sees some of himself in that fighter. When he wins, every Mexican wins.

The sport has a way of uniting the country, a commonality often passed down from one generation to another. In recent times, one Mexican boxer in particular has embodied the values of a nation: one who has triumphed on every level of the sport, one whom Mexican kids grow up idolizing—Julio Cesar Chavez.

The greatest Mexican boxer of all time, Chavez represents the gritty superhero Mexicans relate to—a man of steel with dirt under his fingernails. He was born in Culiacán in 1962, a dirty, drug-infested town in the foothills of the Sierra Madre mountains. Chavez made it a mission at a very young age to take care of his family and clean up the town. He felt destined for a better life than what he could expect selling fruit or drugs.

Chavez's two older brothers were boxers. Julio liked the action in the ring and knew he could make a quick buck at it. His first fight, as an eleven-year-old, was against a fourteen-year-old girl who bullied the younger boys. This girl had a reputation in town as someone who kicked ass. When she fought Chavez, he pounded her developing chest so badly that she gave up boxing. At sixteen, Chavez quit school and was fighting daily for $6 a bout.

Julio Chavez went pro in 1980 and won his first ninety fights. Known as the Lion of Culiacán, he was the WBC super featherweight champion from 1984 to 1987; then he stepped up a weight class and became the reigning lightweight champion from 1989 to 1994. But the un-thinkable was yet to come: Chavez shocked the boxing world when he gained weight and fought for a third world championship at welter-weight. He beat Roger Mayweather in 1989 to become the first Mexican fighter to be a champion at three different weight classes. He solidified the hearts and minds of the Mexican people with a 1993 vic-tory over Greg Haugen in front of 130,000 screaming fans at Mexico City's Estadio Azteca. It was the largest crowd in boxing history.

Chavez realized that with his success came responsibility. The Mexican people looked up to him the way they looked to their saints for guidance and hope. In a *Sports Illustrated* article in 1993, Chavez summed up his reasons for boxing: "I am fighting for a whole family," he said. "I am a sponge for their problems. It has given me many worries, this role, but it has matured me. It has stabilized me. It has made me who I am."

Oscar De La Hoya is also a boxing champion who came from a poor family, but Mexican nationals considered him a traitor. De La Hoya built himself a mansion and became a media darling in later years, a far cry from the hungry fighter who came from an East Los Angeles barrio. After Chavez became wealthy, by contrast, he re-turned to Culiacán and invested in the town, which helped define him as a philanthropist as well as a boxer. De La Hoya loved the finer things. He enjoyed reading and listening to classical music while Chavez preferred sitting in the backyard of his childhood home and chewing the fat with the locals.

Some Mexicans took offense at De La Hoya's behavior. He seemed embarrassed by his roots and took no pride in his culture and heritage; he was a gringo, a U.S. Olympian golden boy. De La Hoya indeed felt like part of the Mexican culture, but he had a hard time selling that image south of the border. And what was more, he became an American hero. Chavez, on the other hand, was first and foremost Mexican, so much so that he never bothered to learn English. It typified his national pride, and the Mexican people treasured his irreverence.

Tom O'Shea and fellow trainer Sean Curtin were Chicago boxing icons. They were known not only for making great fighters but for having a vested interest in assisting inner-city Chicago youths. Students of the old school, they believed that the sweet science doubled as a sure salvation for troubled kids. Their approaches, however, were different.

O'Shea trained Chicago youths to become good amateur boxers, as well as upstanding citizens. His tutelage centered on a grander discipline: staying out of harm's way. O'Shea's idea for a boxing gym evolved from a boxing club he started while he was teaching at King High School, a neighborhood school in the notorious Cabrini-Green housing project.

He was an English teacher, one of only a few white teachers, who had a hard time keeping students' attention. One student in particular, a muscular black football player named Carmi Williams, used to harass O'Shea. He'd murmur racial epithets and threaten him. "Man, if you weren't a teacher, I'd kick your fuckin' ass," he said after class one day in 1977. O'Shea had enough.

"All right. I've got some boxing gloves in the car," he replied. "If you're so tough, meet me in the basement at 3:15. We'll settle this once and for all."

Word spread throughout the school that big, bad Carmi Williams was going to fight a teacher. When the final bell sounded, Carmi had an entourage of football and basketball players follow him into the basement. O'Shea stood by the boiler awaiting his student. He threw Carmi a pair of boxing gloves, rolled up his sleeves, and donned his own pair.

They squared up and Carmi began making rookie mistakes. He went for the knockout shot right out of the gate. The teacher evaded him and countered with a shot to the gut. Carmi doubled over while the students in attendance roared. Carmi tried to land a haymaker, and O'Shea landed another shot to the gut. After the third punch to his breadbasket, cocky Carmi waived off his smaller, older teacher.

The fight was over, and the days of Carmi Williams harassing O'Shea were over too. Other students stepped up and wanted the medium-framed Irishman to teach them to box. Interest was so pervasive that by 1979, about the time Jesus Jr. was swimming the Rio Grande, O'Shea's first boxing gym opened around the corner from Cabrini-Green. Two years later, the gym Gabriel eventually stumbled on opened in the basement of Eckhart Park's recreational complex.

The room that would become the boxing gym was used for training dogs and stank of wet fur and dog urine. But O'Shea didn't care. His after-school project had a home. Now he needed a name. One day some of his students from Cabrini-Green were mulling over potential names. One boxer piped up with a name that stuck: "Coach, you're always telling us to be like a matador. You always say get out of the way, don't get hit." Coach was struck by the image of the lone matador—the solitary man facing a fierce beast. The matador was the crowd's favorite, but he was the vulnerable underdog. The Matador Gym—and the source of Gabriel's eventual namesake— was born.

There was one small ring in the gym, two feet off the floor, but no free weights. There were a couple of punching bags, but O'Shea purposefully kept them to a minimum. The repetitive thumping sound of the heavy bag and the rat-a-tat-tat of the speed bag made too much noise in that basement echo chamber. Boxers learned by hitting focus mitts, sparring, shadowboxing, and mirror work.

O'Shea discouraged fighters from going pro. Sean Curtin, on the other hand, was a more career-oriented trainer. Curtin was a former army boxer, an official, a coach, and in later years, a Chicago boxing commissioner. He was concerned with refining natural ability and discovering whether a pugilist had the tools to become a contender. Despite their conflicting opinions on boxing as a career, they both had a keen eye for talent. And they both remember when a preteen named Gabriel Sandoval started raising eyebrows on the Chicago amateur boxing circuit.

Gabriel did indeed obey his father and his coach. He dutifully walked to the gym every day after school, then again on weekends. Even before he had the boxing skills, he had an incredible will. The older kids from King and Wells High Schools immediately liked Gabriel even though he was the youngest boxer in the gym. He was funny and witty. They admired how hard he tried to perfect his English, and they were even more impressed with his courage. Gabriel would get in the ring and box anyone: young or old, good or bad, the young boy refused to back down, even when he was outclassed by more skilled opponents.

O'Shea noticed that the boy enjoyed the battle. The coach cherished that quality. He could teach someone how to box, but he couldn't teach someone to love and respect the sport. When the boy got hit, he wouldn't back up. He stood in there and fought off the ropes. Gabriel was aggressive, and he absorbed O'Shea's advice.

In boxing, when it comes to a stress point—when a fighter is alone in the ring with an opponent and the coach cannot call time out—the sport takes on an instinctive quality. Again, O'Shea noticed that Gabriel had this sixth sense. He could visualize the match in real time. The boy could tell from an opponent's footwork and other subtle signs which shots were coming, and he'd adjust and counterpunch in kind.

As the years passed and Gabriel matured, he became a recognizable name in Chicago boxing circles at the 112-pound weight class. Sean Curtin was promoting boxing matches around the city and O'Shea called his buddy and asked if Gabriel could fight on an amateur card. Curtin agreed, eager to see this kid in action. O'Shea had gone on at length about his protégé, and the kid did not disappoint.

The coaches got together after the fight and talked about young Gabriel's future. Curtin, who ran the CYO gym on the South Side of Chicago, thought Gabriel—if properly trained—could mature into a professional prospect. O'Shea agreed, but he wasn't about to start encouraging young boxers to go pro. The professional boxer to O'Shea was a sad athlete. "He puts all his eggs in one basket, and the basket usually breaks." They differed on Gabriel's professional future, but they agreed that the kid had a stellar amateur career ahead of him.

Curtin started coming around the Matador Gym and helping coach Gabriel. When he was sixteen, the boy won the Chicago Golden Gloves at 112 pounds. O'Shea and Curtin took the boxer to Springfield, Illinois, to fight in the statewide Golden Gloves. Gabriel drew the defending champion in the first round and gave opponent Patrick Byrd the fight of his life before eventually losing the fight. When Gabriel got to be 119 pounds, some of the other athletes at that weight class willingly left the division. Gabriel had to spar with the bigger boys, the 140-plus pounders.

"He had a drive in him that I never had as a fighter," Curtin recalled. "It was a drive I wish I had. Nothing ever took away his confidence."

O'Shea and Curtin were like second and third fathers to the boy. Because the Sandovals were undocumented immigrants, Gabriel had to be promoted carefully. Curtin had contacts with a Mexican boxing club in Tijuana that staffed the Mexican Olympic boxing team, and he was in talks with a coach to give Gabriel a tryout for the 1992 Olympic squad. Curtin was sure the kid would make the team and showcase his talents to an international audience in Barcelona, Spain. But the trainer was not the only influence pulling on Gabriel.

Chicago's mean streets were beckoning. Gabriel was a tough Mexican kid, good with his fists. Simpleminded neighborhood toughs with street smarts worked on the boxer. They began to show him a life where knowing the right people made you a neighborhood king. O'Shea figured Gabriel was already a rock by this point, that the punks couldn't sway him. Curtin, however, knew better. He observed the boy hanging out with locals who were more than just disreputable. These were gang bangers, and a violent gang to boot. The Harrison Gents, a mob of black and Hispanic West Siders, was a force to be reckoned with. Curtin warned Gabriel to stay away from those guys and concentrate on boxing. But the streets have a way of deviling a boy, even one as talented and streetwise as Gabriel.

2

West Side

C hicago Avenue cuts a broad swath through historically rich and culturally diverse neighborhoods of the city. The thoroughfare borders the city's storied Near North Side, home to a mix of shopping boutiques and high-end restaurants. To the far west, Chicago Avenue bisects the affluent suburban Oak Park, best-known as the stomping grounds of the late architect Frank Lloyd Wright. There, framed by ancient maples and oaks, sit the Bootleg Houses, distinctive dwellings designed by Wright while he was employed by Adler & Sullivan, who forbade the eccentric designer from taking outside commissions. Hence the name.

In between Oak Park and Lake Michigan, however, Chicago Avenue in the 1980s and early 1990s straddled a desolate no-man's land. It was the Midwestern equivalent of inner-city Baltimore or East Harlem or Compton. This was the infamous Near West Side, where black, Hispanic, and Eastern European immigrants lived within a five-mile radius of one another, each ethnic group carving out its own territory along Chicago Avenue. The impoverished surroundings contributed greatly to gang activity.

The nuclear family was a fairy tale. There were no picket fences or pies cooling on the windowsill. Mothers did not always tend to their children, and fathers were not always around. Even families that did live together did not always produce children impervious to delinquency. The best parents on the West Side—the ones who immigrated to the United States, legally or illegally, looking for a better life for their children—also hailed from this area. They worked grueling hours under backbreaking conditions for inadequate pay. Their dedication to their jobs meant that they were not around to ward off the bad influences on their children.

The lure of the streets made it difficult for hardworking parents to consistently keep an eye on their kids. The streets beckoned. They tantalized and titillated. Chicago's West Side, with Chicago Avenue as its main artery, had pothole-riddled streets and dilapidated houses and storefronts. There was no sense of civic pride or community as different ethnicities lived near each other but were incapable of coming together to remedy their common problems.

Foremost, Chicago Avenue offered an escape from domestic discord. When tempers flared at home and parents screamed, kids bolted for the street. When dad got hopped up on Old Style beer after work and mom chain-smoked Dorals in the corner, and the babies wouldn't stop screaming and the third notice on the electricity bill threatened prolonged darkness and there was no retreat and no recourse, Chicago Avenue was a constant. And when dad toiled away as a city maintenance hand, working through rain and sleet and snow and through parent–teacher conferences and stickball games, and when mom was suffering from a heart condition and her lethargic body could not keep up with everyone's comings and goings, the street marauders became a substitute family. These were the groups that welcomed a troubled kid as one of their own. Strife was the binding tie. No matter the harsh realities of home life, there was always a likeminded and like-skinned group of teenagers who understood family friction. They chose their own fate as a gang, and their booty resulted from their own labor. They were a fraternal order with their own initiation rites, their own code of conduct, and their own support system. When a kid was having trouble at home, the gang offered sweet salvation, or so it seemed.

The gangs were self-contained. They preyed on unaffiliated teens like vultures circling fresh carrion, but they didn't want someone to join if he wasn't willing to commit. Gangs were looking for teens with heart who were willing to prove themselves to join and even abandon lifelong friends as they crossed over to "the lifestyle." Someone who wanted in with a gang had to show how down he was. Only then would the gang give him a chance to pledge, as it were. Good deeds don't go unrewarded, and the street code forces crews to honor and return favors, even when the reciprocation has the potential to turn violent or deadly.

The Harrison Gents were one gang among many on Chicago's bandit-ridden West and South Sides. They were daredevils. Renegades. Murderers. Guys who would knife a passerby for fifty cents. They were feared by the neighborhood adults yet revered by many Wells High School teenagers. The students were mostly minorities, and many of the Mexican members came from undocumented immigrant households. They lived a secret life. On the street and in school, they were American, touting stylish urban fashions like Starter jackets and Air Jordans. They listened to rap music.

But messing up on the street and getting mixed up with the authorities brought heat on the whole family. If one got pinched, all got pinched. West Side kids felt alone in the world, afraid to go to their folks—assuming they were around and they cared—with their fears. Moms could offer words of encouragement, but the kids had to stay under the public radar. As for dreams, how big could they be? Each new day brought new risk, not new hope. All they could wish for was to be left alone. Becoming a doctor or a lawyer or a professional athlete was far-fetched for immigrant kids. What happens to a dream deferred? On the West Side, it dries up.

Once a teenager curried favor with the gang and the brothers decided that they wanted him as a member, a metamorphosis took place. His free time became gang time. He began respecting imposed boundaries—don't go south of Chicago Avenue on Damen; avoid

Humboldt Park. When the gang higher-ups deemed him ready for full membership and he had proved his commitment to the gang's mission—whatever it was—initiation rites commenced.

Different gangs had different criteria for new members. Some, like the Two Two Boys and Vice Lords, observed a practice known as "jumping" someone in. The initiate arrived at a designated spot like an alley or an abandoned building, unarmed, and was surrounded by the waiting brothers. They formed a circle around him and several members entered the center. Some words of encouragement were spoken, more Machiavelli than Lombardi, an explanation about how that kid was about to become an associate of a select crew, and how the gang comes before all else: before family, community, God.

Then they beat the teen bloody. It was usually three or more on one and they beat him into their criminal family. This brutal right of passage was an act that all new initiates had in common. Taking a severe beating and having the battle scars to show for it was a way for these kids to prove their bravado, their heart.

Some gangs required an act of burglary or vandalism to join, while others put teens to the ultimate test. Jimmy T wanted to prove to the Vice Lords that he was hard. He was a marked behemoth with scores of tattoos covering his bulging biceps. His eyes were deeply set and when he stared, the dark brown irises swam in the bloodshot whites. In 1992, when Jimmy T was sixteen, the gang instructed him to demonstrate his devotion.

"O.K., it was like this," he told *Time* magazine. "They told me, 'Time to put some work in for your homies. Here's the gun. There's the car. Get up and go, boy.'" Translation: go snuff out some rival gang bangers. He hesitated, as killing another young man in cold blood was significantly more serious than the vandalism and schoolyard fights he'd previously been engaged in for the gang. In the past, his lawless ways were for show. The big, tough gangster was more like a bleary-eyed sheep; like an attention-starved child trying to please his parents. Jimmy T just wanted to impress the gang. The prospect of murder, however, was like an electric jolt to his consciousness. It plunged Jimmy T into the West Side's version of a midlife crisis.

He was so afraid of reprisals if he didn't do what the Vice Lords asked, though, that he pulled together what shards of moxie he could muster, got high, and loaded his TEC-9 handgun. He drove around the West Side streets in a stolen Honda Prelude looking for targets. He rode past his high school, past the park he played in as a kid. One street later, he was behind enemy lines. Jimmy T doggedly observed the speed limits and stalled for time. He was trying to rationalize his actions prior to the moment of truth. "I'm thinking, ohhh, man, this sain't for me. I'm just tired of this gang banging, and I'm like, real scared," he told *Time*.

But the pressure got to him. Jimmy T rolled up to a random group of teenagers in enemy territory—kids who may or may not have been rival gangsters—and fired several 9 millimeter rounds into the unassuming crowd. He wounded three people.

As trying as it was to join a gang, it was doubly hard to leave. When you're a Jet, you're a Jet, all the way—Calling it quits was all but impossible for active members. If a gangster stopped showing up for meetings or refused to hang out with his brethren, some gangs issued a BOS order (beat on sight). The Latin Lovers were more gracious: They at least gave the turncoat a fighting chance, though the ex-member usually left the fight via ambulance or black body bag.

The Latin Lovers were one of the West Side's more vicious Mexican gangs. They battled for turf with the Harrison Gents from time to time, but on the whole, the Lovers respected the Gents territory, and vice versa.

Keith S. informed the Latin Lovers in 1991 that he'd had enough, that his lawlessness had finally run its course. The gang set up a de-initiation ceremony for midnight in the shadows of a local park. Much as the Two Two Boys jumped new members in, the Latin Lovers jumped them out. Keith S. would have to fight four other members—guys he used to break bread with and who swore they'd stick by his side no matter the circumstances—for three minutes. But the gang didn't need that much time. The fifteen-year-old buckled after one minute and then slipped into a coma that lasted fifty-eight days. There was no community uproar. West Side parents didn't scream bloody murder, and school principals didn't coordinate antigang task forces. Keith S. was just another hoodlum who got what he had coming.

Then there was the collateral damage gangs caused. Steven Watts toed the line throughout high school. Staying out of the gangs wasn't easy; life would have had fewer physical confrontations and bullying had he followed his friends and joined up. He lived in a violent and gang-riddled section of Chicago's South Side and was a star football player who had recently received a full athletic scholarship to Iowa State University.

Steven was walking home from a high school dance one night when a carload of gang bangers spotted him and mistook him for a rival gangster. They opened fire.

Steven was a fast runner—one of Julian High School's fastest—but not fast enough. A bullet lodged in his spine. By the time an ambulance arrived and rushed him to the hospital, Steven Watts was DOA.

Gangs on Chicago's streets helped bring down the community. The threat of turf wars and drive-by shootings and the muggings and robberies contributed to local businesses boarding up and fleeing the neighborhood. Gangs were the main reason why glass stayed broken and strewn about the street; why flowers were never planted in the spring; why as many students dropped out of high school as graduated. Getting messed up with the Harrison Gents made Gabriel's boxing future take a dramatic and harrowing turn for the worse, and it ended his formal education.

The Harrison Gents (Gentlemen) was founded by neighborhood toughs from Harrison Street and Chicago Avenue in the mid-1980s. Their call sign was a skeleton wearing a top hat and holding a cane.

At first the gang functioned as a social club. Members got together and smoked weed, passed time in each other's company, and stayed up all night when there was no reason to go home. As Chicago's gang population grew, the Harrison Gents assumed a thuggish persona. They began by marking up their territory with gang graffiti. Then they marked up their skin. Eventually they graduated to robbing the local population, fighting, and selling drugs.

Like many Hispanic kids on the West Side, Gabriel Sandoval discovered the gang when he was sixteen years old. He was known around the neighborhood as "the boxer," a bon mot that eventually served as his gang alias. Gabriel was a standout athlete at Wells High School. His pugilistic talents were known on the schoolyard and throughout the neighborhood. The boxer had friends in the predominantly Latin street gang long before he joined. They hung out on Harrison Street, not far from Wells High School and the Matador Gym. The gang did not come calling Gabriel; he sought them out.

Gang culture was socially cool. Gangsta rap emerged on the national scene with the 1988 release of N.W.A.'s "Straight Outta Compton." The rap group spoke of urban blight and gang warfare in Compton, near Los Angeles, although they could just as easily have been talking about the Bronx or East Cleveland or Chicago's West Side. Their lyrics hit home for urban kids. "When somethin' happens in South Central, nothin' happens," said lyricist Ice Cube. "It's just another nigga dead."

N.W.A. sang of casual sex and killing cops, of living by the gun and dying by the bullets. And city kids everywhere bought it. The Harrison Gents were inspired by N.W.A. and other artists of the time like Ice T and the Ghetto Boys. The Harrison Gents inspired fear in everyone in the neighborhood, an emotion that masqueraded on the streets as respect. They openly smoked marijuana and dealt crack. They got girls by talking like rappers. Gabriel wanted desperately to be one of them.

As he was making his way to the gym one day after school, he observed one of his Harrison Gents buddies getting his ass kicked in a street fight. The sixteen-year-old boxer intervened and rescued his friend, beating up the rival gangster in the process. He was instantly accepted into the Harrison Gents. Gabriel's boxing prowess and name recognition in the neighborhood made him a good catch for a street gang. Of course the gangs didn't want him to know this. They treated Gabriel like any other member so the respect wouldn't go to his head, except when it came to initiation.

Like the Two Two Boys, Harrison Gents jumped new members into the gang. The odds of how many guys would fight the prospect depended on the physical size of the kid and on how badly he wanted to be in the gang. Gabriel, however, was not jumped in, most likely because he could have handled himself against the odds. The Gents might beat him down en masse, but they knew that a few would get severely beaten in the process.

He began hanging out with the gangsters outside of school. Gabriel continued to go to the Matador Gym and train, but he started slacking in the ring. Sometimes he'd bring fellow gang bangers to the gym. They'd sit in the corner and make comments about the other fighters: this one had no talent, that one was a pussy. The Harrison Gents never dared enter the ring themselves; to do so would result in public humiliation.

Tom O'Shea did not notice Gabriel's metamorphosis from ring fighter to street fighter because the boxer continued to work out at the Matador Gym and listened to O'Shea's advice. But Sean Curtin knew that something was wrong even before Gabriel started bringing his hoodlum friends to the gym.

Curtin used to work with gangsters in a Big Brothers–type program. He could sniff out a gang banger. They were a different mold from other teens. Curtin observed Gabriel riding in cars around the neighborhood with some of the known thugs, and then he fingered the criminals when they accompanied Gabriel to the gym as much by their gang colors and appearance as by their surly demeanor. Although O'Shea suspected nothing, Curtin noticed that Gabriel's ring work was off. The trainer used to spar with the boxers, sometimes slipping a hard counterjab to the chin to let them know he was there—that a harder, more precise shot was in store for them if they lost their concentration in the ring. After Gabriel started hanging out with the Gents, Curtin was tattooing him with more hard rights than usual.

He also came down harder on Gabriel than he had in the past. His facial expressions became sterner, and he developed a catch in his voice. But Curtin was not about to tell Gabriel how to live his life. He wasn't his father; he had met Gabriel's father and knew Jesus was a stand-up guy. The boy was grounded enough, the trainer thought, to outgrow those bastards and focus on his boxing. Hopefully the gang was a phase. Gabriel was well aware, he assumed, that he had a future in this sport as a professional.

September 25, 1990, was a particularly nippy Tuesday, though the skies were cloudless and bright. Good September weather for Chicago. The dry cold made the skin crackle, as the weather had been warm and sunny just three weeks earlier. The sun made Chicago Avenue appear misleadingly warm, and students bided their time in the classrooms until the final bell and freedom.

Wells High School had just let out for the day, and the seventeen-year-old boxer was making his way down Chicago Avenue toward Harrison Street to hang out with the gang. He was in fine spirits because of the clear weather. Some days he took the bus to and from school, but today looked too nice. He watched the shadows cast by neighboring buildings from his desk in English class and couldn't wait to go outside. Shadows meant that there was sunlight somewhere in the city. Gabriel figured he'd get some fresh air and stretch his legs after school.

He carried his schoolbooks home with the intent of doing home-work that night. Despite his growing involvement with the Harrison Gents, Gabriel maintained decent grades at Wells. The A's slipped to B's, and the B's to C's, but he wasn't failing any classes. A C student was like a Rhodes scholar in a street gang.

His plan was to sit around with his boys, shoot the shit, and head over to the Matador Gym at 4:00 P.M. and get in a good hour and a half workout before returning home for supper. On the way, Gabriel ran into fellow gang members Bubba and Saito. They were dressed in heavy black hooded sweatshirts and wore thick down coats and baggy black pants. Gabriel wore a hooded sweatshirt, a denim jacket, and his only pair of sneakers. Bubba and Saito had their hoods pulled up over their heads and low enough over their eyes that Gabriel didn't see them coming; they saw him first.

"Yo, Boxer, come over here," Saito called.

Gabriel walked over to the two boys and they exchanged secret handshakes. The duo seemed a little quieter than normal, a little too reserved. Saito carried an old black umbrella, the kind available for a few dollars at the local bodegas. "What you got that here for?" Gabriel asked, as there wasn't a cloud in the sky.

"Check it out," Saito replied. He pulled the polyester fabric open to reveal the muzzle of a sawed-off shotgun. The twin barrels looked like two black eyes peering from within. Gabriel was surprised but not shocked. He had seen his share of guns, even though he'd never fired one. Both Bubba and Saito acted hard, like having that weapon made them invincible. They started talking tough, about how they were going to knock off Edmar's Grocery Store on Chicago Avenue.

"Man, they got a shitload of money in there," Bubba said. "We hit that and we'll be set." Gabriel asked how they planned to do the robbery. Bubba explained that they had stolen a van earlier and he'd be the getaway man. He'd be sitting in front of the store with the engine running. Saito would be the gunman and make whoever was behind the courtesy desk empty the safe into a paper sack. The two didn't mention that they were apprehensive about pulling the caper off in broad daylight. They wanted a third man to stand sentry while Saito did the talking. Gabriel seemed like a perfect choice. He was strong and both gangsters knew the kid had balls. If some customer tried to be John Wayne, the boxer could kick his ass and Saito wouldn't have to discharge his weapon.

"This is gonna be easy," Saito said. "We'll be in and out. You should come along, Boxer. All's you got to do is watch my back, make sure fools don't start trippin'. And then we'll be rich, *ese*. We'll be set up."

Since joining the gang, Gabriel had shoplifted sodas and chips and he smoked marijuana, like the other members. This, however, seemed way different. Saito was talking about a truly violent crime. Armed robbery was nothing to sneeze at. All three teens knew Harrison Gents who'd been sent up for the same crime. But Saito made it sound easy. He spoke with such confidence that Gabriel figured this was the sort of thing he should be begging for a piece of. He thought he must be pretty cool if these guys were asking him to help. "Let's do this thing, Boxer," Bubba said firmly. "Let's get ours."

The adrenaline pumped through the boxer and caused his heart to pound and his chest to hurt. Gabriel was daunted by what he was thinking of doing, but hell, it would only take a matter of minutes. And these guys whom he revered would think he's the baddest. When it was all over, they'd probably tell everyone about how tough Sandoval was. How brave. So Gabriel agreed to go along, his apprehension out-weighed by the excitement of the plan.

Bubba and Saito led the boxer to a delivery van they'd stolen earlier that day. Inside were spare clothes to put on after the holdup and a payload full of fresh bread. The inside smelled pleasant, like a bakery.

The target, Edmar's, was a sprawling storefront with a slew of floor-to-ceiling windows facing Chicago Avenue, and it was relatively quiet at that time of day. There was no view, though, as advertisements for cheap produce and discounted meat were plastered all over the glass. Bubba and Saito had cased the joint earlier. The store's courtesy desk was closest to the front door, making it the closest target because the store's registers were off to the side and set some 20 feet back from the door. Saito's plan was to stick up the person at the courtesy desk and demand that they empty the safe under the counter. If the employee didn't know the combination, then he or she was to empty the register behind the desk. Saito figured if he spoke harshly enough and threatened to use the gun, there shouldn't be a problem. If he needed to use the gun, he could (and would). But he really hoped it wouldn't get to that point.

As the three drove to the store, Bubba and Saito briefed the boxer on what he was to do. Eyes. That's what Saito needed. Keep an eye on everyone in that store. There was probably a button someone would press to automatically call the cops, but they wouldn't be in there long enough for the Chicago Police Department to mobilize. Make sure no one snuck up from behind or, worse, pulled their own piece.

They arrived at the grocery store in the stolen delivery van. Bubba left the engine running. They all had the hoods of their sweatshirts pulled up over their heads. "You ready, Boxer?" Saito asked, shooting a menacing look at Gabriel, as if to say, "You better not fail me!" Gabriel just nodded. "All right. Let's go!" Saito opened the sliding door from the inside and emerged from the van with the sawed-off shotgun—N.W.A.'s weapon of choice—tucked inside the umbrella. Gabriel followed him out and slammed the door closed. His blood was pumping loud enough that he could hear it flowing in his ears. Shock was beginning to set in.

They walked rapidly into the store and made a beeline for the store's courtesy desk. A middle-aged woman stood there by herself. Saito pulled the gun out from the umbrella and pointed it at the lady's head. Her eyes widened and she began to breathe rapidly.

"Empty the fucking safe," Saito said in a level but forceful voice. She complied immediately, sticking stacks of money in a paper sack. Saito kept his eyes trained on her, assuming that the boxer was doing his job and watching his back. But Gabriel was somewhere else. He didn't panic, though he didn't exactly go to great lengths to watch the customers and employees, either. He stood there like a deer in headlights, too dazed to move.

The scene was surreal to him. Customers were going about their shopping, and the people at the checkout counter as well as the shoppers in the aisles seemingly had no idea what was going on. Everyone was calm and unsuspecting in the store's interior while Saito had a loaded sawed-off shotgun aimed at some poor woman's head. She finished loading the bag and placed it on the counter, too afraid to speak. Saito grabbed the loot, took five steps to his right, and was halfway to the getaway van. Gabriel gathered himself and trotted after the gunman. Saito threw open the sliding side door and jumped as far in as he could. Gabriel didn't have a chance to slide the door shut before Bubba threw it in gear and tore out of there.

The streets were starting to fill with rush hour traffic. Bubba made a couple of crafty turns, used the side streets like secret passageways, and maneuvered the stolen van onto a crowded Chicago thoroughfare. In the far distance, the three could hear police sirens, but they were faint and getting fainter. They'd made it. Bubba and Saito whooped it up in the van when they were sure the sirens weren't headed in their direction. The boxer forced a smile. He tried to act just as euphoric as his partners in crime even though inside, his conscience was already hard at work. He could still see the lady's eyes and the fear on her face. The poor thing was absolutely terrified, and she wouldn't recover from that double-barrel shotgun in her mug anytime soon.

They parked in a vacant lot miles from the crime scene and counted their score: $3,600. The money was divided up on the spot: Bubba thought it best to split it right away in case the authorities came looking for it. Each participant received $1,200.

Gabriel told the guys he needed to get to the gym or the trainers might suspect something. The guys agreed and he was dropped off about a block away. The boxer walked in meekly with his head lowered. He went into the locker room and changed, stowed his gym bag—now $1,200 more valuable—and then emerged and jumped in the practice ring, where Curtin stood waiting.

He trained that day, dutifully obeying his coach but not punching very hard. Nor were his movements particularly sharp. Curtin knew something was wrong immediately, though he said nothing. Gabriel could come to him if he needed to talk. And indeed he did, though not for another week and a half, and not until he had spent the robbery money on clothes and boxing equipment.

Both the trainer and the boxer were changing in the locker room after their workout one day. All of a sudden, Gabriel plopped down onto the bench and stared vacantly at the floor. Curtin finally spoke up.

"What's wrong with you, kid?" the trainer asked. Gabriel continued to stare down while he wrestled with his secret. His conscience was killing him. Feelings of guilt and remorse pushed out all other thoughts. He needed to tell someone.

"I can't believe what I did last week," he finally said. Curtin sat down on the bench next to his boxer and leaned his head in close.

"What did you do, Gabriel?" Curtin queried softly but firmly.

"I helped rob Edmar's."

The trainer put a foot up on the bench and grabbed his knee. He let out an exasperated sigh and shook his head. Sean Curtin had been around the streets and around street kids way too long to mince words and feelings. His immediate thought was that he should take this seventeen-year-old to O'Hare and stick him on a plane to Mexico. At least down there the kid could put some distance between himself and the gang while he waited for this thing to blow over. Perhaps after time passed and he got his head screwed back on straight, the boxer could sneak back into the country and resume training. But that's not what came out of the coach's mouth. He knew better than to encourage kids to run from their problems. Sean Curtin spoke in harsh truths.

"Well, what are you going to do now that you're going to jail?" Curtin asked sarcastically. "Because if you keep this shit up, that's exactly where you're heading." A few tears slid down Gabriel's cheeks. He'd let Curtin down, and that pained him as much as the crime itself. The trainer was not about to comfort the boxer. He felt horrible for the kid and wished he could tell him that everything would be all right, but he was foremost a trainer. A coach. He didn't wish jail time on the seventeen-year-old, and he would do everything in his power to help his charge, but at that very moment, he left Gabriel alone to stew in shame. And the boxer did just that.

Gabriel went home that night and tried to avoid his family. He'd been quiet since the robbery, mostly speaking when spoken to. But coming clean to Curtin somehow made the robbery real again, like it had just happened. He was ashamed and didn't want everyone to start asking what was wrong with him. Their lives were hard enough without knowing that the eldest son had just committed a violent crime.

He made it through dinner and went to bed, where he slept scared. The next day he took the bus to school. Wells High was only a few blocks from Edmar's Grocery Store. Gabriel's stomach dropped when the school bus rumbled past the crime scene. Each passing school day, the grocery store was a shadowy reminder of his lawlessness. He tried not to look at it, but there it was. Every day. In his neighborhood.

He got off the bus and made his way into school. He put most of his books in his locker and took one to his criminal justice class. Chicago police arrived at Wells two hours later, pulled the seventeen-year-old out of his criminal justice class and arrested him in the hall-way. Bubba and Saito had already been picked up. Someone had ratted them out.

The school called the Sandoval home, and Rosario Sandoval re-ceived the information in disbelief. She did not know what to do, so she phoned the Chicago Housing Authority and asked to speak with her husband. Jesus answered the phone and tried to calm his wife, who was hyperventilating as she spoke. He managed to discern that Gabriel was in jail. He told her to relax: he was sure it was minor and their son would be home in no time. The U.S. justice system, he assured her, was much more sophisticated than Mexico's.

After work, Jesus went to the local precinct to inquire about his son. The police said there was no Gabriel Sandoval in their jail and sent him to a different station. They were just as rude to him as they were to other people inquiring about their loved ones. They treated him indifferently because he was just another Mexican inquiring about jailed kin.

Jesus was becoming concerned. At the next station, the cops were overly rude. The watch commander said Gabriel wasn't there either. Jesus pleaded in his remedial English with the officer, beseeching him to find out where his son was. A detective overheard the exchange and approached Jesus. He asked the maintenance man if he knew what armed robbery was. Jesus said no.

"It means he took a gun and robbed a store," the detective said.

"What?" Jesus said, shocked and wide-eyed. "No. Not Gabriel." But the detective was insistent. He did not know where Gabriel was moved to, but he warned the boy's father that he was in serious trouble.

Jesus returned home worried. No one was helping him, and his knowledge of the law and of the American criminal justice system was nil. All he was certain of was that jail was no place for his boy.

Jesus knew one other family in the neighborhood where the man was a police officer, and he caught up with the cop two nights later. The officer was surprised to see Jesus and was doubly surprised at how distraught the man was. Jesus begged him to help locate Gabriel. The neighbor made a call and came back with grim news: the boxer was in Cook County Jail, charged with aggravated armed robbery.

The Sandovals couldn't sleep that night. Jesus and Rosario sat in the kitchen and said little until 8:00 A.M., when they left the house and rushed downtown to see their son.

3

Promises

The Sandoval family crowded the visitor's room at Cook County Jail on October 6, 1990. They waited anxiously for the first glimpse of their son in three days. Jesus and Rosario Sandoval held each other as they sat on steel benches attached to a steel table, all anchored to the floor. Cook County Jail was a congested mess.

Hundreds of families waited to spend an hour with their incarcerated loved ones. They shuffled fretfully, and they clamored and bellowed their discontent. Their voices resounded throughout the cavernous visiting room.

Lidia, 15, and Jimmy, 7, sat quietly, too scared to say boo. All they saw were tempers and furrowed foreheads—and those were of the visitors.

Deep inside the CCJ vestibules, hidden from the congregating visitors behind several feet of concrete, three electronically controlled steel doors, and a host of armed guards, were more than 8,000 of Chicago's worst criminals. They were corralled into cells with too many other bodies. They represented all classes, though the vast majority came from streets like the one Gabriel Sandoval hailed from.

CCJ guards made their rounds during visiting days and called out inmates with waiting guests. After three days in the joint—the longest three days of Gabriel's life—the boxer was relieved to hear that he had visitors. While Jesus and Rosario were frantically trying to track down their son, Gabriel himself was frantic because he had no way of alerting his parents to his whereabouts. He was too afraid of the guards to ask for his proverbial one phone call. City kids grew up wary of the law. Cops didn't patrol their neighborhoods out of goodwill. They came to haul kids in. Anyone with a badge and a gun was trouble.

Gabriel was placed in a cell with about ten men, though the numbers fluctuated as inmates were recycled throughout the jail. He buddied up with some Hispanics who were down with the Harrison Gents, which was a lucky break for Gabriel. He was mystified by his surroundings, and the last thing he needed was an intergang conflict during his first few days in the stir. Mexican children are raised to be respectful of their parents, and his mind was busy worrying about his family. The Mexicans among the Harrison Gents were exceptions to that rule, but Gabriel never back-talked Jesus and Rosario. Even with his boxing background, he feared his father. Jesus was stern and fair. He rarely laid a hand on his son while Gabriel was growing up. There were the occasional spankings, but those were meant strictly as a disciplinary measure and not done out of malice.

Mostly, Gabriel didn't want to let his old man down. He feared that his hardworking father was about to get into trouble because of his own stupid crime. His parents—and especially his father—were trying so hard to live out the American dream and make it into a reality for their children. They were on their way to becoming naturalized American citizens, thanks to Ronald Reagan's Immigration Reform and Control Act of 1986 that allowed illegal immigrants to receive permanent residency status as long as they could meet specific requirements. With their paperwork already in the system, the Sandovals had been granted temporary status in 1987. Gabriel worried that his crime would affect their residency applications or that the city might fire his father for having a criminal son.

The imagination works overtime in jail, and the human mind focuses on doomsday scenarios. Factor in Cook County Jail's 3,000 corrections officers, sworn to maintain and preserve order (translation: keep the cons in line), and the wandering mind can convince the soul of damn near anything.

A guard called out "Sandoval" while reading a list of inmate names who had visitors. A feeling of joy momentarily engulfed the seventeen-year-old. Papa had come. He'd set everything straight. He'd tell his son not to worry; everything's gonna be all right; I'll have you out in no time.

Gabriel followed a parade of inmates single file down a whitewashed corridor to holding cages. Prisoners were frisked and then stripped naked so the corrections officer could do a full body search for weapons and contraband. They had to open their mouths and stick out their tongues and then lift them to the roof of their mouths so COs could look for weapons, like razor blades or safety pins. Then they had to turn and face the wall, bend over and grab their ankles so guards could make sure they weren't smuggling illegal imports in their rectums. Finally the inmates put on their dull beige jumpsuits with CCJ stenciled across the back in block letters.

Gabriel donned a boiler suit that was too big for his slender frame. He swam in the garment, looking more like a little kid in his father's city uniform than a violent accused criminal in the Illinois Department of Corrections. He approached the waiting area and began to tremble. How could he look his father in the eye in those surroundings? And his mother: she already had health problems. What would she think when she saw her oldest child wearing prison garb? These thoughts weighed heavily and Gabriel used every ounce of facial strength he had to hold back the tears and to swallow the lump in his throat.

He entered the visitors room where his distraught mother and father stood to receive their boy. Rosario grabbed him first and hugged him tight. She began to sob deeply on his shoulder, her plump tears soaking into the beige jumpsuit and leaving a dark circle around his shoulder. Gabriel held her close and yearned to cry with her. His insides burned with an inexplicable tingling heat. The mucus he tried so hard to keep in his nose now ran down his throat and choked him up. Gabriel gently pushed his mother off him. He didn't want her touch to end, but he knew that the longer he remained in her warm embrace, the weaker he became; he had to hold it together for her sake and his own.

Jesus Sandoval took his son in his arms and hugged him firmly and quickly. Papa knew better than to have a roomful of suspected criminals observing a sappy family reunion. He cried with his wife the night before, but in Gabriel's presence, he had to remain strong. Lidia and Jimmy greeted their brother apprehensively. They didn't know how to act.

Gabriel described to his parents the events that landed him in the joint. He spared no details about how a lapse of reason was to blame— he never intended to hurt anyone. But he read on their faces how deeply hurt they were. The boxer had been in Cook County Jail for only three days, but already he noticed the physical and psychological effects on his mother. He figured she'd get worse the longer he was there.

He explained to his parents that a judge had arraigned him the day before, that the judge said he stood accused of armed robbery and asked him how he pleaded, guilty or not guilty. He told the judge that he was guilty. Gabriel spoke meekly and bowed his head slightly before the judge. The judge, however, didn't budge. Gabriel was issued a public defender and assigned a sentencing date for eight months from that day. Bond was set at $70,000. Gabriel needed to come up with 10 percent, or $7,000, to stay out of jail until his court date. To the seventeen-year-old, that figure might as well have been $7 million. Even if he had not spent his share of the robbery money, there was no way he could have made up the difference.

Jesus Sandoval had a solution. He had recently bought his family a home on Rice Street on the West Side for $30,000. Jesus could take out another mortgage or put his house down as collateral for his son's bond. The Sandovals didn't understand how bond worked, how you put up 10 percent of the established bond, and that it's returned after the suspect stands trial or is sentenced. Jesus thought it meant he'd have to sell his house and the money would be gone.

As Papa pledged his help, Gabriel's face became animated. He could go home, back to his mother's authentic cooking and to play cops and robbers with Jimmy. He could go back to the Matador Gym and square himself with Sean Curtin and Tom O'Shea. Best of all, he could leave that awful Cook County dungeon and its moldering interior and piss-smelling cells.

Gabriel read his father's expression. Indeed, Jesus Sandoval was ready and willing to trade in his taxing hours spent working for the city in some of Chicago's roughest housing projects so that his son could have, at the very least, eight more months of freedom. Gabriel was moved that his father was willing to sacrifice so much for him. His father's gesture separated him from the other inmates and fellow gang bangers. The Sandoval family might have come to America with nothing, but they had an abundance of love for each other.

He briefly weighed the pros and cons of using his father's house to post bail. Despite the ghastly sounds, sights, and smells all around him in CCJ, Gabriel could not let his father do this. Jesus Sandoval risked his life to bring the family to the United States. He swam the Rio Grande too many times to give everything up. The old man spent his working hours cleaning up other people's shit so that Gabriel wouldn't have to later in life. The boxer was devoting his life to the sweet science, and Jesus Sandoval worked doubly hard so that his son could stay in the gym and refine his skills.

"Papa, thank you," the boy said above the reverberating voices in the visiting room. "I know you'd do anything for me. But this is my crime. I screwed up. I messed with the wrong crowd. I was there with the guys in the grocery store. I want to be a man and take my punishment like a man, so I won't let you throw all your hard work away on my crime."

Jesus Sandoval shook his head while his son spoke, awaiting his chance to reply. "You are a man, *mijo*," he said, putting a hand on the back of his boy's neck. "You already confessed. You owned up to your role. But Gabi, eight months until the court date—that's too much time."

"I can handle myself, Papa. I come from a good bloodline," Gabriel replied. "It won't be that bad. I didn't really do anything. I just stood there. I don't think I'll get a big sentence."

Neither did the court-appointed defense attorney. Gabriel's friends had been in trouble before, but he'd never been arrested. He had decent grades, which his attorney said would bode well with the judge, as it would demonstrate that he was a dedicated student and not someone who used the city's schools as a host body for parasitic gang banging activity. He was a promising boxer, the pride of his neighborhood.

True boxing aficionados often talked about the time Gabriel was fifteen and fought a former prisoner-turned-boxer at the Golden Gloves regional tournament. The guy was ten years older but Gabi took him to school. And they often talked about the fight between Gabriel and Raul Diaz at a suburban Chicago country club. Curtin and O'Shea arranged an amateur fight for their boy against a fellow 119 pounder. The country club hosted the fight as a cheap thrill for the rich golfers. When Gabriel showed up, there was no one at 119 or at 126 pounds for him to fight. But he really wanted to fight. The only match near his weight class was up at 136.

Raul Diaz was a natural 136-pound fighter who outweighed his younger opponent by seventeen pounds. Gabriel told Curtin that he wanted to fight Diaz, and Curtin let him get in the ring because of the supreme confidence he had in the rising star. The fight was scheduled for three rounds. The sauced, rich golfers laughed at Gabriel as he entered the ring. He was so small compared to Diaz, who chuckled when Gabriel started to stare him down from across the ring. When the bell rang, the smaller Sandoval was the aggressor. He put so much pressure on Diaz that the older, heavier boxer spent all three minutes fighting off the ropes. Round two was more of the same, and Gabriel hammered away, never stopping for moment. In the third round, Diaz started tying up his opponent and leaning on him. The weight of his bigger body took strength out of Gabriel's legs, and the tired 119 pounder started getting belted around. But he survived the round and racked up enough points in the first two rounds to win the fight. The moment was as sobering for Raul Diaz as it was for the rich golfers.

This fresh-faced kid, the court-appointed attorney said, would certainly convince the judge that the court's time would be better spent pursuing real gangsters. Mostly the defense was banking on the fact that Gabriel was a first-time offender and a juvenile. The court usually showed leniency in those situations. He might get a lot of community service and maybe a year in juvenile hall to scare him straight. And of course he'd be on probation for the next five to seven years. But the court would probably not unleash its full wrath on a first-time juvie. At least that's what the court-appointed defense attorney thought.

———

Cook County Jail was a jumbled, overcrowded mess in 1990 and 1991, thanks in large part to the soaring murder rate. In 1990 and 1991, Chicago set a record for murders in two consecutive years with more than 1,200. Police superintendent LeRoy Martin attributed that figure to increased street violence and stepped-up gang activity. Mayor Richard M. Daley tried to pass the buck, attributing Chicago's woes on the federal government's failure to stop drugs and illegal aliens on the Mexican-U.S. border. In essence, Mayor Daley said that undocumented Mexican immigrants equal drugs, and drugs equal crime. During that two-year period, Chicago saw more than 32,000 burglaries and thefts. Regardless of who was at fault, Cook County Jail housed the suspects.

An austere structure, it held twice as many bodies as it was designed to, under deplorable conditions. In 1988 a U.S. District Court judge fined Cook County Jail for failing to address its overcrowding problem even though the top brass had been promising to do so since 1974. But the number of inmates was skyrocketing and administrators could only pay the fines and watch the jail burst at the seams. More rooms and more bars were the only answers to the congestion question. However, as is typically the case with overcrowded prisons, the need to expand butted up against budget constraints.

Gabriel waited for his court date in that problematic prison. He tried to keep his head down and stay off the radar of prison officials and other inmates. To screw up in Cook County Jail was to screw yourself. Judges gladly tacked time onto sentences of inmates who were discipline problems. For inmates facing long sentences, that did not matter. Cook County Jail was one rough joint and inmates were more concerned with earning other prisoners' respect than following rules.

From the outside, it looked clean and orderly. Four stories of white concrete and two rows of chain-link fence topped with razor wire formed the perimeter. Four corner guard towers monitored all outside activity. The interior was another story. Bare white walls were anything but. Graffiti and dirt buildup made the ramparts look menacing. The bars were rusted and the cells were crowded.

CCJ was at 131 percent capacity, and over 1,100 of the detainees were accused of murder: they'd end up at Stateville maximum security prison upon conviction. Roughly 2,000 inmates did not have cots. They slept on old, stained mattresses on the floor.

While the jail exceeded capacity, CCJ came under public scrutiny for another crisis. In the early 1990s, corrections officers and detectives reportedly used dishonest tactics when trying to extract information from suspects. The county was accused of employing crooked cops, and Cook County Jail corrections officers would beat statements out of their detainees. In Area Four on Chicago's West Side, which included Gabriel's stomping grounds on Chicago Avenue, cops made indiscriminate arrests.

Police officers and detectives had a tough job. Mayor Daley wanted a crackdown on city street violence, and the Chicago Police Department responded by increasing patrols and hauling in more suspects for questioning. There was a thin line between tough questioning and brutality. Many suspects accused their interrogators of being overly rough with them, threatening severe bodily harm if they didn't "confess" to whatever they were being charged with, and in some cases being severely beaten. Two years before Gabriel found himself sitting in the clink, the city of Chicago paid almost $160,000 to settle lawsuits brought by four men alleging they'd been assaulted during questioning.

Guys like Detective Kriston Kato brought heat down on the force. Between 1988 and 1991, twenty-five criminal suspects testified in open court that Kato either threatened them with violence or actually beat them up if they didn't give the military veteran what he wanted. They accused the detective of keeping suspects up for nights on end, refusing to give them food or water, and punching and kicking them. "Detective Kato, for some reason known only to himself, uses physical abuse in order to obtain statements and close his cases," assistant public defender Anthony Eben Jr. told a judge during a March 1991 hearing. As a result, CCJ was full of angry, wronged suspects as well as legitimate criminals.

Chicago's criminal justice system was spiraling out of control when Gabriel confessed to aiding in the grocery store robbery. He was categorized as a violent gang member when he went in and was made to spend his eight months in a savage CCJ wing known on the inside as gladiator school. He was grouped with suspected murderers, rapists, and pedophiles. Luckily for him, there were other Harrison Gents in gladiator school. Gabriel posseed up with his gang brethren and managed to avoid inmate-on-inmate confrontations.

CCJ brass noticed the seventeen-year-old's model behavior. For a violent offender in gladiator school, he was rather disciplined in the joint. Gabriel was asked to partake in a Scared Straight–style program, counseling troubled teens and warning them what lay ahead if they didn't clean up their act on the street. He enjoyed this work. The boxer was still ashamed of his actions, but he channeled his self-pity by working with at-risk black and Mexican youths.

As his time in Cook County Jail slowly drew to a close and his sentencing neared, Gabriel had more frequent meetings with his public defender. His situation was looking grim, the PD said. Chicago authorities, under Mayor Daley, were instructed to come down hard on street gangs and crimes associated with gangs. Strike one.

Daley blamed Chicago street violence on a porous southern U.S. border and the steady stream of illegal immigrants flowing into the country. These immigrants, he said, brought drugs and crime to Chicagoland. Strike two.

And there was a 1984 law on the books that required juveniles fifteen years old and up to be tried as adults if they were accused of the most violent of crimes: murder, aggravated sexual assault, or armed robbery. Strike three.

The judge planned on sentencing Gabriel as an adult and the state was going to come after him with guns blazing. He was staring at a thirty-year prison sentence, which was essentially a life sentence to a seventeen-year-old who dreamed of a future as a professional athlete.

The lawyer advised Gabriel to take a deal if the prosecutor offered one. A deal is what the boxer got: in exchange for a guilty plea, the district attorney's office was willing to charge Gabriel with a lesser count of armed robbery. He would be required to serve seven and a half years in a level 3 high-medium security state penitentiary, though he would be eligible for parole in half that time. At the lawyer's urging, Gabriel agreed to the terms and spent one last night in Cook County Jail before getting transferred to the Illinois River Correctional Center.

Seven and a half years earlier, Gabriel had been living in his grandparents' humble flat in Delicias, Mexico, while his mother recovered from heart surgery. And that seemed like a lifetime ago. Back there, he walked the dusty streets and played with the kids his age at the *gimnasio municipal*. He couldn't even remember all the years in between; that's how long seven and a half years is.

Gabriel became overwhelmed at the prospect that he might not emerge from prison until he was twenty-four and a half years old. And what then? He hadn't finished high school, and his only job had been flipping burgers at McDonalds, which was honest labor but not much money. And he'd have a felony on his record. Gabriel made a pact with himself on that last night in Cook County Jail that he would use the seven plus years—or however long he would be in the joint—to get in top-flight condition and recommit to a life of boxing. He called his father collect from CCJ that night.

"Papa," Gabriel said to a surprised voice on the other end. "It won't be so bad. I'm going to make you a promise: When I get outta this place, I'm going to be the champion of the world. You'll see: I'll make you proud yet."

Illinois River Correctional Center in Canton, Illinois, was the type of prison violent criminals hoped to do time in. Built in 1989, the complex showed no wear and tear. The guard towers loomed but the grounds were handsome. The sprawling lawns and lush trees of Canton in May were the most green Gabriel had ever seen in one place.

Inside, all the cells were opened electronically by a central circuit. The walls were clean of graffiti and the toilets didn't look like someone spray painted them with urine and feces. Illinois River was the antithesis of the Cook County Jail.

Gabriel was grateful that he didn't get sentenced to Pontiac, Menard, or, worst of all, Stateville. In fact, the Illinois River Correctional Center paid the most attention to the inmates' welfare. In 1991 the complex spent over $20,000 per inmate annually, by far the highest total in the state, much to the taxpayer's chagrin.

The biggest gripe of inmates—the same complaint inmates all over the state had—was that the place was too crowded. Gabriel got a taste of that. Designed for just over 1,000 inmates, Illinois River had twice that number. Cells designed for single occupancy were doubled up. Gabriel shared one such cell with a fellow gangster—a member of the Latin Disciples. The two got along well.

Life inside was not without its provocations and dustups. Gangs roamed the corridors in packs. They were escorted by corrections officers, but the prisoners were in the majority. Gabriel found himself caught between gang rivalries. Mostly, though, he passed the time by hanging out with fellow Harrison Gents in their cells and smoking cigarettes and marijuana. For all the security measures prison wardens took to ensure order, drugs passed easily through their checkpoints. Due in part to the creative efforts of prison visitors and in part to crooked prison staff, drugs were currency in prison. The Harrison Gents would offer, say, protection for a nonaffiliated inmate in exchange for some reefer. Marijuana was a sweet escape for inmates. Getting high meant diverting the mind. A convict could smoke a joint and get lost inside his own head. If he had to do his time completely straight, the monotony of it all became maddening.

The boxer was just over a year in and was making good time. He spent his days working out in the prison yard and lounging with fellow gang members. High-medium security prisons afforded inmates that luxury. Around the time Gabriel was becoming regimented to a prison routine, a fight broke out between the Harrison Gents and a black gang. The boxer took some shots and dished out even more before corrections officers suppressed the insurrection. Members from both gangs—including Gabriel—were written up for prison rule infractions. In January 1992, when gangs caused problems in high-medium security prisons, they were given one warning. The next step was to ship them to a level 1 maximum security facility.

At the time, there was one prison in Illinois that housed the worst criminals: Stateville. Not long after his fighting infraction, Gabriel got caught smoking marijuana and received a one-way ticket to Joliet, Illinois.

4

Stateville

He was just a boy when he was incarcerated: young and dumb, small and scared. Gabriel came from a loving family of illegal though law-abiding residents who belonged to the growing Mexican population in inner-city Chicago. He was known around the neighborhood as a good kid, making good grades. But the Windy City's mean streets have a way of corrupting even motivated youth.

Gabriel Sandoval felt queasy: days like these made him nauseous. He ate two square meals earlier on, but the food wouldn't settle. The twenty-year-old was on high alert; his senses were heightened.

He monitored his surroundings at all times. Even at lights out, his sleep was nervous. Lots of things go bump in the night, especially when a thousand souls are packed into a fortified concrete structure with steel bars and filmed-over bulletproof windows, where every sound reverberates. The rustling of bed sheets and deep guttural snores resonated throughout the 150-yard-long, five-story structure. During the wee hours, when the majority of men were in deep repose, a dispute occasionally erupted between two "guests," and the sounds of hand-to-hand combat in close quarters traveled throughout the

building and roused the snoozing men. Scuffles broke out when someone's roommate snored too loud or the man on the upper bunk bed
tossed too much and the squeaking metal springs annoyed the man on
the lower bunk. These were eerie noises, though at least they were
predictable.

But lights out was still five hours away. Gabriel was biding time, trying to get through the day. On days like this—when Stateville maximum security prison was ghostly quiet and nary a voice was audible
among the thousand inmates in the Bravo Housing Unit, the thousand
in the Edward Housing Unit, and thousand more in F-House and
X-House—Gabriel knew that something was about to go down. They
all knew it: the cons, the guards, the administration. Somewhere in that
giant prison, gang linchpins decided to attack their rivals. It was to be a
glorious day of victory for some and a day of reckoning for others.

The air was electric. Currents of tension, coupled with anticipation
and fear, permeated the ninety-year-old concrete structure surrounded
by fifty-foot yellowing limestone walls. Stateville was an island of sorts.
It was tucked away from the freeway and situated on Route 53, a rural
road constructed to get prison personnel in and out. The road also
separated the prison from the community, so law-abiding citizens
wouldn't have to think about what went on there—out of sight, out of
mind. High walls and barbed wire, reinforced by a second tier of
barbed wire and buffered by acres of prison farmland gave the
compound a vast, hulking presence. As did the pervasive illumination.
When the sun wasn't providing natural light, scores of high-voltage
fluorescent floodlights cast an unnatural glow on all the buildings and
surrounding farmland. Corrections officers with night scopes and
binoculars, and others with shotguns and high-powered rifles, scanned
the grounds.

A noisy prison was a normal prison. Even at Stateville, a level 1 correctional compound designed to house the baddest of the bad, the
shouts and threats and general racket seemingly didn't disturb the prisoners. Three thousand souls crammed into eight-by-twelve cells,
stacked one atop the other for five stories, inevitably produce noise.

Factor out sound-dampening elements like carpets or drapes and factor in the reality that nearly all of the men were dangerous criminals and half of them were convicted murderers serving life sentences who didn't care about societal or institutional rules, and you have the perfect formula for violence.

Many of these men never finished junior high or high school, and their aptitude was forged on the street. The average inmate probably would not be able to spell "Stateville" were it not stenciled on his jumpsuit, but he could sniff out a soft target from a sniper's distance; he could identify vulnerable prey in the time it took for that sheep to walk fifty yards from B-House to the south yard. Tellingly, street smart convicts subscribe to the safety-in-numbers mentality. Likeminded and same-race men seek each other out and form prison gangs. On the Chicago streets, many of these men were in rival and warring factions, and in Stateville they naturally joined the corresponding prison gangs. Members protected one another's backs and were ready to strike hard (or strike first) to capitalize on another inmate's momentary lack of awareness.

Many prisoners demanded respect, and the slightest hint of irreverence could trigger intergang conflicts. During yard time, as gangs would congregate on their declared section of State and Madison—a long open walkway like those that span freeways—hard stares often resulted in violent clashes. The corrections officers, understaffed and outnumbered, would come rushing into the fray and swing away with billy clubs and open fire with tasers, but they rarely contained a gang fight. Not until the riot squad arrived on the scene five to fifteen minutes later would the inmates peel off the pile and scatter back among the general population. In the time it took for a gang to mobilize and plan a retaliatory attack against a rival, the lines became blurred as to who started what and who was to blame. Conflicts that made men murderous in prison might have been overlooked on the outside. But with few activities to keep them busy, their desire for revenge festered and bubbled over. Inmates anxiously awaited another lull in yard time, when the COs would be talking among themselves and neglecting their patrolling duties. Then the gang would pounce.

What had Gabriel so apprehensive was the calm. The quiet. The seemingly restored order. These sensations had no place at Stateville maximum security prison. All the prisoners and COs and wardens who ever passed through the aging brick threshold—under the barbed wire and into the processing center with "STATEVILLE" carved in limestone above their heads—understood the basic truth: a quiet prison is a deadly environment. When the noise stopped reverberating off the concrete walls and steel bars, inmates used the silence to make peace with God. For on days like these, whether he expected to or not, a Stateville convict might very well meet his maker.

———————

The boy's future was bright even amid Chicago's many temptations. He had a talent. A gift. The kid could box, and even at the tender age of sixteen, both his trainers and the greater Chicago boxing community recognized that Gabriel Sandoval was a promising pugilistic prospect. But Gabriel wanted to be accepted by his neighborhood gang and he began to listen to them more than his elders.

His boxing coaches told him in no uncertain terms: "Keep working hard in the gym. Keep learning. Keep winning, and the money will come. You'll have plenty of time later in life to worry about a living. For now, you have only three responsibilities: stay in school, stay in the gym, and stay off the streets."

He listened until he turned sixteen, achieving in the gym and in the classroom. Why, then, was he so stupid that he went along on the robbery of Edmar's Grocery Store? Why did he succumb to the gang's criminal ways and hold up a store in his own neighborhood? Damn them. Damn them all.

He did the crime: there was no denying it. Gabriel was planning on hanging out on Harrison Street in his neighborhood with his buddies that day in 1990. At least a couple of his buddies, however, had other plans. Harrison Street was in decay. Once a charming neighborhood with century-old stone and Chicago-style raised homes on the adjacent streets, years of neglect wore out the masonry and severely stressed the intricate, antiquated interior woodworking. The neighborhood infrastructure was also diminishing. Businesses were moving out—not in—and the city failed to curb the rat problem. The once-striking single family homes, separated from each other by gangways— a Chicago term for alleyways—now looked menacing rather than charming. Sunset signaled the hoods to take to the streets and lurk in the gangways.

His buddies, the Harrison Gents were tough and violent. Gabriel wasn't planning on joining in criminal activity on the day in question, not violent criminal activity, anyway. They'd hang out on a stoop and talk shit and catcall women. Someone would probably bring a joint and it'd get passed around and the gangsters would get high and talk more shit. So goes gang life.

But Gabriel did not make it to Harrison Street on Chicago's dangerous West Side that day. Instead, he encountered gang bangers Bubba and Saito. And he agreed to act as their lookout while they robbed Edmar's Grocery Store in broad daylight.

All of that was a memory as young Gabriel, three and a half years into a seven-year stretch, sat stewing in Stateville. He had lived in two different cell houses since he arrived there almost a year earlier. Although most short-timers (inmates serving less than twenty-five years) don't do a turn at Stateville, those who were discipline cases at other prisons were shuttled to Joliet to serve out the rest of their sentence. Punishment for the already punished. Gabriel became a problem for officials at the high-medium security Illinois River Correctional Center in central Illinois. He didn't incite violence, but he never backed down from it. That and he liked marijuana. When the fighting became too commonplace at Illinois River, prison officials tried to break up the known gangs, and Gabriel and some other Harrison Gents were sent to Stateville.

The Illinois Department of Corrections bus ride to Joliet was frightening. Gabriel sat in a blue jumpsuit with "IDOC" stenciled across his back. At 5 feet 6 inches, he was shorter than his bus mates. He weighed about 160 pounds, though. At Illinois River, Gabriel packed on the pounds, figuring he needed the extra mass to fend off the larger convicts. He was right.

The school bus, converted to a mobile holding cell, rumbled north along Interstate 55, passing signs for Chicago as it did. Gabriel longed for home—for his mother's warm and loving embrace. He longed for the morning walks to school with his father, for the lengthy conversations with his sister, for playing tag with his younger brother. What he got instead was a steerage-class one-way ticket—at the taxpayer's expense—to arguably the roughest prison in America.

The first complex Gabriel arrived at in Joliet was the R&C Center, or the receiving center. It was bunker-esque but new. The steel-colored concrete and transparent windows—filmless and clear—did not look all too different from Illinois River. The linoleum hallways smelled of bleach and disinfectant. Corrections officers came across as cordial and almost friendly.

But like the concrete shell of the structure that looked benign and impenetrable from the outside, the R&C Center was a tease of a building. A half mile due east lay the real prison, noticeable from the street only by the giant water tower rising from the center of the penal complex, announcing "Stateville" in brown-painted block letters to all new arrivals.

A convict work detail was picking up trash from the side of the roadway while another detail was tending to a large prison farm. That too was a tease for young Gabriel. Down the road from the level 1 complex was a minimum security prison. Inmates from that minimum security facility essentially kept the prison town looking clean from the outside. They were the frontline custodians for a town that hosted three prisons that employed most of the local residents.

After he was processed at the R&C Center, Gabriel took his newly issued Stateville prison blues, his set of sheets, one towel, and a toothbrush, and reboarded the rolling jail cell bound for his new home. The bus approached the faded red brick front gate and a guard came aboard and handed the driver a clipboard. Gabriel tried to take a mental photograph of his surroundings. He sighed aloud as he realized that this would be the last free air he'd breathe in a while. He had heard stories about his new home, stories of other inmates boarding the bus to Stateville never to return. Or they'd return a paraplegic or a quadriplegic. Or brain dead. Or insane. He knew that survival was paramount and that all other aspects of his shattered life would have to wait for one to four years. He took in the surroundings one last time before being locked behind those colossal limestone prison walls.

Back in Chicago, Jesus and Rosario Sandoval, his parents, were preoccupied with their son's fate. They knew about Stateville. Most of Chicago's inner-city dwellers knew someone doing hard time in the level 1 maximum security joint.

Jesus Sandoval wanted to reach out to his son—to do whatever was in his power to help young Gabriel. But he was poor and he was ignorant about America's criminal justice system; he didn't know the right questions to ask. All he knew was that his oldest child was about to serve the remainder of his sentence in the one place on earth that frightened the neighborhood punks. He silently hoped and prayed that his boy had the grit to get through there, that the twenty-year-old who managed to get through two years of high-medium security prison had learned enough on the inside and on Chicago Avenue to survive among so many career criminals.

Rosario Sandoval, on the other hand, was inconsolable. She was a small, frail woman with sad brown eyes. Her face was frequently red from sobbing, causing her pretty and defined features to fade. Sometimes she became overwhelmed with sadness and retreated to her cramped bedroom in the family's two bedroom house on West Rice Street. Her husband remained outwardly vigilant—most likely for her benefit—but she knew he felt as scared and empty as she. When there were family occasions and happy times, as when her youngest child, Jimmy, brought home an outstanding report card, or even when the U.S. Department of Immigration approved the Sandoval family for permanent residency status, Rosario's bliss was tempered. Her family was incomplete. Gabriel was off in a dungeon enduring God knows what. This weighed on her heart constantly. Even when Rosario was happy, she could not help but to cry.

Opened in 1925, Stateville was created to house the burgeoning Illinois prison population. The state's three other level 1 maximum security prisons, the Joliet Correctional Center (built in 1858), the Pontiac Correctional Center (1871), and the Menard Correctional Center in southern Illinois (1878), could not keep up with the steady influx of inmates.

Stateville was supposed to be the answer, but over time it became part of the problem. Designed to hold 1,500 inmates, Stateville housed more than 3,000 when Gabriel Sandoval arrived in 1992. The prison was at nearly 100 percent double-cell occupancy: everyone had a roommate, whether compatible or not. The lone exception was I-House, the solitary unit.

U.S. prisons do not concern themselves with decor, yet Stateville is perhaps worse than most. The towering limestone walls were all an inmate saw when gazing outward from the complex. And the exterior of Stateville was as drab as the interior.

When Gabriel was an inmate, Stateville's interior had a muted color pattern. The walls were an eggshell blue-gray from floor to waist, then gray-white from waist to ceiling. The bland tones were intentional, as the two-toned paint was supposed to make inmates feel melancholic. And indeed it did, coupled with the blue jumpsuits inmates wore. Living in a pervasively despondent state was supposed to deter rage among inmates, which in turn was supposed to deter violence. But when Gabriel arrived there, the prison was a pressure cooker threatening to explode.

Since the 1970s Stateville has been associated with gang violence. In 1979, *Newsweek* magazine ran a story chronicling the rise in prison gang activity and identified Stateville as having one of the worst problems. The drug trade in the prison was as brisk as it was on the streets of Chicago, and financial disputes among inmates were settled by whatever means necessary. The country was shocked to learn of this rampant disorder, as inmates were supposed to be locked in their cells twenty-two hours a day. During one Stateville shakedown in 1979, corrections officers confiscated hundreds of illegal drugs, 391 knives, eighty-one clubs, fourteen saw blades, two guns, two gas masks, and two copies of the infamous how-to text on explosives, *The Anarchist Cookbook.*

Ironically, Stateville's problems were the result of a citywide crackdown on Chicago youth violence in the 1970s. Authorities were successful in rounding up the hoods and getting them tried and convicted as adults in court. But then they were sentenced to Stateville, where they received an education in all types of illegal activities. The courts were inadvertently sentencing Chicago youth to Larry Hoover's Stateville Gang University.

Born in Mississippi in 1950, Larry Hoover grew up in Chicago's rough Englewood neighborhood on the South Side. He witnessed racial and interracial brutality firsthand and was no stranger to gang violence. He felt the pull of the streets at the age of thirteen, joining up with a black gang called the Supreme Gangsters. Hoover was shot in the thigh when he was fourteen in 1965. He was expelled from school the same year.

Come 1969, while America was consumed by the war in Vietnam and engulfed by the cultural war at home, the Supreme Gangsters were cutting a swath through Chicago's South and West Sides. A gang linchpin, Larry Hoover merged his 5,000-member gang with another gang kingpin, David Barksdale, and his 10,000-strong Disciples, thus forming the Black Gangster Disciple Nation. Hoover and Barksdale served as crowned kings, adopting the crown as their gang insignia.

The BGD organized drug and prostitution rackets, and they wreaked havoc on rival gangs and local authorities. Hoover considered himself virtually untouchable and routinely ordered robberies and executions of gang enemies. The hit ordered on William "Pookey" Young, a drug addict who robbed one of Hoover's drug houses, however, landed the gang leader in Stateville.

He was marched into the prison in 1973 at the age of twenty-three. Hoover gravitated to the predatory nature of Stateville, where rapes and riots were as common as morning chow and midmorning counts. A fairly good cross-section of the prison population was Disciples, and the street-smart Hoover thus hatched a plan for institutional domination.

Barksdale died in 1975 and the Disciples split. Hoover's followers became the Gangster Disciples while one of Barksdale's gang protégés, Jerome "Shorty" Freeman, formed the Black Disciples. The gangs jockeyed for control of the prison drug trade and prison turf, much as they fought turf wars outside the limestone walls. Hoover seized on the "safety in numbers" mentality and commenced talks with jailed leaders of three other prison gangs: the Latin Kings, El Rukns, and Vice Lords. They formed a mass alliance known as the "People," while Shorty Freeman's Black Disciples formed alliances with the Latin Disciples, the Cobras, and the Two Two Boys, and became known collectively as the "Folk." Less than a decade later, the Harrison Gents moved under the Folk umbrella.

As he plotted a way for his gang to run Stateville, Hoover inadvertently inspired a gang culture that spread from coast to coast. In 1978, he successfully organized a strike of prisoners to protest lousy food, an act of disobedience that marked him as a chief instigator at Stateville. He was then transferred to the Pontiac maximum security prison, where he was later accused (but never convicted) of inciting a riot in 1979 that left three guards dead. Word spread through the prison grapevine of Hoover's actions at Pontiac and of subsequent guard retaliations against gangsters under the People umbrella, and inmates at Stateville turned their animosity towards guards as well as rival gangs.

The prison gang culture that Hoover created in the 1970s exploded in the 1980s and 1990s. Stories of riots, infighting, and killing filled the newspapers and evening newscasts. None of the prisons made more news than Stateville.

In the summer of 1991, just before Gabriel arrived, a corrections officer shot and killed an inmate who attacked a guard. The inmate was under the Folk's umbrella, and the consolidated gang responded by taking three guards hostage the following day. The prisoners reacted to the standoff between authorities and hostage takers by rioting in their cellblocks. Toilet paper and newspapers were set afire and gangs attacked rival gangs. When the insurgency was finally quashed after two days of carnage, Illinois authorities at long last recognized that they had a full-blown epidemic on their hands at Stateville.

Tony Godinez, a respected lawman from the same West Side neighborhood as Gabriel, was promoted to warden at Stateville two months later. The prison was still on lockdown when he started. He brought the prison back to regular working order and ended lockdown five days later. Lockdown, he determined, would be used as a deterrent, commissionable at the first sign of trouble. Each time tempers flared among inmates, Godinez would drop the hammer: twenty-four-hour confinement for everybody. Although Godinez restored a semblance of order, he could not control the gangs and gang violence. All he did was spread it around, like a kid who moves food around the plate to give the impression that he ate his supper.

Gang attacks on guards did decrease, which was the lasting legacy of Godinez. Gang-on-gang violence, however, didn't cease, and some inmates and corrections officers complained that it increased.

Gabriel Sandoval arrived at Stateville on a day when the prisoners were on lockdown. That nauseous feeling in the pit of his belly was one of his defining sensations when he checked in.

His first home at Stateville was a lockdown within a lockdown. Because of his involvement in a fracas at Illinois River and because he was caught with contraband, the twenty-year-old moved right into solitary confinement.

I-House was reserved for Stateville's worst. It was the solitary confinement unit, serving as the prison's dungeon for troublemakers ever since Stateville stopped using real-life basement dungeons in the 1930s. The prison administration threw suspected gang leaders in I-House to stem the tide of gang violence. Some men were serving life sentences in the decaying wing. In lieu of metal bars, as in B-House or E-House, and even instead of caged doors as in F-House, the solitary unit had one big steel door with a slot-hinged door for guards to pass inmates their daily meals. The men were confined to their cells twenty-four hours a day, with one hour of yard and shower time per week if they behaved. I-House was the only wing of the prison where inmates had their own cells. While that might have seemed like a luxury, being completely alone was designed to be a torment. That's where Gabriel Sandoval began his time at Stateville.

He stepped into his eight-by-twelve cell in I-House and initially felt somewhat relieved. For the first time since he arrived in prison two years ago, he had his own space. The cell had a window, even though it yielded no view, as it was blackened from the outside by either years of neglected grime or intentionally by the COs.

There was a single steel-framed military-style cot and a flimsy yellowing mattress, with a toilet and a sink built into the corner. It was dirty, just like the Cook County Jail in downtown Chicago. In Stateville, a man in solitary didn't mind if his cell was messy or not. No roommate was around to complain.

A CO waited until Gabriel was securely inside the cell with the door closed and locked before he instructed the inmate to stick his cuffed hands through the hole in the door. Then the guard removed the cuffs and disappeared without a word. Moments later, the fear set in.

The single-occupancy cell became a suffocation chamber. Gabriel's ears and psyche were no longer accustomed to quiet, and the silence of his cell developed a sound of its own, a loud buzzing; a ringing in the ears similar to the animated sounds after a heavy metal concert. Gabriel honed in on the drone of the fluorescent lights above; on a guard's rubber-soled shoes scuffing on the linoleum hall floor; on the leaking faucet; the toilet in the next cell flushing by way of a reverberating echo in his own. He became preoccupied with how air got into his cell, as the slot in the door was just big enough for a lunch tray and barely big enough for his hands to fit through. He thought his breath was shortening, that he wasn't taking in enough air. He thought he might suffocate.

The quiet was surreal. The fluorescent lights buzzed above until they sounded like a swarm of bees: an angry horde locked in that single cell with him. He sensed that the walls were breathing—imagined that the blue-gray and gray-white two-toned paint had come to life. He watched the walls contracting when he inhaled, expanding when he exhaled. Gabriel tensed: the walls breathed in perfect timing with his own lungs. He wished he hadn't started smoking cigarettes at Illinois River because he was paying the price now. He became crazed at the thought of doing hard time in solitary. He was getting anxious. Fidgety. Destined for an anxiety attack. Gabriel's nervous system was beginning to seize up. His mind teetered between madness and rational thought. He tried to steady himself; he needed to figure out a way to deal with his desperate confinement.

"Easy," he said to himself. "Breathe easy. Controlled. Think. You freak out, they'll think you're a bug and keep you locked in here. You lie low and don't make a fuss, and they'll let you out; they'll need this cell for someone who really deserves it. Be cool. Stay calm. It's just you in here: don't need to watch your ass now. You're finally safe."

Gabriel decided to pass the solitary hours by exercising in his cell. The convict was determined to become a boxer again. He vowed to make good on a pledge he made to his father before sentencing: "Papa, I'll be the champion of the world one day, and all of this will seem like a bad dream. I promise."

Gabriel went to prison a boy and became a man inside, mentally and physically. He told himself repeatedly in that single cell that he could deal with the solitude. Harness it. Make the most of it. He started working out every waking hour. First came the hundreds of push-ups and sit-ups. Gabriel used his body as its own fitness center. He didn't keep count of his repetitions, as assigning numbers or any sort of measure to a prison day made time stand still. He wanted time to pass, and numbers only kept track of time.

Then came the flurry of jumping jacks and dips: Gabriel put his hands on the cell floor and propped his feet up on the steel toilet. He pushed his weight up and down until his lats and triceps felt hot enough to burn through his skin.

After a few weeks in solitary, when Gabriel established himself as a quiet, cooperative inmate, a CO granted his request for a broom to address the daily dirt buildup. He took plastic garbage bags, filled them with water from his sink, and affixed them to the ends of his broomstick. Gabriel did curls for hours on end.

He was transforming from a chubby kid into a well-conditioned young athlete. Except for his addiction to nicotine, he was in excellent physical shape. His back and shoulders broadened, his neck thickened, his lats assumed the shape of lengthy rods. His biceps became rock hard and his triceps resembled a dragon's claw. As inmates in solitary confinement didn't have the privilege of yard time, Gabriel could not get a cardiovascular workout. So again, he improvised.

At lights out, when all was finally quiet among Stateville's sprawling complex and the humming fluorescent lights overhead finally darkened and yielded to the prison's red security night lights, eerie shadows filled his cell. In his solitary unit in I-House, the coming of the red lights signaled the commencement of Gabriel's ad hoc yard time. He'd rise from his steel cot to fight his silhouette. His labored breathing softly reverberated off the concrete walls and steel door, and Gabriel fought himself until he was exhausted or through the night until morning count.

When he did sleep, he dreamed of standing in the middle of the boxing ring, slugging it out with the best the boxing world had to offer. He dreamed of flashbulbs and cheering crowds, of money and freedom. When the fight was over, Gabriel dreamed about being hoisted atop high shoulders, bloodied and battered, tired and spent. Victorious.

———————

Something was about to go down. He just knew it. B-House was too quiet. Gabriel had been moved to general population only weeks earlier, and in that short time, he learned what the various sounds of Stateville meant. When the prison was an echo chamber—like it was on most days and nights—all was well. Quiet, however, meant trouble. It usually signaled that one of his fellow inmates, or perhaps even a guard—or maybe a friend—was about to take a shank in his neck. Prisoners carved these homemade weapons out of everyday items: toothbrushes, hairbrushes, boosted screwdrivers or wood scraps from the prison factory, even the plastic tips of their shoelaces. Gabriel carried a shank everywhere he went in Stateville. His was a nail wrapped in tape and cloth so just the pointy part showed through. It was always tucked away in his jumpsuit when he went to chow, yard time, and especially when he went to the showers, where he'd tuck it away in his towel. On ghostly quiet days like that one, his shank was his sidearm.

Gabriel's cellmate knew something was up also. Shorty G was his running mate. A Chicago gang banger also, Shorty G was a Cobra, and fortunately for them, both the Cobras and the Harrison Gents were Folk: they fell under the Latin Disciples' umbrella in Stateville. Bear, another Harrison Gent, was only two cells down. The *tres hombres* traveled through prison like a pack of feral dogs. One ate while the others stood watch. One lifted weights while the others stood watch. And when they showered, they showered quickly.

On that day in 1993, something indeed did go down. A gangster from the People and one from the Folk got into it in the mess hall. High above the steel tables and chairs that were bolted to the floor, three guards in an interior watchtower sprung into action. The tower contained three guns, two shotguns, and a mini 14, a smaller, more accurate rifle. When the inmates started fighting and additional prisoners jumped into the fray, the first guard fired one of the shotguns into an adjacent box. The loud blast resounded inside the mess hall and signaled a high-powered warning to the feuding prisoners. But the fighting continued, and a second shotgun shell blasted into a second box adjacent to the watchtower. Warning number two. Inmates had been told at processing that should a fight or riot break out, they'd hear two warning shots before the mini 14 was locked and loaded. That was the kill gun. After two warning shots, the next discharge they heard would mean someone's life.

The inmates ceased their fighting and were subsequently hauled off to solitary confinement. That fight wasn't for Gabriel, but with one to four years left on his Stateville sentence, he was sure there'd be others.

———————

Illinois River Correctional Center and even Cook County Jail were soft compared to Stateville, where gangs ran the show. Doing time there was a game of survival, and Gabriel had no choice but to play.

The prison gang culture was similar to street gang culture. They competed for turf, control of the prison drug trade, and bragging rights. Sometimes gang members got into fights because of a hard stare or an incidental bump in the lunch line. If a gang member thought he was being disrespected by a rival, it was common for one gang member to "call out" the other. Regardless of any size differential, when one called out the other, he had no choice but to accept. Declining such an invitation would be an admission of fear: That's when you really got beat down in Stateville.

A gangster would either get in another's face and call him out or send a message through the prison grapevine. During open cell time, when the inmates were free to lounge around the Bravo housing unit, the two would go into an empty cell and shut the door behind them. A representative from each gang then stood watch outside the cell for guards or other gang members.

Inside the cell, the two gangsters fought a war of attrition until one was knocked unconscious or until the sentries called for them to cease because of a patrolling guard. The cells were so confined that the fighters' heads got knocked by the sink, the toilet, the steel cots, and the steel prison bars, in addition to each other's fists. Because of the back-and-forth momentum, inmates adopted a nickname for this kind of fighting: ping-pong. Gabriel played his share of ping-pong in Stateville. Sometimes he won. Other times, he'd regain consciousness in his eight-by-twelve cell with his roommate's hand on his carotid. It was Shorty G checking to make sure the boxer was still alive.

Those sorts of scenes played out in Stateville for nearly two years. Gabriel tried to avoid getting in fights, but if someone came looking for a beef, he was ready. The boxer packed on the pounds, eating as much as he could. Extra mass helped fend off some of the bigger inmates. It also made his punches harder, as he was good at putting his weight behind his fists. Gabriel was a short-timer: even if he served out the remainder of his sentence, he'd be out in three years. There were over a thousand men in Stateville serving life sentences. The lifers usually stayed away from other lifers. Having a raging felon on your case for the rest of your life got old real quick. But the short-timers, like Gabriel, were fair game. Target practice, as it were.

He was making it through his time, but it was hard. The isolation was maddening in solitary, yet he felt isolated in the general population as well. Inmates could only move within their own cliques. The fighting was always scary: Gabriel always figured his opponent had a shank, since he had one. The question was, would they duke it out like men, or would the losing fighter draw his weapon and get that upper hand?

Hardest, though, was the distance from his family. Regardless of how many times Gabriel tried to console them, telling them he was making it through and not to worry, Jesus and Rosario fretted about what was happening to their son behind Stateville's limestone walls.

It was hard for them to make the forty-five-mile drive to Joliet. They did it once, when Gabriel's grandparents, Hermila and Jesus Sandoval Sr., made the trip up from Delicias, Mexico, at the beginning of his sentence. His grandmother cried so much when she saw her grandson incarcerated that the family temporarily halted their visits.

His father worked all the time while his mother's health continued to fluctuate. They also debated about whether to bring Lidia and Jimmy to Stateville. Jesus wanted his other children to see their big brother, but not necessarily in that situation. They limited their visits to special occasions like birthdays and Christmas. Jesus worked on Christmas Eve, but like all city employees, he had Christmas Day off. When he punched out around 6:00 P.M., Chicago's streets were iced over and the streetlamps glowed softly in the subzero December air. He walked home, sometimes slipping on the frozen sidewalk, and made it in time for supper. In a corner of the small house was a stack of blankets and extra socks gathered for the trip. The Sandovals ate together in glum solitude. Few words were spoken. There was a small Christmas tree and presents underneath, but it was tough to celebrate while Gabriel was locked away.

They stalled until the midnight hour rolled around. Then the whole family piled into the family car and hoped that the engine would turn over. Jesus maneuvered the bulky Dodge south onto Interstate 55 and to

Joliet. They drove slowly. The streets were empty and extremely slick, as the Illinois Department of Transportation was down to a skeleton crew on Christmas Eve. The old Dodge occasionally caught a patch of black ice and the rear kicked out a little. Jesus pressed on, going between thirty-five and fifty miles per hour. He hunched over the wheel and strained to see as snow blanketed the highway. The high beams didn't help at all. They only illuminated the flakes, making them brighter.

They finally arrived at Stateville in the wee hours. Rosario passed out blankets to her children and husband as they did not have enough money for a motel room. The rates were jacked up by managers looking to make a fast buck off families visiting their incarcerated sons. After all, families spending Christmas Day in an institution didn't matter to the hotel keeps. Fuck 'em; they're convicts.

The car was freezing that night, but they wanted to see Gabriel at the 7:30 A.M. commencement of Christmas Day visiting hours. It was frigid and everyone was sniffling, but they'd rather suffer any indignity than leave their son alone on Christmas.

In the visiting room, as they were among the first to arrive, Gabriel chose a table in the corner of the stale blue and gray room. He'd sit in the corner and have his family face him—face the wall. As the room steadily filled throughout the day, inmates became publicly affectionate with their lovers. Women performed oral sex on their incarcerated boyfriends and the men groped their ladies in front of anyone who cared to watch. Gabriel was aware of what to expect, as he'd heard fellow cons crowing about what they'd do when they saw so-and-so.

Christmas 1993 was bittersweet, but it was potentially the last one Gabriel would serve in Stateville. He was up for parole, having served half of his sentence. Despite the infractions at Illinois River, he was cautiously optimistic that the parole board would look favorably on him since he had not been written up once at Stateville.

As his release neared, the Immigration and Naturalization Service initiated deportation proceedings. The Sandovals had finally been issued green cards in October 1990 for their 1987 amnesty applications. But Gabriel was in jail. His papers came through too, but the government would not validate his green card because he was accused and later convicted of a violent crime. Both he and his parents were notified that the boxer, who had not spent a day in Mexico in over a decade, would be deported immediately upon parole. During a subsequent visit as the parole date neared, Jesus and his son decided to meet at the El Paso airport: that's where the INS agent told Jesus that Gabriel would land. From there, the INS—with Jesus now tagging along—would escort the boxer to the El Paso–Juarez border and watch him walk across.

After serving almost four years in three different institutions, the hulking steel doors of the toughest prison in Illinois swung open for Gabriel Sandoval. He was paroled from Stateville on April 1, 1994. April Fools' Day.

5

Stranger in a Strange Land

As a bell rang to signal the opening of Stateville's front gate, Gabriel Sandoval surveyed the surroundings. The grass was a vibrant green and freshly cut. It made the heavy spring Illinois air smell lush and fragrant. He heard the leaves rustling and felt the bright sunshine. In prison the boxer had avoided the sunlight on bright days. It made him feel depressed.

Free air smelled sweeter. Free ears tuned into sounds that institutional ears couldn't hear, or chose not to. Distant car horns and train whistles sounded pleasant. His spirits were high. Even the guards seemed cordial. "So long, kid," one familiar face said. "Good luck on the outside. Stay out of trouble."

"Aw, man," Gabriel said, his vocabulary now seasoned with prison slang. "You know it."

He was wearing the same clothes he wore on the day of his incarceration. His blue jeans fit more snugly, the result of prison cooking and confinement, coupled with weight training and a limited cardiovascular regime. His black hooded sweatshirt and jean jacket smelled like mothballs. His pockets were empty, save for some family pictures he had stuck into the springs of the above bunk and some get-out-of-town money, a $50 bill, courtesy of the Illinois Department of Corrections.

Among the various corrections officers monitoring the front gate, one man stood out. He was wearing a brown suit and paisley tie, an outfit that contrasted with the officers' blues. The only suit prisoners saw was the warden's, and they averted their eyes when he walked by.

The man approached the free boxer and cordially introduced himself. He was a representative of the INS, sent to escort the twenty-one-year-old ex-con to O'Hare International Airport and a waiting flight. None of this was a surprise. Gabriel and his parents had been informed by the government that he'd be deported on release from prison. The suited man casually requested that the boxer produce his hands, wrist to wrist. Out came the handcuffs. Freedom would have to wait.

The INS agent opened the front door of his tan Oldsmobile sedan and told the boxer to watch his head as he entered. The man got behind the wheel, started the car, and steered it north along Route 53 toward Chicago.

"Gabriel, I've been dispatched to transport you to O'Hare International Airport and an American Airlines flight to Mexico City," he said in a formal tone.

"Mexico City?" Gabriel asked in amazement. "I thought I was going to El Paso."

"I apologize if you were told something different," the man in the suit replied. "But I have my orders."

They rode in virtual silence for the next hour. Gabriel observed the outside while the agent observed Gabriel. The boxer couldn't believe how much Chicago had grown in four years. Traffic seemed brisk and modern buildings seemed to grow from the city's outskirts. The boxer realized in the Oldsmobile that life had gone on without him. He didn't even think about the government custody and the handcuffs he was in. The boxer was preoccupied with thoughts of what he'd do when he arrived in Mexico City, how long that $50 would last, how he would find his father, how he would start his new life, and how he would get back to Chicago.

The man in the suit pulled into an airport short-term parking lot and killed the engine. "Gabriel, you seem like a good guy," he said to his passenger. "So I'm going to take these cuffs off, if you promise to behave."

"I will," the twenty-one-year-old replied. "I just got out of the joint. I don't wanna go back in."

"Good man. Just don't do anything stupid, that's all I ask."

They walked side by side through the airport and to the international departures wing. The man in the suit explained to the American Airlines employee working the counter that this was Gabriel Sandoval, a scheduled passenger on the flight and a recently released prisoner. The lady regarded him cautiously. Gabriel was about 160 pounds and as wide as he was tall. His black hair was cropped close to his head, and his clothes smelled old. His neck was thick and his eyes seemed to stare straight ahead. When Gabriel blinked, it was a pronounced opening and closing of the eyes. The tic he'd had since childhood became more prominent in Stateville. His upper lip curled up a little as he did and his forehead and eyelids scrunched. When Gabriel reopened his eyes, they went briefly wide while adjusting to the light. The boxer looked scary, but he was polite. He thanked the lady when she gave him the boarding pass and called her ma'am.

Gabriel and the suited man were the first to board the airplane. The boxer took his window seat and buckled up while the INS agent approached the flight attendants and the pilots in the front of the plane and said something inaudible to the boxer. They all looked back at him and nodded in agreement to the agent. Then the agent returned to his assignment.

"Okay, Gabriel, you're on your own now. Don't give these people a hard time, stay in your seat, and good luck to you."

"Thank you, sir," was his reply. "I'll be good."

"Seems to me like you will be, son."

The airplane filled and Gabriel stared out the window. He never liked flying; it seemed unnatural. He'd been on several planes, flying to Chicago as a young boy and later to St. Louis and Miami for Golden Gloves competitions. From Chicago to Mexico City was a long flight, though. He would be completely alone and lost when he touched down, a stranger in a strange land and speaking a strange language. He had been born in Mexico and lived there as a child, but he grew up in Chicago. His Spanish was fluent but his accent awful. To the Mexican nationals, Gabriel Sandoval was a *pocho*, an American-born Mexican, used interchangeably to mean "traitor." His life was about to take another bewildering turn.

The flight attendants began making their way down the aisle with the beverage cart. Fellow passengers ordered Coke and Pepsi, and some ordered beer. When the flight attendant asked Gabriel what he was drinking, he matter-of-factly said, "Can I have a beer please, ma'am?" The flight attendant knew this passenger just got out of prison, but he was sitting quietly and asked so politely. She handed him a Budweiser while he dug into his tight denim pockets for the $50 bill. Before he could produce it, the flight attendant was already a row back.

He drank his beer slowly, the first he'd had in four years; the first he'd had legally. It calmed his nerves, and the flight attendant noticed. When she made her next round with the drink cart, she handed Gabriel another Budweiser. Same thing for rounds three and four. When the plane touched down five hours later, Gabriel was sauced. He waited in line behind the other deplaning passengers—he was the only one with no carry-on or checked luggage—and offered the flight attendant his $50 bill as she stood at the plane's threshold. She looked at him warmly and patted his shoulder, refusing the money. "Take care of yourself, you hear?"

The U.S. Immigration and Naturalization Service was grossly understaffed for the task at hand. Undocumented immigrants were streaming across the border in record numbers. Every year, the problem got worse. According to the 2000 U.S. Census Bureau, 38.8 million Hispanics lived in the United States, or more than 12 percent of the population. Of that number, 66 percent, or 25.3 million people, reported as being of Mexican heritage. Analysis suggested that at least 5.3 million were illegal immigrants.

Between 1990 and 2002, the legal population of Mexicans living in the United States roughly doubled while the undocumented population grew by 165 percent. And in that time, the frequency and technique of deportations changed. In the early and mid-1990s, at border checkpoints that separated Calexico, California, from Mexicali, Mexico; Nogales, Arizona, from Nogales, Mexico; and El Paso from Juarez, hundreds of deportees left the custody of the U.S. federal government and crossed back into Mexico with little formality every day. On the other side of the border, depending on the location, a Mexican government official was waiting to ask about citizenship, and a local charity usually offered sandwiches to the repatriated citizens. Within minutes of crossing the border, those who were illegal in the United States were now on bona fide legal ground and disappeared into the Mexican interior.

If an illegal was caught in the further reaches of the United States, like New York, Boston, and Chicago, and if it was cheaper to fly the Mexican back to Mexico City rather than El Paso or Tucson, then the INS did just that. If the undocumented immigrant was wanted by authorities back in Mexico, a formal exchange was set up. The converse was that many immigrants wanted by U.S. authorities would simply flee back into Mexico. People can walk freely into Mexico from the United States. Coming back is the hard part.

In 1994, some 70,000 illegal entrants were sent back to Mexico. That was almost never a deterrent. Like Jesus Sandoval in the 1970s, Mexicans committed to coming to the United States would continue to make clandestine crossings. When they got rounded up by border agents patrolling or "cutting" the desert, and when they were forced back to Mexico, they'd wait a few days and try again. It was a nonstop game of cat and mouse.

Mexico City's Benito Juarez International Airport is Latin America's biggest and busiest. It is the world's gateway to Mexico. In 1994, Mexico City (Distrito Federal to the locals) was the most populated city in the world, though still a third world city in a third world country. Old diesel and leaded-fuel cars and buses coughed up exhaust that settled between the surrounding mountain ranges and covered the city in a blanket of smog.

Gabriel descended a steep metal staircase and stepped onto the sweltering tarmac. He followed the other passengers like a lost lamb, baggage-less and disoriented. The airport was bustling with thousands of Mexicans hurriedly walking in every direction. They looked foreign to him. Much as his father looked for that one Mexican face among a sea of Chicagoans, Gabriel searched for that one American face among the Mexicans. But there was none.

He still had the $50 and a stash of peanuts from the flight. Gabriel asked some passersby in his American-accented Spanish where the bus station was. The central station was in the heart of Mexico City, some eight miles from the airport. He knew of only one place to go in that country: his grandparents' house in Delicias, in the northern Mexican state of Chihuahua, some 880 miles away. And he figured that when he didn't show up in El Paso, Jesus would assume his son was flown directly to Mexico and that he'd make his way to Delicias. Gabriel couldn't call to ask, as he couldn't remember the phone number. He decided not to waste time and started heading toward the bus station.

That $50 seemed like an insult at the time. "How is the state gonna give me this and expect me to make it?" he wondered. "I guess it don't matter now. I'm not in the state. I'm not even in the country. Got to survive, man. Just got to survive."

As the sun began to set on Ciudad de Mexico, that $50 was all the boxer had between life and starvation. A taxi would cost a good $10. So Gabriel started walking in the general direction of central Mexico City, asking pedestrians every mile if he was heading in the right direction.

Four hours and several wrong turns later, Gabriel stood in the center of the huge station, akin to Grand Central in New York City in terms of size and traffic. He was tired and thirsty. The beers had long since worn off. Yet he didn't want to break the $50. Gabriel sucked down water from the bathroom sink and snacked on his peanuts from the flight.

The station was divided into four terminals with buses leaving for points throughout Mexico. He made his way from counter to counter trying to find a line that ran to Delicias or Chihuahua City. Sure, plenty of bus companies made the trip, but not even the third class buses did it for less than $70. Gabriel tried to explain his predicament to some employees, but none would budge. Apparently they were immune to smooth-talking travelers.

He switched into street mode. Gabriel observed which buses destined for Delicias left from which terminal. He spotted a second class bus that had recently arrived and was fueling up for the return trip. Gabriel approached the driver and started bargaining with him.

"*Hola, amigo*. Listen, I have a problem. I just got out of the joint, and this here $50 is all I have to my name. I need to get to Delicias. Can we work something out?" he queried the seemingly unimpressed bus driver.

"Sorry, pal," the bus driver said. "I could lose my job if I got caught. I'd like to help you out, but there's nothing I can do."

"Okay. But what if the bus isn't that crowded and you have many empty seats. I'll give you most of this money. All I ask is you give me back some pesos for a little food. You stick the rest right in your pocket." The driver thought for a minute.

"Hang out near the terminal," the driver said. "If there's not too many people, I'll give you a nod. You can pay me then."

Customers began forming a line in front of the coach. The driver stood at ground level checking tickets and loading luggage into the belly of the bus. He took a count and shot a glance at Gabriel. Then he nodded.

Gabriel trotted up to the driver and eagerly produced his $50 bill. The driver briefly studied his face and could tell the kid wasn't trying to pull one over on him. That and he didn't have any luggage. Most guys fresh out of prison don't.

The driver gave him back 150 pesos (about $15) for food and incidentals along the way. But he didn't say anything. It would take two and a half days to drive 880 miles. The boxer figured he could stretch his remaining money until the bus pulled up to Delicias. He hoped he remembered where his grandparents lived—it had been so long since Gabriel had been in their house. All he remembered was that it was lime green and a fifteen-minute jog from the *gimnasio municipal*. And he remembered his grandmother's kitchen always smelled of savory Mexican food. He thought he was as excited to eat his first home-cooked meal in nearly four years as he was to see his family. And he hoped his arrival in Mexico City rather than El Paso wouldn't worry Papa, though he was fairly confident that it would. Regardless, Jesus Sandoval was a resilient and resourceful man, Gabriel thought. He'll figure it out.

Right before departure, Gabriel tried hard to remember his grandparents' number. It had been years since he made a phone call to someone other than his parents, but phone numbers were streaming in real time through his head. One in particular lodged in his memory. He wasn't completely sure, but thought he remembered it being the number of his grandparent's house in Delicias. He asked the bus driver if he had five minutes to spare before departure. He did.

The boxer darted back into the bus station and used fifty pesos to buy a phone card. He found a phone and frantically dialed the number. His grandmother's soft voice sounded on the other end. She could barely contain her feelings while he rattled off his travel itinerary. He didn't have much time to talk, since fifty pesos doesn't go far over long-distance TelMex phone lines. He told his grandmother that he'd be in the Delicias bus station in just over two days. Would someone come meet him?

Of course someone would. Grandma had not heard from her son yet, so Gabriel still fretted about his father's fate. But at least someone in his family knew he was in Mexico. He was finally expected and would be among familiar faces. He hung up and allowed himself a little smile.

As he made his way back to the bus and took the same seat toward the rear, Gabriel tried to think two and a half days into the future, to a day when he'd be embraced and received—with hugs rather than handcuffs.

———

Central Mexico was magical. Colors and people seemed to mesh among the vast expanses. Every twenty miles, the winding road skirted by bustling metropolitan areas or rolling meadows with poor people taking their goods to market. Mexico's highways were decidedly third world, and no interstate connected the cities and towns. The old converted school bus he rode—one like the rolling jail cell that transported Gabriel from Illinois River Correctional Center to Stateville—rumbled along, coughing diesel fumes into the dusty air. This was a beautiful country, Gabriel mused, the land of his father and grandfather. The great irony was that the United States, the country he knew and loved, had disowned him. Uncle Sam was through with Gabriel Sandoval, kicking him out of the country he identified with and putting him on the first jet out of town, back to the country of his birth. Mexico was his country now.

Hour after hour, he peered out the window. The chatter slowly subsided as road-weary passengers slipped into sleep. Jagged mountain peaks were illuminated by an intense southern sun and then silhouetted by an orange setting orb. No one attempted to talk to him, and he didn't attempt to talk to anyone. Gabriel's bootlegged bus ride was all business: he wasn't there for fun.

The openness of central Mexico frightened him a little while it zipped past his window. He tried to listen to her sounds and somehow find a causal link between the land he was birthed in and the land before his eyes. But there was nothing. The boxer was completely out of his element. Any element. He related no better to the people he was doing road time with than the people he did hard time with. In fact, he related better to the latter. Gabriel had known poverty before, but the deficiencies of the industrial Midwest were unlike those of southern, central, or northern Mexico. Despite the various towns and municipalities along the way, there was no infrastructure. Fruit stands were randomly thrown up along the side of the road, as were taco stands and bodegas. And the road hadn't been repaired in decades. From his seat at the rear of the bus, Gabriel experienced firsthand the poor condition of the road. The other passengers were immune to the frequent potholed jolts and so was he, but for other reasons. He'd never had a smooth ride in his life.

Gabriel was used to prison sleep. A few hours here and a few minutes there was all he needed to function. He was also experiencing too many emotions for the first time in years for his nerves to stand down and let his eyes rest. It was his first time in those parts of Mexico (he'd never been south of Saucillo before, a tiny town just south of Delicias), the first time he'd traveled alone for so far, and his first time on a bus since the one that deposited him at Stateville. The ex-convict's introduction to the country that he now found himself in was a two and a half day bus ride only two and a half days removed from his release from an American prison.

Right about the time road sickness started surfacing, he saw a roadside sign for Delicias: fifty-four kilometers away. "How far is that?" he wondered. "Even the measurements in this place are foreign." He was starving and his mouth was parched. He wanted a cigarette and dreadfully needed to stretch his legs. The anxiety he felt in solitary confinement reared up again. The bus made him claustrophobic and made his mind race. "Where is Papa?" he asked himself. "Did he get a hold of my grandmother, or is he still waiting for me in El Paso?"

Jesus Sandoval walked from gate to gate at the El Paso airport. It was small, especially compared to O'Hare, so it didn't take him long to check the central screens for arriving flights and then head to the gates that had arriving planes. Then he scanned the arriving passengers. He also was unsure which airline Gabriel was on: Jesus didn't know if he'd be connecting anywhere or if he caught one of the few direct flights from Chicago to El Paso. He decided to check them all. But his son was not among the deplaning people. He became worried.

Jesus called his house in Chicago and Lidia answered the phone. No, she had not heard from Gabriel, and she called her grandparents' house in Delicias already, just in case. Jesus told her to keep working the phones and said he'd check in later.

The passing hours made him increasingly tense. He wondered if something had gone wrong—maybe Gabriel wasn't paroled on time.

Had something happened in Stateville on his last few nights that made him miss his flight? He feared the worst, like maybe a big prison fight sent his son to the infirmary. Or maybe the prison administrators forgot that April 1 was the day Gabriel was scheduled to be released. That would be the meanest of April Fools' jokes, he thought.

The planes kept arriving and emptying their passengers, and Jesus surveyed the crowds person by person. For good measure, he had "Gabriel Sandoval" paged over the airport's loud speaker several times. Come 8:00 P.M., with only two more flights scheduled to land at the airfield, Jesus was certain that something happened: his son would not be in El Paso on that night.

He called Chicago again and Lidia answered on the first ring.

"Papa, I talked to grandmother," she said excitedly. "His plane landed in Ciudad de Mexico! He is on a bus right now to Delicias!"

Jesus Sandoval closed his eyes and leaned against the pay phone. A sigh escaped his lips and his jowls relaxed for the first time since he arrived in El Paso the day before. "He's out," the father said into the phone. "He's safe now. Call your grandmother and tell her I'm getting on a bus and will be in Delicias first thing in the morning."

He rushed out of the airport and hailed a taxi to the El Paso bus station downtown. The cab rolled along Interstate 10 and into the heart of old El Paso. The bus station was a gateway for wayward wanderers. Folks could get to all major Texas cities from the station, and it serviced dozens of buses from Juarez every day. People taking the Juarez/El Paso bus were playing border roulette. The bus would leave the central Juarez station and wind around the Mexican city's busy streets until it hit one of three bridges linking the old world to the new one. Then everyone got off the bus and stood in line with their passports or work permits—some real, some forged—and waited to clear the U.S. border patrol agents who stood patiently awaiting their arrival. The agents wore freshly pressed uniforms with holstered sidearms and many wore gloves to protect their hands should they need to riffle through a bag or should they cross some-one so desperate to get into America that they'd attempt to breach the agent's security. Border agents saw all kinds of people pulling all kinds of tricks. Jesus Sandoval thought of the cat and mouse game going on at the border posts as he saw the millions of twinkling lights of Juarez—right there across the border—from his cab window.

The buses from Juarez would park at the border for inspection, the driver's papers would be checked, and then the driver and the bus waited for an hour on the U.S. side for the customs-clearing passengers to reboard. Then the bus started off for the El Paso bus station. Often the bus would be significantly less crowded after the checkpoint than when it arrived.

Jesus glimpsed hundreds of people waiting in line to come into the United States. He thumbed around in his pockets for his green card, just to be sure. He walked into the El Paso bus station and bought a ticket to Juarez. Once inside Mexico, he would buy a ticket to Chihuahua and once there, he'd buy a local ticket to Delicias.

In just a few minutes, he thought, he'd be on an air-conditioned American bus that would transport him unmolested and undisturbed back into Mexico. The sensation struck him as funny. He'd made so many attempts at sneaking into the United States only to bus right back in—past the very agents he tried so desperately to avoid years earlier. And he couldn't help but chuckle aloud when contemplating his return trip: his clothes would be dry.

But those jovial minutes were fleeting. Jesus had to think of a way to bring his son back into America and then back to Chicago. He would be permitted entry, but Gabriel had no papers. His son was persona non grata. Jesus was determined that sooner or later, though, they'd make it back to the West Side together. He had three bus rides and five hours to draft a plan.

———

Gabriel rolled into the Delicias bus station two and a half days after departing from a terminal in Mexico City. Delicias was as he remembered it: charming but dusty. He was one of the first people in the aisle of the bus, anxiously wanting to get off.

He descended the bus's narrow stairwell and heard a small scream. It was his grandmother, flanked by his grandfather and Papa. Jesus Sandoval Jr. had made it to Delicias after all. Gabriel's face burst into a smile and his eyes teared up. He was overwhelmed as all three family members embraced him at the same time. He was free, though not in the right country. They returned to the family house on Avenida Poniente and broke bread together. His first meal as a free man in four years was more than he ever dared to wish for in prison, as the Sandovals sat in the parlor room with the 1950s furniture and tiled floor and chatted late into the twilight. After the grandparents went to sleep, Jesus and Gabriel stayed up until first light and discussed their options for returning to the United States.

They talked about going into the underworld and contacting coyotes. Gabriel was open to that suggestion, but Jesus was more reluctant. Many Mexicans looking to sneak into the United States employed coyotes, or guides, whose unprincipled character often resulted in the demise rather than the salvation of their hapless clients. Coyotes also employed their own distinct lingo. They referred to their clients as *pollos*, or chickens. Tellingly, they referred to themselves as *polleros*, or chicken wranglers.

The guides were usually Mexican toughs who earned about a hundred dollars a head. They were the workhorses of a corrupt black market empire that straddled both sides of the border and trafficked in people. Despite the financial rewards for *polleros* with each successful crossing, a misstep or misroute in the unforgiving desert often meant an anonymous death for the desperate coyote and his customers. Jesus thought coyotes should be considered only as a last resort.

Gabriel inquired about swimming the Rio Grande the way his father had more than a decade ago. That was a possibility. Jesus kept that option on the table. But he had an alternative he wanted to attempt first.

Jesus Sandoval was a card-carrying permanent resident. Gabriel did not have papers, but he spoke perfect English. He also knew U.S. geography. Perhaps when Jesus presented his papers, if Gabriel spoke some English and presented himself to the border patrol as the man's son—as a boy—maybe the agents would wave him through. After all, Gabriel's English was better than his father's. They might assume that Gabriel was an American-born Hispanic. Then it would be relatively easy to get on a plane to Chicago. The El Paso airport saw its share of Mexican Americans. Jesus figured that if they spoke English well enough when in the presence of airline employees that they would rubber-stamp the Sandoval boys aboard.

Father and son agreed that they'd try to walk through a port of entry into the United States. They had two known backup methods of gaining access should the first attempt fail. Jesus told his son to rest for a couple days: spend some time with his grandparents and ingest some fresh country air. When the color returned to his son's face and the road weariness wore off, they would take the bus from Delicias to Juarez.

April is the most pleasant month in the American Southwest and northern Mexico. The temperature tops out in the mid-eighties and a light breeze tempers the sun's intensity. The air is so mild that people waiting for hours in the lengthy lines on the Mexican-U.S. border remain in good spirits.

The roads leading into the United States are always packed, as is the pedestrian traffic waiting to cross a point of entry, but the congestion and the gasoline smells are more tolerable in April. Especially for those Mexicans waiting in line with work visas. Between 18,000 and 21,000 people walk across the border legally into Los Estados Unidos each day, and the lines are anywhere from an hour and a half to three and a half hours long. Jesus and Gabriel took their place among the waiting masses and acted as though they belonged there—as if they'd walked the border a million times. Jesus had a small suitcase with his clothes in it. Gabriel carried nothing.

The plan was to act normal. Jesus would present his green card to the questioning agent while Gabriel stood silently. When he was asked direct questions, he was to make eye contact and speak in clear and unaccented English. He was going to consciously suppress the nearly four years of prison slang that crept into his vocabulary.

As they approached a border agent checking papers, a pang of fear stabbed at Gabriel's gut. The boxer made a promise to himself in prison that the lawlessness was behind him, but here he was, less than a week after being paroled from Stateville, attempting to break the law. He felt, however, that crossing into America illegally was essential to his future as a prize fighter. And he couldn't fathom a life so far from his family. He wanted to see his mother and siblings so badly that his desire overran the consequences.

At long last, it was their turn to face off with the agents. The border patrol is, above all else, fiercely proud of being American. Many of them have military backgrounds, and a certain patriotism brews in former soldiers. They are willing to sacrifice their lives if need be for their country. When they join the world of law enforcement, the expression "to protect and to serve" takes on an American connotation.

Jesus Sandoval had his green card in hand and was ready to produce it, along with a tooth-bearing smile. The agent, a forty-something-thing blond-haired officer with cleanly shaven cheeks, a mustache, and eyes bluer than those usually found on the border, summoned the two to step forward with a flick of the wrist. "ID, please, sir," the agent said to Jesus. Gabriel stood silently at his father's side, hands in pockets.

"How are you this afternoon, officer?" Jesus asked, making sure to smile as he did.

"Not too bad," he replied while studying Jesus' green card, looking up from time to time to make sure the face on the I.D. and the one in front of him were the same. "And how are you all today, Mr.—Sandoval?"

"Oh, pretty good. Looking forward to getting home."

"You are a United States citizen, Mr. Sandoval?"

"Yes I am. We are. We live in Chicago."

"And who is this you brought with you?"

"This is my son, Gabriel. He's fifteen." Gabriel tried not to blush and not to giggle when his father introduced him as a teenager. The twenty-one-year-old was much shorter than his father, and the mass he packed on in prison sort of had the appearance of baby fat. He looked up at the officer and smiled.

"What were you and your father doing in Mexico?" the agent asked Gabriel, sounding a little suspicious as he did.

"We were in Delicias visiting my grandma and grandpa," Gabriel responded while making eye contact and speaking in his best English.

"Oh yeah?" said the officer. "Did you have a nice visit?"

"Yes, we did," he replied. "But I'm ready to go home now also."

"Are you bringing anything back with you?" the agent asked, still looking at Gabriel.

"I have both of our luggage here," Jesus chimed in, tapping the suitcase. The agent shifted his glance to Jesus and directly questioned him.

"Are you bringing back any fruits or vegetables?"

"No, sir. Just our laundry," he responded, still with a smile.

"Thank-you, gentlemen," the agent said, handing Jesus back his green card. "Have a nice trip home."

"Thank-you," both Gabriel and Jesus said in unison. And just like that, Gabriel was back in the United States. Jesus put a hand on the back of his son's neck and gently massaged it as they walked. He could tell Gabriel was nervous, and his father's touch reassured Gabriel that he was safe.

"Very good, *mijo*," Jesus said in a soft and sincere voice when they were a safe distance from the border. "Let's catch a taxi to the airport and get you home."

Gabriel relaxed once he was in the taxi. His father briefed him on all that was going on back home: Jimmy was growing like a weed and had developed an interest in boxing; Lidia was prettier than ever and had been dating a guy rather seriously; Mama's health had been up and down, but knowing that her son was on his way home, she'd never felt better.

Jesus bought two one-way tickets on an American Airlines flight direct from El Paso to Chicago. Again, they walked right on the plane without questioning or raised eyebrows. Gabriel took the window seat, Jesus the aisle seat right next to his son.

The one direct flight from El Paso to Chicago on American Airlines usually follows a strict flight path. The aircraft takes off to the east and cuts north over, ironically, Hobbs, New Mexico, the same town Jesus spent seven days hiking to when he was fifteen. From there, the plane gradually flies northeast, crossing the Texas panhandle in Amarillo, then over Oklahoma City and Wichita, Kansas. Then on to Kansas City, Springfield, Illinois, and into Chicago.

For some reason never explained, that particular flight took off from El Paso to the east and flew southeast for about an hour into the heart of Texas before making its northbound turn. What was more, the plane flew unusually low over the West Texas wasteland, where the sloping mountains seemed irregularly close to Gabriel's wingtip and the shadow cast by the plane on the ground glided flatly over the desert valleys.

Like a mirage, a city popped up under the plane. The plane was so low that from his window seat, Gabriel made out the shapes of individual buildings and cast his gaze on the perfectly manicured lawns and copious trees that were greener and lusher than the ones of central Illinois. From overhead, the pilot's voice came on the loudspeaker.

"Folks, we're flying over Austin, Texas, right now, the state capital and home of the University of Texas Longhorns."

Gabriel turned to his father and casually spoke his first words of the flight. "Hey, Papa, Austin looks real nice."

"*Si*. You got an uncle there, you know. Uncle Julio lives in Austin. He likes it very much."

The plane made its turn north and back on course to the Windy City.

———————

Reuniting with Lidia, Jimmy, and his mother was beautiful and heartfelt, but the honeymoon didn't last long. Word quickly spread around the neighborhood that Gabriel had returned and the phone started ringing off the hook. The Harrison Gents were looking for him. Gabriel had survived Stateville, thus propelling him to rock star status in the gang. For his part, Gabriel loved the attention.

He started going out all the time and staying out until all hours. His personality changed and the once dutiful son became irreverent toward his father. He no longer referred to him as "Papa." Now, it was "pops," and the tone he used was disrespectful.

It only took a few weeks of hanging out with the gang again for Gabriel to revert back to lock-up mode. His father feared that the joint might have permanently messed up his mind. He was talking crazy. And he was acting lawless.

"Pops, let me take your wheels," Gabriel often demanded.

"Where you gonna go?" was his father's usual response.

"I don't know. We're gonna drive around. What difference does it make?"

Jesus reluctantly lent his son his car, though he got noticeably more agitated with each repeat performance.

Then the phone calls got more and more discourteous.

"Hello?"

"Yo, I wanna talk to Boxer."

"He's no here," Jesus responded. "You talking to his father."

"Yeah, I know," spoke the thug's voice on the other end. "So where the fuck is he?"

"What kind of language you using when you talk to me?" was the amazed response. "Someone needs to teach you some manners."

"Yeah, okay. Whatever."

Click.

Jesus started running out of patience. His son's behavior was driving him nuts, was worrying his mother sick, and was a horrible example for young Jimmy. Jesus decided he was going to give Gabriel an ultimatum: clean up your act or get the hell out.

"This ain't gonna work, *mijo*," Jesus said one night when Gabriel finally returned home with the car. "You're killing your mama. You ain't gonna kill me, but I don't want to see you hurt her. And you gonna kill yourself."

"I know what I'm doin'," was his son's reply.

"If you wanna go back to that same shit with those same guys, I can't help you. You gonna wind up right back in Stateville." Gabriel gave his father a look that Jesus had never seen before. It was a fiery, angry stare, the kind developed in prison, not on Chicago Avenue and certainly not in that house.

"Well, what the fuck you want me to do?" he said, looking squarely in his father's eyes. For Jesus, that was the last act of defiance he was willing to take.

"Who the fuck do you think you talking to!" he shouted back. "You think you so bad? We can go outside right now, you little punk. I'll teach you a fucking lesson!"

Gabriel immediately humbled himself. He'd never seen his father that upset, the rage bubbling in his eyes. The boxer bowed his head. "Papa," he said solemnly. "I don't know what to do. I don't know how to act anymore."

Jesus was still red hot from the exchange, but he detected his son's sincerity. "*Mijo*," he said warmly but sternly, "you got to get the fuck outta here. The way you going, you gonna end up right back on the streets. That life's not for you. If you want a car, we'll get you a car and you can go somewhere."

"You don't have any money. How you gonna get a car?"

"I can find money," was the reply. "I got a garage filled with tools. I can sell my tools. If you want to start fresh and start boxing again, I'll help you, *mijo*. But you can't stay here. There's nothing but trouble for you here."

Gabriel took a moment to collect his thoughts. "You're right, Papa. I need to leave," he said remorsefully.

"Okay. Then I'll help you. We have family in Los Angeles, Las Vegas, and Austin. You decide where you want to go and I'll make a phone call."

His son stood there and thought. Briefly. He didn't need more than a minute to make up his mind. The plane ride from El Paso was still a vivid memory. Gabriel chose Austin.

6

House of Lord

G abriel Sandoval arrived in Austin in May 1994, overweight and out of shape. The relocation was rough on him at first. He moved into a relative's cramped house in East Austin, where four people occupied two bedrooms. Gabriel's cousin had lined up a job for him as a maintenance hand for Motorola on their construction sites. The boxer was a hard worker, and he'd regularly wake at 4:30 A.M. and head to the day's location. Once there, he'd load large pieces of debris onto eighteen-wheelers, push the broom, and mop up the scene before he punched out. When he finally left at 3:30 P.M., Gabriel headed straight to the local gym for a workout. He was smoking two packs of cigarettes a day.

Gabriel first went to the Montopolis Recreation Center, which consisted of free weights and a basketball court with a cramped room off to the side designated for boxing, complete with a couple of heavy bags and a small ring. Although the quarters were restricted to a handful of amateurs, they packed themselves in and fumbled around with the equipment. There were some University of Texas students and a few local roughnecks, but no serious boxers to work out with. Gabriel came to Austin weighing close to 170 pounds, significantly more than his 5-foot-6 frame could carry gracefully.

He was committed, however, to getting in shape and getting back on a training schedule. The boxer made a call to Tom O'Shea, his former trainers at the Matador Gym in Chicago, and asked if he could help him scout out a gym. O'Shea was surprised to get this call. His budding protégé had been out of touch for several months, and they had spoken only sporadically since he'd been paroled.

He was pleased to hear that Gabriel was adapting well to life out of prison and to his new Texas surroundings. He was even more gratified to learn that Gabriel wanted to get back into boxing, a sport that he was convinced would keep the fighter from street brawls and essentially out of trouble. Gabriel told O'Shea that the Montopolis Recreation Center had decent equipment, but no true boxers. O'Shea said he'd try to help.

The Chicago trainer called some boxers he knew in Chicago who had fought on the Texas circuit, and he called some other trainers as well. Then he remembered a guy in Texas named Doug Lord with a son who used to hang out with the welterweight champion of the world back in the 1960s and 1970s. All queries led to the same answer: R. Lord's Boxing Gym in North Austin.

Lord's Gym was an Austin staple, and Richard Lord, a Dallas native and the gym's owner, was the closest thing to a celebrity that the Austin boxing community had. He was well-known around town because of two distinctions: He aggressively promoted fights—without the sleaze—eventually transforming his Friday night amateur bouts into a series of "Brawl in the Hall" matches, where professionals did battle in the local music hall. Lord single-handedly made boxing an occasion in a town where the University of Texas Longhorns dominated the sports pages. And he was one of the first boxing trainers in the state of Texas to welcome women into his gym.

Lord's Gym had an unusual clientele in the mid-1990s, an eclectic group that included newspaper editors and FBI agents, ex-convicts and university students. "Ninety percent of the people at the gym don't fight, but there is the 10 percent that do," he said casually. "The others just want to learn the skills, everything except get their nose broke. So we can accommodate them on that. But if they want to get their nose broke, we can do that too."

He is a soft-spoken man, the polar opposite of what comes to mind when one thinks of a boxing coach. Richard Lord is compact—5 feet 7—with a medium build that is all muscle. Even at fifty, Lord looks quick and crafty. His hair has been messy and disheveled ever since high school, and he has a salt-and-pepper goatee. He sports a long strand of hair in the back, braided at the base, which has been his rebellious Samson-esque calling card since his days as a Golden Gloves competitor. He speaks in a choppy monotone, and while his manner has the telltale signs of a punch-drunk, his words are eloquent and well chosen. That's because he learned a thing or two when he studied psychology at the University of Texas in the 1970s and graduated cum laude.

Richard was at his desk, a battered writing table squeezed into his cramped office at the back of the gym, going over the day's training schedule one early morning in September 1994 when his phone rang. A voice on the other line asked to speak with the gym's owner.

"Richard," the voice said. "Tom O'Shea here in Chicago. I'm a trainer at the Matador Gym. I got a kid up here who's really a talented fighter. Knows his stuff and can really work the bags. The thing is, he got in a little trouble up here, and he's moved down there. The kid's got a lot of promise and could really use your direction. He's trying to get his shit together, and you come highly recommended, and your father and I were acquaintances. Is it all right if I send him your way?"

"You say the kid can move?" Lord asked.

"He's quick, even for a featherweight. Richard, you'll appreciate what you have with this kid."

"Okay. Send him over and I'll take a look at him."

"Thanks, Richard. I appreciate it. By the way, the kid's name is Sandoval. Gabriel Sandoval."

Lord went back to his schedule and forgot about the conversation. The trainer had been around the sport long enough to know that recommendations—even one as good as this—don't always measure up to the hype. Maybe the kid would show, maybe he wouldn't. Boxers are not the most punctual people. If he did come in through the garage door that doubled as the front door, Lord would uphold his end of the bargain and judge for himself if the kid was worthy. Boxing trainers move in small circles. There's a fraternal code among them: you help the other guy out. If a coach says his boy can fight, you give him the benefit of the doubt. Don't judge him on first appearance, as many boxers are shy and introverted. Get him on the heavy bag or in the ring and see how he moves. Then there was the fact that O'Shea was an acquaintance of Richard's dad. That's old school. Boxers respect their elders, and Richard couldn't refuse a guy who knew his old man.

An hour later Lord went to run the stairs at the University of Texas football stadium. While he was gone, a short, overweight Hispanic timidly ducked his head under the low-hanging garage door and shuffled into the gym. He carefully examined the joint and took in the numerous posters on the walls. The young man had a bit of an eye twitch and smelled like an ashtray. He was met in the middle of the gym by Abel Davila, one of the local fighters who made the gym a second home.

Abel didn't look twice at the visitor, taking him for just another work hand who wanted a cheap place to work out. Or maybe he was looking for work. Abel told the visitor that Lord was out, but he'd be happy to take a message. When Lord returned later that day, he took Abel's message and called the stranger.

Gabriel answered the phone at his relative's house when Lord rang. He said he'd make it to the gym as soon as possible. The boxer didn't want to tell the trainer exactly when he'd be in, since he was at the mercy of Austin's public transportation system. Lord said he'd see him around and then retreated to his office and commenced poring over his daily training schedule. But Gabriel returned to the gym that day and once again stood in the middle of the warehouse and looked around.

Lord peered from behind his desk and figured the stranger for a local who mistook the gym for the Goodwill store in front. He shouted to his visitor over the noise of a transistor radio that blasted an Austin rock station.

"Can I help you?"

"I'm looking for Mr. Lord," the visitor said.

"Well, you can stop looking. You found him. Something I can do for you?"

"My name is Gabriel Sandoval," the man said with a muffled tone in perfect English. "I'm here to box."

Richard Lord grew up on the sport. His earliest childhood memories include talking and watching boxing with his father, Doug Lord. Father and son would go to Fair Park in Dallas and watch the amateurs fight when Richard was only six, and his father tried to instill an appreciation for the sport in his eldest son's head.

Doug Lord was raised in an orphanage in Fort Worth. He grew up tough. The other boys from the orphanage in a Masonic home were coarse, always looking for something to get in to. In the 1950s, Fort Worth was still an outpost town, stepsister of Dallas to the west. There was a viable cattle trade, and the cowboy way of life was the model for young men. Except, of course, the young men growing up fatherless.

Doug Lord and some friends went to see some amateur boxing in East Fort Worth when the boys were teens. They didn't have any money and looked for ways to sneak into the venue. The fight promoter caught on to the scheme, and he approached Doug and his friends.

"Boys, there's two ways to get in here: Pay or play." Beg money in the streets for a ticket or get in the ring and be part of the show. This wasn't a well-organized amateur competition but ragtag and without sanctioning. Nevertheless, Doug and his friends chose the latter.

They went back to the orphanage and found some soiled rags. These boys were no strangers to street brawls, but they figured that boxing was more sophisticated than that. Doug led by example, taking two tattered rags and wrapping them around his hands. The other boys followed suit, and they had makeshift boxing gloves. For the rest of that afternoon, the orphans beat shit out of each other while trying to develop a style.

Later that night, Doug and the boys got in the ring. They were the only participants who actually looked worse before the fight because of their earlier "training." From that day, Doug Lord devoted himself to the sport, and when Richard was born in 1954, he was baptized into the world of boxing.

Texas has always been a big boxing state, producing some talented and storied fighters. Old-timers love to tell the tales of yesteryear while occupying barstools and gathering around card tables. There was that time in 1972 when a thug from Fort Worth's notorious Stop Six neighborhood named Elmo Henderson knocked out Muhammad Ali during a San Antonio exhibition match. They regale themselves with stories of a vicious heavyweight from the tiny town of Orange named Randall "Tex" Cobb, who tore up the division in the late 1970s and throughout the 1980s, culminating with a 43-7-1 record. They still talk about his one big loss, a savage beating from Larry Holmes in Houston's Astrodome in 1982. Cobb was beaten so bloody on that November night that TV announcer Howard Cosell retired from boxing commentary. "I am tired of the hypocrisy and sleaziness of the boxing scene," Cosell quipped. He never called another fight. Devout fans of the sport like to tell tales of Roy "Cut-and-Shoot" Harris, a West Texas great white hope who lost a title shot to former heavyweight champ Floyd Patterson in 1958. And of course there was Jack Johnson, the first African American heavyweight champion and arguably the greatest fighter ever, who was born and raised in the poor black section of Galveston.

For Richard Lord, the Texas boxer of choice was undisputed welterweight champion of the world Curtis Cokes, who reigned over the division from 1966 to 1969. Cokes ran a boxing club in Fair Park, an inner-city Dallas neighborhood. Lord was a Dallas kid who hung around the gym and fought on the amateur circuit. He recalls being the sole white fighter in an area steeped in tension caused by the Jim Crow South, but he was never ostracized. Nor did he ever feel superior to his black counterparts, despite the social inequities of the time.

Cokes took a liking to Richard. As a teen, Richard was a fearless and tenacious fighter. He loved the craft of the sport as well as the action.

Richard was a very visual person with a photographic memory. He studied Cokes's movements and tried to mimic them in the ring. Even though Lord was built for speed, his ring presence was more that of a bruiser than a boxer. Cokes saw an opportunity to refine Lord's raw talent. He tutored the white boy, teaching as much by instruction as by example. Cokes took Lord around the world as he defended his title, putting the teenager to work in his corner. For a poor kid from East Dallas, the opportunities that Cokes showed Lord were unfathomable. Lord had never been east of Shreveport, but here he was, traveling to far off lands like France and Italy, Saudi Arabia and South Africa.

Cokes gave Lord attention, but it was Coke's trainer who took an interest in Lord's professional future. Tiger Reed encouraged Lord to pursue boxing full-time. Richard liked that idea, but he promised his father that school would come first. Doug Lord demanded that his son finish high school, and he envisioned his book-smart son going to college. Richard kept his promise and graduated from Bryan Adams High School in 1974, then he made a move to Austin and the University of Texas.

Austin did not have much of a boxing community in the 1970s. There was one noteworthy gym on Sixth Street, right above Big State Pawn Shop. The gym was built by Dr. Jerry Baugh, the local heart surgeon and an avid boxing fan. Dr. Baugh spent his free time working on his conditioning with the few regulars, one of whom was a compact amateur from Dallas with a bushy mustache and a long strand of hair growing from the back of his head and braided at the base.

Lord spent as much time in the gym as he did in the classroom. He aspired to become a pro fighter when college was over and, like any dedicated athlete, trained hard. Yet Dr. Baugh's boxing gym did not turn out boxers with a competitive spirit the way Curtis Coke's Boxing Club did in Dallas. Lord needed to maintain his competitive fighting edge, and he needed to spar. Boxers may have been scarce in Austin in the 1970s, but the University of Texas had a plethora of fraternities, and Austin had an overabundance of bars. Lord and a buddy, Cowboy Schwan, would go trolling up and down the infamous Sixth Street as well as Fraternity Row looking for frat guys under the influence and feeling strong. Lord would fight anyone under 160 pounds, Cowboy would fight anyone over 160. Those sessions managed to keep Lord in top physical condition and also served as a recruiting tool for the gym. Even the proudest, toughest fraternity guy couldn't deny that there was skill associated with ring work.

Lord graduated from the University of Texas in 1978 and registered to be a professional boxer. He was a natural lightweight and he cut a deep swath through the division, culminating with a professional record of 18-1-1. He believes he could have won a championship, but the years were stacked against him. Lord has always been a man of his word, and he retired from professional fighting at twenty-nine, thereby keeping a promise he made to his mother, Opal, that he would not fight beyond his thirtieth birthday. He was ranked number eight in the world.

When Lord retired from boxing, he joined the nine-to-five world at Threadgill's, the North Lamar Street landmark that had been around since the 1930s. Starting in 1983, he worked as a restaurant manager for eight years, switching from working out and punching people to ninety-hour work weeks and smiling customer service. The current location of R. Lord's Boxing Gym was Threadgill's old dry goods warehouse. Richard used to make trips back and forth between the restaurant and the dry goods supply warehouse when he noticed the spaciousness of the stockroom. He'd been working out at the Sixth Street gym and out of his home garage when he realized that there was plenty of space in Threadgill's warehouse for some heavy bags. And maybe a speed bag or two. After a couple of years, when the hotdog buns had been cleared out, there was room for a boxing ring.

Lord and some of the restaurant workers would go over to the warehouse—tucked neatly behind the Goodwill store on North Lamar—and run through a boxing workout. Ever the egalitarian, Lord didn't care who among Threadgill's staff came along; everyone was welcome. For the most part, the Mexican cooks and busboys would go along for the workout, fortunate to have not only a free place to condition but a former pro boxer as a trainer. This went on for years. And with each passing season, more and more people started showing up at Threadgill's dry goods warehouse to box.

By 1991, Lord knew he was on to something. The warehouse was bustling, even when he wasn't around. There was always someone bodied-up to the heavy bag and the speed bag was constantly being pounded. Someone had also installed a double-end bag—an inflated leather bag that was suspended between rubber ropes and anchored to the floor and ceiling—and the small but functional seven-by-seven ring always seemed occupied. Lord was now training all the time for fun. "Work really interferes with a guy's life," he says. "I figured out a way how not to work while still working." Lord decided that he would make a living on his schedule, doing what he loved.

Although the "R. Lord" shingle hanging on the gym signified a new way of life for the former contender, the gym itself denoted a new chapter in Texas boxing history, and the advent of Austin as a boxing city. Richard made an offer to buy the warehouse from the owner of Threadgill's and soon R. Lord's Boxing Gym was a reality. He put little effort into marketing the business. To this day, the gym has never had a commercial phone, nor has Lord ever spent a dime on advertising. He puts his effort into running a clean, safe place.

"I've always been surprised with the success. People work out for different reasons, reasons that I don't know all about. I guess a lot of people take pleasure in punching something, be it a leather bag or a person," he says in his monotone.

Most of the clientele were rank amateurs: people who might get in the ring and spar—might even fight in amateur events—but mostly wanted to be part of the boxing scene, or just part of a community. As time progressed, women became a common sight around the gym.

In 1992, Lord's Gym got its first professional boxer, and Richard became a professional trainer by default. Joe De La Cruz was a name in Texas boxing circles. A no-frills speedy Mexican featherweight with strong legs and quick jabs, De La Cruz was in the market for a new place to train. Lord had been around the pros all his life, so managing a pro fighter seemed like the next logical step. That and there wasn't another gym in town as focused on boxing.

Lord trained De La Cruz hard and, using trial and error, developed a skill for promoting and scheduling fights. He managed to get De La Cruz a fight against Louie Leija in Waco, Texas. By then, De La Cruz's talent had peaked. Lord wasn't expecting Joe to become an international success. Nevertheless, he was enjoying his new role as pro trainer. And training other pro fighters was on Lord's mind the day he got the phone call from Tom O'Shea in Chicago.

Standing before him, though—just about an hour after he hung up with the eager boxer—was a guy who looked like a couch potato. Gabriel Sandoval said he was here to box, yet Lord wasn't so sure. Were it not for the promise he made to O'Shea, Lord may never have tested the skills of the stout ex-con.

Gabriel Sandoval stood in the middle of Lord's gym—head slightly bowed, hands in the pockets of his faded, soiled blue jeans—and fielded questions from the trainer. Yes, he was the fighter that Tom O'Shea called about. Yes, he'd been in some trouble with the law, but he was committed to turning his life around. And yes, he would train hard and do what was asked of him, anything to get back into boxing. Gabriel had big dreams, honed in a prison cell every minute of every hour of every day for nearly four years. Dreams born in prison manifest into obsession quite easily, and Gabriel was obsessed.

In prison, case workers and jailhouse shrinks encouraged inmates to think ahead to their future on the outside as a way of avoiding temptation once paroled. To the true dreamer—and prison has its fair share of them—this was a dangerous prospect, since it set up the inmate for failure and dashed hopes.

Gabriel had at best a rudimentary education. Were he to fail at boxing, he would likely take his place alongside the scores of undocumented Mexican immigrants doing menial, off-the-books jobs while fretting over the prospect of discovery and deportation. He would succeed at boxing, he told himself repeatedly. He had to.

Lord was confused by his visitor. This guy looked terrible, and his ragged appearance was slightly less offensive than his body odor. Heavy cigarette smoke mingled with human grime—the result of laboriously toiling away at a construction site in the relentless central Texas heat—and he gave off a stench that stood out even in a boxing gym. While Lord could manage to see through the dirt, he could not ignore the weight. Gabriel was no featherweight as he'd been told. This man weighed enough to be a light heavyweight, and his walk was more of a hobble. How on earth was this guy going to be able to fight? He looked like many things, but a fighter wasn't one of them.

Sill, Lord was moved by the man's modesty. He politely said he wanted to box; that's what he knew. The trainer told Gabriel to grab some gloves off a shelf, lace up, and get on the heavy bag.

It didn't take long for Richard Lord to recognize the raw talent and power of his new charge. Gabriel hit the heavy bag with precision. He moved the bag around like a crafty veteran, and he fought off the balls of his feet, resisting the temptation a lot of fighters have to stand there and plant themselves. In fact, Lord recognized that this overweight, out-of-shape young man was gifted. The moves and continuity were extraordinary. His breathing was rough and labored, but that attributable to the two packs of Marlboros the fighter puffed each day.

Lord's enthusiasm grew with each crack of the heavy bag. Never before had a fighter of such caliber graced his gym. The boxer's stance was proficient and unique. Lord had never seen a fighter keep his guard up around his head and still advance forward, and he hadn't even heard of someone using such a posture since the days of John L. Sullivan. Gabriel's moves were fluid, much like the pros.

Lord had crossed ex-con fighters before, and prison helped brand a fearless mentality in boxers. One thing prison didn't always teach, though, was heart. This kid looked like he had plenty of heart. He stuck the heavy bag and moved, stuck and moved again. And again. And again. For the time being, Lord cast aside Gabriel's troubled past and mulled over ways to get him in shape.

As a trainer, Lord usually didn't concern himself with an athlete's personal problems unless he was approached for advice. But Tom

O'Shea had planted that seed in his head, and Lord felt compelled to have "the talk."

Gabriel explained to Lord that boxing had always been his true passion: his life as well as his livelihood. He talked about the Harrison Gents and the lure of Latino gang life on Chicago's West Side. He talked about Stateville and the severity of the place. He told Lord everything—except that he was in the country illegally.

Lord might not have cared anyway. He was more concerned with smoothing the boxer's rough edges than outing him to authorities. But because Gabriel withheld that information, Lord almost got him in trouble.

Richard Lord is a suspicious person, probably because of corruption in the ranks of the sport he prizes. Several police officers, FBI, and CIA agents were regulars at the gym. Lord asked Gabriel for his social security number, then handed it off to one of the boys to do a little background checking. Gabriel gave him a number that a friend instructed him to use if anyone came asking.

That number was attached to a criminal record as long as any pulp novel, detailing crimes much more severe than armed robbery. According to the social security number Gabriel provided, the boxer was a convicted rapist from California. A legal resident, yes, but a violent sex offender. This info befuddled Lord. He had received a call from Chicago telling him about a kid who'd gotten into some trouble. By the boxer's own admission, he was in the Harrison Gents street gang and Stateville maximum security prison. Now he's also a California rapist! The trainer didn't know what to believe. On the one hand, he was excited about his talented new boxer. On the other, Lord had made a name for himself around town by welcoming the female clientele. Lord decided to allow the boxer to train but quietly told gym goers to keep an eye on Gabriel.

Months of intense training passed before Lord questioned Gabriel about the California rape. The trainer was hesitant to bother the boxer about his legal conundrum because he was so impressed with Gabriel's work ethic. Each day, like clockwork, the boxer arrived at the gym in the soiled blue jeans and T-shirt that he wore at his day job. The cigarette smoke had long since disappeared. A boxer on a Richard Lord training schedule can't afford to pollute his lungs. He'd shower before he worked out to accommodate the others in training.

"How could a guy who worries about smelling bad around boxers be a violent sex offender?" Lord wondered. When he finally confronted the boxer with his burning curiosity, Gabriel fielded the question with shock. No, it was a robbery in Chicago, not a rape in California. He finally confessed that the social security number was a fraud: he was just an ex-con who wanted a second chance. The trainer sympathized. "This kid's had a real rough run at it," he thought. Lord figured if he were to take Gabriel Sandoval pro, then the robbery would eventually catch up to him. He needed a new ring name.

The boxer had been christened Jesus Gabriel Sandoval Chavez, Jesus being his father's first name and Sandoval his last. Gabriel was what his mother named him, and Chavez was her last name. As fate would have it, all four names would come in handy.

Gabriel Sandoval was an illegal alien. Gabriel Sandoval spent four years in the Illinois prison system and was then deported to Mexico. Gabriel Sandoval had an amateur record of 95-5, topped off with three Golden Glove titles.

Jesus Chavez, on the other hand, was a no-name. An unknown. Clean slate, fresh start. Jesus Chavez was a strong name. A fighting name, close to Julio Cesar Chavez, a Mexican lightweight boxing champion and national hero who was in the prime of his career. Gabriel Sandoval would become Jesus Chavez.

The boxer was a new man. The name change enabled Lord to register his charge as a pro without anyone batting an eye. And that's what happened in the summer of 1994.

Lewis Wood was a hard-hitting Houston native who had lost in the last round of the U.S. Olympic tryouts in 1992 to Oscar De La Hoya. He'd gone undefeated since the De La Hoya fight, and his people scheduled this new Austin professional named Chavez at the last minute; he was to be an automatic mark in Wood's win column.

Lord fielded a call from Kenny Weldon, one of Wood's promoters, who asked if his fighter wanted to have a shot at the former Olympic hopeful in Houston in two weeks. Wood's people wanted to use this fight as his coming out party—welcome to the pros—with a decisive victory in front of his hometown audience. Chavez, however, would use this as a coming out party unto himself, and he won a split decision over the favorite. Lewis Wood didn't know what the hell hit him. Richard Lord knew his fighter would give the Houstonian the fight of his life. Eleven years later, Lewis Wood hadn't lost a fight since that night in Houston.

———————

By this point, Chavez ate, slept, and breathed boxing, and Lord grew to enjoy having Jesus around. Student and teacher learned much from each other and together about the world of professional boxing: the politics, policy, rules of thumb, and the shadiness. Jesus was slimming down fast, and Lord conceived an entire persona for the fighter. Gabriel Sandoval was Jesus Chavez, and Lord nicknamed him El Matador, a tribute more to the Matador Gym in Chicago than to his Mexican roots. Lord had opened his heart and his mind to his protégé, and now he opened the backroom of his gym to the hungry fighter.

El Matador lived there for more than two years starting in late 1994. His room and battered mattress lay downwind from the practice ring, heavy bags, and free weights; it smelled awful. And BO isn't the easiest odor to eliminate, especially when it's renewed every day for eight hours straight.

The Texas heat didn't help much either. When it was 100 degrees outside in the summer, it was 105 degrees in the gym. El Matador would go outside to cool off. When he was hungry, he'd eat canned tuna, fast food, or Ramen noodles. The warehouse/dry storage/boxing gym was home, and while the quarters were stuffy and uncomfortable, they kept Chavez's mind trained on the task at hand: becoming a boxing champion.

Lord's Gym is a classic. The building itself—a warehouse with a two-car garage door as the front door—is hidden from Lamar Street by a shopping complex that includes Austin's most popular Goodwill store. The aluminum siding and cement floor convert the place into an echo chamber. The smallest sound resonates throughout. Even outside, trainers can be heard barking instructions.

Inside, every inch of wall space is covered with boxing paraphernalia. There are hundreds of posters promoting the great fights of yesteryear: Holyfield versus Lewis, Mercer versus Holmes, De La Hoya versus Trinidad. But as El Matador progressively won each match Lord scheduled, the gym became more or less a shrine to the undocumented immigrant, who was rapidly becoming the best boxer ever to come out of Austin. Every one of Chavez's promotional pictures hangs throughout the gym, as do all of the newspaper clippings written about him over the years. It was within those walls that a transformation was under way.

7

King of Britannia

The fighter now officially known as Jesus Chavez was adapting well to his new Austin home. Nights in the gym were still eerie, when the twenty-three-year-old was alone with his thoughts. The wind whistled through the aluminum siding and cause the building to creak. As he lay on his beaten-up mattress downwind from the heavy bags and free weights, the blown insulation on the steel ceiling beams took on a whole new persona. The ceiling looked furry, and in the dark, after a prolonged stare, Chavez's eyes played tricks on him. The beams appeared to move in time with the creaks.

Outside his room, the weight machines became intruders lurking in the shadows. He eventually grew accustomed to his tomblike residence. When the morning finally came and the albatross above him turned back into a ceiling, he didn't have far to travel to begin training.

Chavez continued to help Lord with the gym's day-to-day operations. When he wasn't training, the boxer conducted personal training sessions with the clientele.

One autumn day in 1995, a tall man with a dark goatee and subtle crow's feet at the side of his eyes walked into Lord's and peered around cautiously. His hair was cropped close to his head, save for a long strand in the back that was braided and rubber-banded at the base. He wore a silver necklace with a silver snake attached, and a silver hoop earring.

He stood out from the other trainees not only because of his unique appearance—he carried himself with an air of confidence that was appropriate to the proudest fighters—but because he was a stranger.

The differences between Richard Garriott and the other fighters, though, were much deeper than that. Unknown to Lord or Chavez, one of Austin's most important and successful entrepreneurs strode into the gym that day. Garriott was the millionaire eccentric who lived in a mansion atop Austin's highest hill and drove around town in a black Lamborghini. This was not an ordinary businessman working off a time clock and climbing the corporate ladder. Richard Garriott invented the local video game marketplace and brought the gaming pulse of the world deep into the heart of Texas, to a place that was formerly known only as the state capital and a premier college town.

Garriott, along with brother Robert, was responsible for putting Austin on the international video game map. He was the creator of Origin Systems and, more specifically, the Ultima line of video role-playing games.

Richard had become tired of the traditional way of staying in shape: those nightly trips to the gym just weren't lighting his burner. A former girlfriend told him he should give boxing a try. But boxing was considered passé in sporting circles, even to a guy as creative and open-minded as Garriott, and one as athletic. In college, Richard was the seventh best fencer in the state.

"Before I came in here, I thought to myself, 'Boxing? Why would I want to get into boxing,'" Garriott mused. "It's a sport where these economically and socially disadvantaged people—who have no other thing to do with their lives—are willing to do each other bodily harm for the entertainment of others." His disdain for boxing was quashed only by the gym and by its most talented fighter: Chavez.

Garriott had no way of knowing that the boxer introducing himself as Jesus Chavez would impact his life as much as he would the boxer's.

The gym would serve as the binding tie, and the two, even though they were from such divergent backgrounds, would foster a friendship that confounded expectations and transcended borders.

The third of four children, Garriott was born and raised in Houston, just down the block from the Johnson Space Center. His mother, Helen, was a professional artist and his father, Owen, an astronaut.

Helen always encouraged her son to tap into his artistic roots. Owen, a man of science, expected that his offspring be educated. He encouraged their schooling, even when he wasn't around. In 1974, when Owen was in space on SkyLab 2, Richard knew he could count on his dad to help him with homework. When long division gave him problems in middle school, Richard would casually walk into his mother's bedroom and pick up the receiver on a curious black phone. He'd push the phone's only button and would be immediately connected to NASA's central command at neighboring Johnson Space Center, where he would then be patched through to his dad.

Garriott competed in science fairs from kindergarten until high school graduation because mom and dad encouraged him to get involved with "big projects." First it was upstaging fellow Cub and Boy Scouts with his elaborately designed model airplanes and soapbox derby cars. Later it was constructing extravagant haunted houses for Halloween. Always think big, they instructed.

Computers fascinated Garriott, even though they were relatively inaccessible—at least to high school students—in the 1970s before the advent of the personal computer. His high school, Clear Creek in Houston, only had one terminal connected via an acoustic modem to PDP 11 desktops. Although archaic and slow, even by 1970s standards, he fell in love with the infinite and untapped world of computer programming.

At about the same time Garriott was making his acquaintance with computers in 1974, he was also discovering the world of fantasy fiction. *The Lord of the Rings* by J. R. R. Tolkien left an indelible mark on his imagination the first time he read it, as did the introduction of the now legendary Dungeons and Dragons board game that same year. Garriott became mystified by the surreal creatures and magical quests, how the line between despair and destruction was narrowly separated from success and victory. He liked the idea of limitless pitfalls and pariahs, of warrior princes and enchanted fairies. And he liked the idea that he too could create such worlds with his vivid imagination and a few key strokes. Having a general understanding of the computer language Basic, he decided to create his own kingdoms on the school's lone computer.

There were, however, no computer classes at school. Garriott worked on his dreamworlds in between classes, after school, or whenever he could get access. But he needed more consecutive hours to write his programs and if he was lucky enough, to finish one and iron out all the glitches. And of course, to test-pilot his games.

Garriott was already a name around the faculty lounge. Teachers knew he was a self-starter from his science fair projects and from his coursework. So they weren't surprised when he petitioned the school to let him work on the computer for school credit. At first, Clear Creek High School officials were receptive but apprehensive. The district regimented the students to a lockstep curriculum: math, science, English, foreign language, history, gym.

The more he persisted, though, the more the faculty recognized that they had a computer prodigy in the making. By his sophomore year, Garriott convinced the school to give him his own class. Literally. He persuaded the faculty that the computer language, Basic, was indeed a foreign language, as most Americans could not speak it in the genuine sense. By having time to play around in the language, he managed to avoid traditional high school foreign language requirements and learned Basic instead.

Garriott was permitted to work in the computer room with no other students present, no teacher and no curriculum. All he had to do for three years of high school for an hour and a half a day was sit in that room and teach himself how to write games on that old teletype. For a final grade, he would present the games he created to the faculty at the end of each semester. And it was a premium credit class to boot, guaranteeing him premium credit A's so long as he stayed the course.

When he was a senior, Apple introduced the Apple 2, the first mass-produced personal computer with graphics. Richard struck a deal with his father to go in fifty-fifty on an Apple 2, a necessity if he was to continue writing games after high school graduation. Each of the programs Richard wrote in high school was done on teletype, which was cumbersome to use, and the acoustic modem was prone to failure. Richard found it easier to write the programs longhand in a spiral notebook. He labeled the games "D&D 1, D&D 2 . . . etc." after his favorite board game, Dungeons and Dragons. When he worked out the technical kinks on paper and in his head, he'd start writing the programs on the teletype. That got old fast. Most of the games he started writing in the notebook never made it to the teletype. The Apple 2 he bought with his father both started and saved his future.

Garriott tried to test the capabilities of his new Apple by programming the last game he wrote longhand, D&D 28, which he renamed 28 B. It worked great, the graphics were measurably better than on the teletype, and the encoding ease made the whole process smoother.

The nineteen-year-old had something here. 28 B, which he renamed as Akalabeth—a made-up name—worked. It was a medieval hack-and-slash game that caught the attention of a local game shop owner who employed Garriott one summer. The shop owner persuaded Garriott to publish his game, a process that was decidedly easier back then.

In 1979, a published video game consisted of some disks in plastic bags, a manual, a cover sheet, and a pegboard to display them on. His mother helped him with the artwork, and Richard invested what was to him a fortune, $200. He used the money for plastic baggies and disks, produced several copies of Akalabeth on his Apple 2, and stuck them on the pegboard at the game shop, thereby publishing his game.

The video game world has always belonged to the insiders. Even in contemporary society, despite the corporate megaproducers, the principal designers and programmers all know one another. One of Houston's lone video game stores sold all the copies of Akalabeth, one of which made its way out west. Three days after the games first graced the pegboard, Garriott got a call from California Pacific, one of the first national distributors of video games, expressing interest in representing the teenager and his hobby, Akalabeth. Within weeks, the distributor flew the nineteen-year-old to California and signed him to a contract, agreeing to pay him $5 in royalties for every game sold. California Pacific sold 30,000 copies, and Akalabeth became the prequel of the nine Ultima games, eventually becoming the longest-running fiction in digital media.

Before his twenty-first birthday, Garriott was making more money in a month than his father was making in a year. The family was stunned and impressed, and they encouraged Garriott to make more . . . as side projects. Garriott was college age and, as he puts it, "I come from a painfully overeducated family." His father has two doctorate degrees, his mother has two master's, one older brother is a doctor, the other has two master's, the younger sister has a master's, and then there was Richard, struggling to make grades at the University of Texas–Austin. His parents figured his gaming money was a fluke, that it wouldn't last. Go to college, they insisted. Get your ticket punched.

UT had a computer science major, but it was geared toward the financial world, software and databases, not video games. Garriott continued making games in his dorm room, and two things happened: his income rose and his grade point average dropped. Midway through his sophomore year, the once stellar student who had his own foreign language class in high school failed his first college class. Ironically, it was a computer programming class.

Right around that time, Richard decided to take a hiatus from college life. He realized that he could pursue either school or video game programming, but not both. He wasn't enjoying school all that much anyway. Games and money tickled his fancy.

Meanwhile, older brother Robert was fresh off his second master's from MIT's Sloan School of Business (his first master's was in engineering from Stanford) and was working as an intern at a venture capital firm, studying the investment patterns of software companies. Robert had become particularly disposed to the video game industry by reading the various business plans of those seeking start-up money. For Richard's part, the first two companies that he published through ended up going out of business while owing him money. It didn't take long for the brothers to form a union.

"Robert said to me one day, 'You know, I at least know how to pay you. Why don't we go into business together, and when the checks come in from your games, I'll make sure to pay you first.'"

In 1983, the brothers created Origin Systems. Over the next eight years, they built a top 10 company in the video game business. The Garriott boys realized that this was a do-or-die industry: Only the top five companies would be able to survive the enormous hardware and software shakeout. By 1990, the industry was Apple, IBM PC, Commodore 64, Atari ST, and Amiga. To be a software maker in the late 1980s and early 1990s, you had to double as a prognosticator—you needed to predict who would be around next year, as it was too costly and time-consuming to produce a game for each company.

The industry was extremely volatile. The Garriott boys needed a strategic partner. By 1992, they couldn't afford to make the wrong decision, as they employed more than 250 people in Austin and were responsible for transforming the state capital into the video game programming epicenter between New York and Los Angeles. That same year, they made the decision to sell Origin Systems to the highest-caliber suitor. Electronic Arts of Redwood City, California, was—and is—the premiere independent publisher and distributor of computer and advanced entertainment software. It pioneered the industry for interactive graphic design and has produced some of the most popular video games in history, including MVP Baseball, Madden Football, and NCAA March Madness. EA came knocking in 1992 and bought Origin Systems for $35 million.

The money was parlayed into more money through wise investments, and Richard Garriott assumed a rather mystical role around town. In his Ultima games, he was known as Lord British, ruler of mythical Britannia, beholder of all befitting a surreal aristocracy. And he developed some rather strange quirks in real life too. He built himself a three-story mansion on Austin's highest hill, incorporating creature comforts old and new, coupled with a haunted air that would make even the Addams family envious.

Entering the elaborate and enormous foyer of "Britannia Manor II" (Britannia Manor I was a sizable home in New Hampshire), one notices a curious assembly of ancient crossbows and assorted medieval weapons. A daunting astronomical observatory occupies much of the ceiling. Lower down, the careful observer notices a bullet hole in the grand staircase at nose level. Indeed, Lord British built himself a castle, one with secret passageways, hidden rooms, a dungeon, antique mechanical toys, an original vampire fighting kit, a shrunken head from South America, a pine coffin, an extensive gun collection, and numerous statues of gremlins and gargoyles.

And then something else started happening. Like a Hollywood horror star, Garriott got letters from all sorts of religious movements calling him a satanist and the Antichrist because of his Dungeons and Dragon–like games. At the same time, he got thousands of letters from fans all but worshiping him as King of Britannia.

One crazed fan claimed that Lord British was instructing him telepathically to finish his quest, and the man followed an effervescent image of the game character to the threshold of Britannia Manor. The fanatic broke into Garriott's Gothic foyer late one night and was lucky that Lord British wasn't in a vendetta kind of mood. Richard was upstairs in his bedroom when a downstairs window shattered and he heard the sound of footsteps crunching on glass.

He had an arsenal of guns in Britannia Manor, but he could only find ammunition for one at that crucial moment: an Uzi. Garriott mounted the landing at the top of his staircase, Uzi at the ready, as an intruder ascended the staircase toward him. Richard shouted at the intruder to stop or he'd shoot. The man stopped, but there was a two-minute standoff on the staircase. Garriott had his Uzi locked and loaded, and the intruder stood there watching Lord British, waiting for him to say something. Finally the intruder turned to leave and started walking back down the staircase. Garriott didn't want to shoot the guy in the back, but he had also instructed his unwanted guest not to move. Lord British discharged a warning shot at the floor to show he meant business, and the shot ricocheted off the floor and lodged in the stair-case (hence the bullet hole). Police apprehended the man minutes later.

Halloween is Garriott's Christmas, and he decks out Britannia Manor to the nines. He regularly pours in over $200,000 to make the already creepy house even creepier, which in turn draws scores of ad-miring Austin residents. They are permitted to come tour the haunted house for free, which turns into quite the spectacle. People camp out for days at a time to be among the first to enter. On some nights, Garriott donates go-to-the-front-of-the-line passes to charities—like the Wild Basin Preserve or Bat Conservation International—and they in turn auction them off and raise thousands of dollars.

Britannia Manor II was completed before Garriott ran out of reno-vation ideas, so the forty-four-year-old Lord British decided to build yet another medieval manor, this one a 25,000 square foot castle with even more outlandish features. Britannia Manor III will consist of three structures. The first is a gatehouse/guest house that will confuse passersby into thinking it's just a regular old house. Behind that mod-est structure is the main house with a grand banquet hall, and the third structure is an even grander banquet hall behind the main house. All three will be connected via secret tunnels and passageways.

The main house will be equipped with an underwater cave attached to the indoor pool, a room that acts as an elevator (à la Disneyland's Haunted Mansion), and rotating walls with beds attached, so that guests in the main house might find themselves going to bed in one room and waking up in a different one.

Garriott's master bedroom will have enough mechanical gadgets and hydraulics to be its own amusement park ride. His lavish king-size bed will be set up to be lifted through the roof so that Lord British can sleep under the stars if he wishes.

When Richard Garriott walked into Lord's Gym in 1995 looking for a new way to get in shape, he was somewhat apprehensive about what he might find. Not that he was scared to be around people who punch other people for a living. On the contrary, Richard was a tough who could handle himself. It was the savage reputation of the sport and the idea of the disadvantaged being exploited by unscrupulous handlers that perturbed him.

Garriott is a confirmed thrill seeker. He's been to Antarctica twice, to the bottom of the sea—6,000 meters down—in deep-diving submersibles four times. He's dived into hydrothermal vents, visited the Titanic, searched for buried treasure. Africa. Amazon. Airplanes. No adventure is too daunting. Yet despite the inherent dangers associated with adrenalin sports, and notwithstanding the interesting and sometimes volatile people Garriott would meet, say, on safari, the world of boxing seemed too savage for him initially.

Chavez boxed out of a life of poverty on the West Side of Chicago, and he exhibited many of the objectionable traits that made Garriott apprehensive about the sport in the first place. He was an ex-con, he'd been deported, and he used his fists to earn a living at the expense of someone else's well-being. Yet Lord's Gym and, more accurately, Chavez's thriving talent at that gym, transformed Garriott's mind-set.

Lord's Gym was not much to look at, especially to a stranger who has not experienced other boxing facilities. The ring was worn but functional. The metal dumbbells were old and rusty, with flecks of metal littering the cement floor. And the clientele was a rough bunch. Some were students, but many were amateur boxers who dreamed of going pro and had a history of run-ins with the law.

Garriott was out of their league economically and intellectually. He could buy the gym and its contents without breaking a sweat. The boxers—and Richard Lord too—did not prejudge Garriott the way he did them when he made his first appearance at the gym. They casually regarded the stranger as sticking out, but that did not impede the hospitality they had for a fellow boxer. Nor did they hesitate to take the gaming guru under their collective wing.

When the fighters weren't taking shots at each other during sparring sessions, they were working on their fundamentals. People who would not talk to each other on the street were all home team at Lord's; an ex-con would hold the feet of a university student while he did sit-ups. An FBI agent held the heavy bag while a newspaper reporter unloaded combination punches.

Garriott squeezed into the cramped, lone bathroom, changed into shorts and a T-shirt, and emerged to be formally greeted by some boxers. "Everybody gets to know everybody else fairly quickly," he recalled. "And everybody supported everybody else without regard to their level of athleticism or their experience. The dedicated amateurs as well as the professionals in here all share a level of dedication. They all want to better themselves, as boxers and as individuals. These guys were not just a bunch of losers. They were hardworking, high-achieving people who were very well aware of what they were doing in here."

It didn't take long before Garriott was hooked. He soon realized that it takes a disciplined person to spend hours jumping rope, lifting weights, and working the heavy bag. That says nothing, however, for the amount of commitment it takes to step inside the squared circle and spar. To go three rounds in a ring against an opponent, the boxer needs to be a good runner, have strong lung capacity and endurance, be physically fit, and understand the ground rules. And these fighters, who were stigmatized as intellectually unsophisticated, were practiced tacticians. They made split-second calculations of their opponent's strength and speed compounded by their endurance. They noted which hand threw more punches and when. What combinations did the opponent string together? Did he come out charging hard, or did he try to wear out an opponent before surging toward the end of the round?

Boxing, Garriott learned quickly, requires more intelligence, skill, and athleticism than he had ever imagined as a bystander. The pure synergy fostered in the gym worked on his consciousness and made Garriott want to be in there day after day. After the first few weeks in the gym, he noticed something about himself: the cyber whiz was stronger. Faster. He went from questioning the idea of ring work to passionately anticipating getting in there with a trainer and working the focus mitts. Garriott learned that Lord's Gym was a family place, fostering the same social element as his elaborate communal video games. And his interest continued to grow on the realization that the hard work and dedication these athletes exhibited in the gym were punctuated by boxing matches.

Here's boxer A, who has worked his whole life for this one golden moment. He's always had the heart, but at times he's been over-matched and outclassed. He has struggled to hold on to his winning record so that promoters will continue his path toward a title shot and not cast him into that inferior class of opponents who are scheduled as automatic marks in someone else's win column. This is to be the fight of his life. If he loses, it will signal the end of his career. If he wins, he lives to fight another day. So you hope that he wins.

Now here's boxer B. Same story. Let's say you are a fan looking for a reason to like one boxer over the other. Maybe he comes from a city in Mexico or from a working-class American town that you relate to. Or maybe you like the fact that he's a little bit older than boxer A and is fighting the intrinsic aging process as well as an opponent. Meanwhile, both fighters walk a razor-thin wire of success. The winner will make substantially more money than the loser. The loser, in addition to making less money, will also have that scarlet *L* on his permanent record. So who do you root for? In Richard's case, it was the underdog, the guy who was so dedicated to the sport that he ate, slept, lived, and breathed it. To Lord British, it was the guy he had a causal connection to: the guy who worked out in the same gym. Garriott became a Jesus Chavez fan even before he knew his whole checkered past.

Chavez was a big part of Garriott's newfound respect and zeal for the sport. Garriott met the boxer for the first time after he'd been in the gym for a little over a week. He needed a trainer. Always a glutton for physical punishment, Chavez worked Garriott hard. The ab workout alone was enough to keep Lord British hunched over the next day. But Garriott developed a high threshold for pain, and he kept coming back to Chavez and his brutal training regimen.

It took a few weeks before Garriott heard from Chavez and then Lord how the boxer happened upon the gym. It was no coincidence that Chavez was in the gym every time Garriott popped by. The boxer trained and lived there.

Just by being around and working out with Chavez, Garriott became a confidant. He was told about Chicago, Mexico, prison, and the name change.

While he was hearing Chavez's story, Garriott was seeing things happen. Austin police officers were bringing East Austin children into the gym to meet Chavez. The police may or may not have known about his illegal status, but, nevertheless, here was a Mexican boxing around Austin and his name was appearing in the newspapers and his face on TV. The cops wanted to show the kids a success story. Chavez genuinely cared about their future, so he gave "the lecture" about the perils of gangs and gang violence, doing a job that most of their parents avoided. The message: stay out of them. They're guaranteed to land you in Huntsville (Texan equivalent of Stateville). Or worse yet, they'll land you in your Sunday clothes six feet under ground.

Garriott observed the pugilist speaking with confidence and personal knowledge. He was impressed by the way Chavez handled himself among the children who regarded him as an icon. He started asking Chavez more questions about his background, and Chavez spelled it out for him during a training session.

"I'm not a Mexican," Chavez told Garriott. "I was born in Mexico, but my family and my career are here. I screwed up one time, and I paid for that mistake." It wouldn't be until years later that Chavez would refine that statement. He was indeed a Mexican, and an American.

———————

Garriott and Chavez started to hang out together outside the gym. They went to movies and hiked at Enchanted Rock Park in the Texas hill country. Richard Lord continued to schedule fights for his boxer, and Garriott started attending each one.

In March 1996, Chavez fought slick southpaw Cedric Mingo (22-5) in Brownsville, Texas, for the vacant WBC continental America featherweight title. The boxer was on edge the whole night. Not only was the fight and the thought of a championship belt weighing on him, but the location was rather intimidating. Brownsville is the southernmost town in Texas, flush against the Mexican border and sister city Matamoros, Mexico. The boxer was less than a mile from the country he was supposed to be living in.

Mingo was four inches taller than El Matador. He did not have the same strength, though his longer reach and hard jabs worked like a cattle prod. In the past, he'd used his reach to keep opponents at bay. In the opening rounds, Cedric connected at will with Chavez's head and put a gash above his left eye. El Matador took each punch well and walked through the jabs to find his opponent's long torso. He hammered away at Mingo's ribs and took precious wind out of his lungs with shots to the sternum. In the sixth and seventh rounds, when the taller boxer's blows lost their sting, Jesus started punching above his head, finding Mingo's face at will. He won a lopsided twelve-round decision. Richard Garriott watched with delight from the front row.

El Matador was now recognized beyond Austin's boxing circles. Lord scheduled more fights, first throughout the state, and later throughout the country and the world. And for each bout, there was Garriott, sitting in the VIP section with a camera, a hobby he'd taken up.

Chavez's body was getting stronger, and the prison fat was long gone. He stayed lean, but muscle weighs more than fat, and the boxer could no longer fight at 126 pounds. He moved up to super featherweight (130 pounds), a division he's been in for almost a decade, and started fighting bigger, stronger opponents. In August 1996, Chavez fought another title match against fierce San Antonio boxer Luis Leija, who at the time was 18-2-1. At stake was another championship title: the North American Boxing Federation super featherweight belt. Garriott watched with pride as Chavez commanded the fight from the bell. Leija could not adjust to Chavez's unique stance, and the Austin boxer dazed his opponent with powerful left hooks to the body. The referee stopped the punishment in the sixth round, and Garriott made his way into the ring to celebrate with Chavez and Lord.

From there, it was on to Atlantic City, New Jersey, where Chavez defended his titles against two-time world champion Louie Espinoza, a fight that was stopped in the eighth because of a cut sustained by Espinoza during a clash of heads. Garriott watched two more title defenses in Austin, where Chavez outlasted New Jersey bad boy John Brown to win a twelve-round unanimous decision, and he watched the boxer rock Puerto Rican Wilfredo Negron.

By October 1997, El Matador was ranked fifth in the world by the WBC. His exciting style and his throng of Austin fight fans drew the attention of Lou Duva and Main Event promotions. Duva scheduled an NABF title defense in Atlantic City against former International Boxing Federation champion Troy Dorsey. This was the big time. The Chavez versus Dorsey fight was the undercard of the Andrew Golota versus Lennox Lewis fight on pay-per-view, yet it wound up being the more interesting bout. Lewis stopped Golota in the first round, but Chavez and Dorsey went seven rounds of all-out brawling before the referee stopped the fight in the seventh and El Matador prevailed.

Chavez's inner circle was jubilant, as was Lou Duva. Chavez was soaring in the weight class, with a number one ranking not far off in the distance. There is a provision in the WBC's rulebook that says a champion must schedule a bout with the number one challenger within a year of winning the title. As such, Chavez had a mandatory fight with the WBC super featherweight champion in his future. But the INS was on to him.

Garriott stood next to his friend and trainer in Atlantic City as fans crowded into the ring and as Dorsey looked on in stunned amazement. Chavez was bloody and swollen, but he and Garriott embraced nonetheless. They shared a victorious moment, hoping that the best was yet to come. El Matador would give the boxing world his best in due time, but Garriott would prove to be instrumental in making that future a reality for the young boxer.

8

Terri

Before Jesus Chavez was "El Matador," and even before Jesus Chavez was Jesus Chavez, there was Gabriel, the soft-spoken ex-con trying to put his life back together through training and a commitment to an ambition loftier and more concrete than any prison wall. As the boxer exercised at a fevered pace and dropped pound after bulky pound, R. Lord's Boxing Gym began to service a growing number of clients. They came to know Gabriel first through his skills on the speed bag and heavy bag, and later through his omnipresence. He was the king of the gym, sharing his reign with Anissa Zamarron. Anissa was a two-time women's Golden Gloves champion from San Antonio who was living in Austin and working as a lab technician while training at the gym and getting ready to turn pro. The gym regulars had great faith in their two boxers because the home team sticks together. That, and Richard Lord was a taskmaster. When the Texas sun was blazing and the industrial-size fans only managed to stir the heat around the gym, there were Sandoval and Zamarron, toiling away in the stifling heat.

As Lord's resident contenders were preparing for professional boxing careers, a nineteen-year-old sophomore coed at the University of
Texas was trying to find a major and a personal identity. She was quiet
and reserved, petite and pretty. Her look was akin to those found in
high-end fashion magazines. She had a trendy fashion sense with her
short black bob hairdo and just-right accessories. Beyond the clothes,
the petite 5-foot-2-inch tall student had cheeks that were soft white
and rosy. Her almond eyes seemed to slant up, a sign that she smiled a
lot. Terri Glanger was bookish but hip, the kind of girl who could hunker down in the Perry-Castaneda main library on a Friday night just as
easily as she could hunker down at the bar for cocktails at Armadillo
World on Sixth Street.

By 1994, Terri was adrift; she was at a crossroads many nineteen-
and twenty-year-olds face as they near the halfway mark of their
college experience. She was taking a lot of art classes, throwing pots,
and studying theory and history. But she desperately wanted to take a
class in photography. The photo department at UT is known around
the world, and some of the Southwest's best photographers, like
Martin J. Harris and Gerald Peters, kicked off their careers with a
University of Texas photography degree. Terri thought that a career
behind the lens might be right for her too, but she wouldn't know for
sure unless she sampled some of UT's photography classes. That
proved to be a task in itself.

Because of the photo department's fine reputation, the classes filled
up quickly. Terri was shut out of the photography courses she longed
to take her sophomore year. She registered for classes in her other area
of interest, philosophy, but the colossal amount of reading and memo-
rization associated with that major turned her off. Terri wanted to
learn photographic skills, and nothing was going to stop her.

Photography was in her blood. Grandpa Jack Glanger and her late
Uncle Maurice Glanger were renowned photographers, the chairman
of the Photographic Society in South Africa and a professional
cameraman, respectively. Terri looked up to her elder relatives. Their
photos of Johannesburg were enchanting. With a twist of a lens and
click of a button, Grandpa Jack and Uncle Maurice captured the spirit

of the continent's southernmost cities. Terri treasured their multihued images of landscapes and seascapes, towns and cities, architecture and people, flora and fauna. They portrayed the inherent beauty of South Africa—and even its glints of old-world European sophistication.

That was the lifestyle Terri aspired to as a nineteen-year-old sophomore. Even though the department shut her out from registering, Terri showed up for the classes she wanted anyway. The professor would take attendance, and there was a stowaway. She approached the professor after a couple of classes and asked him straight out: "If I keep showing up for class, will you let me in?" Initially the answer was no. The professor was flattered, but what sort of example would that set? The university had a policy, and a student who wasn't registered for a class couldn't attend.

After all, the University of Texas in the mid-1990s was experiencing a student explosion. Not only were Texas high school students attempting to get in at an unprecedented rate, but the grand university became a hot destination school for out-of-state applicants. When Terri was a sophomore, UT had an enrollment of 48,000, making it the second largest university in the country behind Ohio State. The faculty and class offerings at UT had not grown as fast as the student body. But Terri didn't let that technicality stand in her way. She persisted, and when a fellow classmate dropped out of a photography class and a seat opened, Terri's doggedness paid off and she was the heir apparent.

She was a natural photographer. Terri's work was defined by her eye for subtle color as much as her conceptual vision. She knew the diffraction grating and what hues worked best in a given situation the way parents knew which subjects their children excelled in. She liked to snap shots of impoverished South Austin residents as much as she liked to shoot the stunning autumn foliage flanking the Katy Trail and Colorado River.

As Terri continued to explore Travis County looking for photoworthy subjects, Travis County continued to redefine itself and expand in every direction. By 1994, Austin had over half a million residents, up fivefold from thirty years earlier. The infrastructure was growing, as were the music, cultural, and, as she'd soon learn, athletic scenes.

The university's student recreation center was always slammed. Terri and her friends often became frustrated with long lines of students jockeying for position to get on a weight bench or a Stairmaster. They ventured out of university confines, as Austin's growing population and infrastructure meant more variety: more stores, better shopping, and alternative methods of working out. Rock climbing became trendy, and climbing gyms began popping up all over the Southwest. Mountain biking was also gaining popularity, especially with the advent of the X-Games and extreme cycling. But both those cardiovascular exercises were expensive and demanding, especially for college students who didn't have the financial means to pursue them.

Terri's older brother, Gary, had a few buddies who were boxers in Austin, fighting on some amateur cards. And boxing an amateur circuit in Austin meant an inevitable stop at R. Lord's Boxing Gym. The facility started to double as a physical education building in the mid-1990s, especially when word spread among the university's cramped recreation center of Richard Lord's strenuous yet rewarding training routine. Then there was the legend of Lord and Bowie, which carried little weight with devout boxers but was an essential validating element for college students.

In 1983, British rock star David Bowie was recording his *Let's Dance* album in The Studio at Las Colinas, a suburb just north of Dallas. As was Bowie's style, he was also preparing for an extensive road tour to promote his album. The Serious Moonlight tour promised to keep the thirty-six-year-old rocker traveling for the better part of a year, spanning the globe with giant arena shows that demanded tremendous physical stamina. One of Bowie's local handlers heard about Richard Lord, the professional boxer from Dallas, running up and down the steps at University of Texas stadium. Lord would climb the hundreds of steps, turn around and run down, making sure to hit each stair. Then he'd do dozens of push-ups and sit-ups.

When Ziggy Stardust called Lord, the trainer nonchalantly agreed to take the rocker under his wing, and the two trained together for a couple of months. Bowie ran the steps and then worked the heavy bags at an old gym on 12th and Jefferson streets in downtown Austin. Bowie developed such an affinity for boxing that he even tried his hand at sparring. "I'm one of the few people that punched David Bowie in the face and didn't get the shit beat out of me for it," Lord said. Bowie was photographed for the cover of his *Let's Dance* album wearing boxing gloves and striking a pose that was quite similar to the stance Lord used when fighting on the pro circuit.

Terri decided to pay Lord's Gym a visit in the spring of 1994. She admits that the sport attracted her, although she couldn't name fighters other than Tyson and Ali. The participants she'd occasionally see while channel surfing on TNT and USA and HBO were conditioned in extremis. Their bodies were hard, their physiques defined, and their shoulder and back muscles seemed to be carved out of onyx or alabaster. This, she figured, was a convincing workout.

One cloudy day, when the skies threatened any outdoor activities she would otherwise have engaged in, Terri got in her Honda Accord and went looking for Lord's. It took a while: finding the gym among the other warehouses on North Lamar Street is akin to finding Waldo. But when she finally caught a glimpse of the life-size statuette of a flexing boxer atop Lord's roof, she navigated her Honda Accord through the pot-holed parking lot and settled on a spot near the garage door. The gym was eclectic. The warehouse facade was unintentionally chic, as warehouse dwellings and urban lofts were the posh taste of the time. From the outside, she heard grunts, and not just from men. Women's voices were distinguishable too, and the photography student figured she had stumbled on yet another idiosyncratic quirk in the state's capital city.

Terri ducked to clear the low-hanging garage door and ambled into the unventilated gym. Nobody thought to look twice at the attractive college student, as open-door had long been the policy at Lord's. She looked around, and she liked what she saw: unbridled training. The place was awash in character. The athletes, the setting, the decor. It was rustic, yet cozy and inviting. Terri walked past the practice ring, where a boxer was doing focus mitt work with a trainer. She strolled past the free weights and heavy bags that had men and women occupying them, and she walked into the office of Richard Lord, who was, as usual, musing over that day's training schedule.

Terri introduced herself, and Lord was characteristically noncommital. Not everyone who checks out the gym ends up staying, and Lord was, for the most part, a good judge of first appearances as to who would stay to train and who would be a one- or two-workout wonder. The college student looked sheepish but determined, and Lord gave her the spiel about the various classes he offered. Terri thought that the ab and bag workout sounded appealing. Appealing indeed, but as tough as they come, especially for someone who was not used to a grueling, full-throttle workout, as David Bowie would attest.

Terri got her gym bag out of her car, changed into some sweats, and an hour later was in the ring with a half dozen men and women about to start Lord's punishing rotation. To get boxers in the mood, Lord had them do three continuous minutes of sit-ups and crunches. That was round one. When the horn sounded, the students moved to the heavy bags for three minutes of form work. Round two. Then it was back to the ring for more sit-ups and some footwork. Round three. In between rounds, rather than taking a minute break as fighters do, Lord instructed participants to get on their faces and push the floor. Everyone aches their first time doing abs and bags. Even athletes who are in top shape learn the morning after their first Richard Lord workout that the body has muscles free weights can't strengthen. This point is hammered home when an athlete tries to brush her teeth or her hair twelve hours later. Not only does it hurt to raise an arm above her head, but it even hurts to wince.

Terri made it through her first boxing workout, exhausted and sweaty. She put her arms above her head—per Lord's instructions—and tried to remember to breathe. Her face was flushed and her black hair appeared even blacker from sweat. Her sweatpants and T-shirt clung to her body as she struggled to regain her composure. The student wasn't thinking about how she looked, nor was she surveying the other boxers in the vicinity. Terri was focused on keeping her rapidly palpitating heart from jumping out of her chest. What she didn't know was that someone was watching her.

Jesus was in the back of the gym. He had popped his head out from his room to watch the abs and bags workout. To the fighter, watching the hell Lord put trainees through was better than watching TV. "Who is that new girl?" he mused. "Man, she's pretty. Haven't seen her before. Hopefully she'll stick around."

She didn't have a boyfriend when she arrived in Austin in 1992, but Terri half figured that she'd have one by the time she left. That's just how college works. Her brother Gary didn't go to Austin two years earlier looking for love, but there he was, in a serious relationship with his roommate's sister.

Terri Glanger was born in 1974 in Johannesburg, South Africa, the second child of Trevor and Karen. She didn't spend much time there as her parents moved to Richardson, Texas, in 1977. The Glangers did not leave because they disliked their native land or because they wanted to improve their economic status, but because of the volatile South African political climate.

The struggle against South Africa's apartheid system of racial inequality was more than just a war of words. Theirs was a bloody conflict, with centuries of racial divergence that begat more than nine thousand political killings in the three years since the system began dismantling in 1990. But in the 1970s, the atmosphere was terrifying, especially after South Africa's black spiritual leader, Steven Biko, died during a police interrogation in 1977. The Glangers realized that the South African situation was about to get worse and they wanted a better life for their children. They felt the United States could offer such an existence.

Trevor asked around and learned that the climate in Dallas was similar to what they were used to. The Metroplex would serve as a home away from home. He was a savvy businessman and an avid adventurer. Trevor loved to bike, hike, and run. He liked fast cars and adrenalin sports. In the 1980s, Trevor opened his first business, Videoland (a precursor to Blockbuster), and later switched gears to an industry he thought was more him. Trevor opened Wheels In Motion, a bicycle shop that would eventually pave the way for a chain of cycle and fitness stores throughout Texas.

Daddy's little girl had some natural athletic ability but excelled in the arts. Terri grew up in an environment that fostered the sound-of-mind-and-body mentality that people like Richard Garriott staked their livelihoods on.

The Glangers were a traditional Jewish family. They tried to attend synagogue regularly, and always made it for the high holidays. The family held Friday night Shabbat dinners at their house with friends and family. Though Terri didn't date much while a student at J. J. Pierce High School, it was not due to a lack of advances from nice Jewish boys. Richardson, Texas, had an affluent Jewish community, and, as is the case with other religions, Jewish adolescents move in Jewish circles. That's not to say Terri wasn't friends with people of other nationalities and creeds. Some of her closest friends were Indian and Asian and African American. Jewish girls, however, are reared with an understanding that they'll inevitably grow up to marry nice Jewish boys.

Yet even the most agreeable child experiences a rebellious stage. Terri says she wasn't intentionally rebelling against her parents or her faith when she first started boxing, nor was she trying to make a statement the day she accepted an invitation to a Golden Gloves competition from a Mexican fighter who lived in Lord's Gym. Love is strange. Terri was an upper-middle-class Jewish girl from an affluent Dallas suburb. Jesus was an ex-con deportee, a professional fighter, an undocumented immigrant, and a Catholic—a nice Jewish girl's parents' worst nightmare.

———

Richard Lord had Terri pegged. She was no quitter, and she had an iron constitution. He worked her hard on purpose to test her will. She passed muster and was welcomed to R. Lord's Boxing Gym.

The sober surroundings of a working boxing gym had a profound effect on Terri's physicality and her psyche. Much like Richard Garriott, she too began to appreciate the inherent dedication boxers exhibit. She respected the workout as much as the concept of two people willingly entering an enclosure with the express intent of knocking the other off his or her feet.

She bought her own wraps and gloves and worked out at the gym several times a week. Terri also began to befriend the gym goers. The women were helpful, especially the experienced ones. Many of the men also offered to help her train. Despite the concentration she put into her workout, she couldn't help but watch the agile Mexican boxer who seemed to command the gym's attention with each move. He was soft-spoken but highly charismatic. He was clearly the most skilled boxer at Lord's, and the most mysterious. It was rumored that he lived in the gym and that he was a professional boxer, not one of the people who came in before or after work.

She liked his boyish complexion and the way he was entranced in his workout. He was only four inches taller than she, and yet he seemed larger than life. Everything about the boxer intrigued Terri, especially the fact that half the gym goers called him Gabriel and the other half called him Jesus. The man was a walking enigma. A riddle. And Terri liked the way he looked at her.

She'd often catch him stealing glimpses while she trained with Lord. On several occasions, Lord would employ Gabriel's training services, and he was only too eager to assist when Terri was in the gym. They flirted with each other the way schoolchildren do. He'd make all sorts of excuses to get close to her, like offering to hold the heavy bag while she hit it or help her lace up her new gloves. She'd ask him for tips on how to throw a right cross even though she already knew the answer. They made eyes at each other. Gabriel would work the heavy bag to the right so he could look at Terri. Terri would do sit-ups in his direction. All the while, Richard Lord saw what was happening. Lord couldn't deny his fighter's crush, but he also subscribed to the old adage that women make boxers' legs weak. He didn't say anything openly as the two continued to flirt and their gym association progressed into a personal relationship.

Terri and Gabriel seemed destined to become a couple. The boxer had introduced himself as Gabriel rather than Jesus, which was a bold move as he was letting her see his true self and not just his boxing persona. Besides, it would have been awkward for a nice Jewish girl to be referring to her boyfriend as Jesus.

When the Golden Gloves amateur competition came to Austin, Terri decided to photograph the event. Richard Lord had several fighters in the tournament, and El Matador was dutifully helping his trainer. Lord offered Terri a ride to the Music Hall, where the competition was to be held, and Gabriel meekly asked Richard if he could ride along. Terri sensed what was going on, flattered by the shy boxer's subtle yet obvious move. Later that night, Gabriel made a more obvious pass at the pretty college student. He played the I-don't-know-anyone-in-town card, which was a half truth. He knew people, as he had family on the East Side and acquaintances from the gym. But maybe she could introduce him to some of her friends? Again Terri sensed what he was doing, though she took the bait. He asked her in between bouts if she'd be good for lunch or a movie in the near future—prefacing the invitation with a "you guys," so as not to come across as too forward. An invitation to hang out in a group was more benign than actually asking her out on a date.

Then he tried to be a fatherly figure. "I don't think you should box," Gabriel said to Terri on one occasion.

"Why not? I'm loving it!" she replied.

"Because you're so pretty that I don't want anyone to mess up your face."

And again, Terri bit. She didn't know about her crush's past. As far as she was concerned, he was just a sweet, timid guy. Gabriel had a quality that made present company forget that he punched people for a living. He aptly distinguished between his ring role and his personal life. Terri had a unique insight into the two, but she never figured him for an undocumented immigrant, and certainly not for an ex-convict.

They socialized in a group at first, and as the attraction grew, Gabriel became comfortable asking her—just her—out on dates. Theirs was a typical college romance, except that he hadn't finished high school. They went to burger joints and movies. Sometimes he met her for coffee on campus, which was a strain since he had to run or bike everywhere. Terri's Honda Accord was the lone car in the relationship, so when she couldn't make it across town to pick him up at his gym residence, he had no choice but to improvise his transportation.

Chronologically speaking, Terri learned about Gabriel's past quickly. She gathered early on that he lived in the gym. An oddity, yes, but not unheard of. Rents in Austin were skyrocketing in the mid-1990s. He told her the family house was crowded, and that was a logical enough reason. Plus he was in training, and there was something alluring about an athlete so dedicated to his craft that he was willing to reside on the site of his daily labors.

Gabriel told Terri that he was from Chicago and that his family was still in the Windy City. Terri reasoned that Austin was a fine town to launch a professional boxing career. Terri was familiar enough with Chicago to know that the West Side, where Chicago and Damen Avenues meet, is rough. When Gabriel wasn't battling violent winters, he was fending off violent gang bangers. Austin was a different kind of town. She figured that the state capital was at the very least a break from the bustle of city living—the sort of place where a man could slow down, take life in full measure. It was when they went on their first dinner date that Gabriel divulged his past.

Terri picked her soon-to-be boyfriend up one Friday evening and they went to the Kerbey Lane Café for burgers. Gabriel was a stand-up guy, and his new life of freedom included an honesty pledge. "Terri," the boxer humbly started, "there's something I've got to tell you. I want you to know about my past and where I'm from."

Gabriel tried to justify his former life by maintaining that he was a good kid, making good grades. He was a dutiful son and a devout Catholic who got mixed up with the wrong crowd. There were a couple of older guys, he explained, who hatched a plan to rob a grocery store on Chicago Avenue. He emphasized that he participated in the heist as a sentry, not a robber. Then Gabriel told Terri about the plea bargain, about doing a year in Cook County Jail, a year and a half at Illinois River medium security, and another year and a half in the infamous Stateville maximum security prison.

She was shocked. This was an incredible story, one that Terri couldn't relate to on any level. She sort of appreciated his lesser role in the crime, though the idea that her boyfriend was an ex-con raised her awareness. Still, she couldn't help but like the boxer. The crime took place several years ago and didn't in and of itself make him a bad person. Terri pitied Gabriel and his past environment. After all, what kind of situation could have made an otherwise resilient person susceptible to that kind of peer pressure? She wanted to help him, to care for him. He was making great strides toward higher ground in life, and she was willing to help him negotiate life's pitfalls.

Terri had thousands of questions, but she thought better than to drill him there at Kerbey's. She decided to continue dating him, and she was willing to wait. When he was comfortable, then she would ask him about life on the inside. For the time being, she was satisfied with the information he volunteered. Gabriel told her almost everything. They spoke of Eva, his Chicago girlfriend whose name he had inked on his wrist while in the joint, only to remove it with a razor blade and lemon juice. He was forthcoming about his former life; like with Richard Lord, however, Gabriel reserved the most private part. He did not tell Terri that he was an illegal immigrant, nor did he utter a word about his deportation. Some things, he thought, were best left unspoken.

At twenty and twenty-two respectively, Terri and Jesus became virtually inseparable. They trained at the same gym, they ran stride for stride on the Katy Trail, and they spent day after day with each other, enjoying the quaint college atmosphere and leviathan Texas moons. Gabriel biked from his gym to Terri's house off campus, and then they'd go traipsing around Austin. They couldn't deny where this was heading: they were falling in love. In the beginning, neither of them figured the relationship would become so intimate. There were just too many variables working against them. But they just clicked, physically and mentally. On Sundays, they'd rise at dawn and run the stairs at the University of Texas stadium. Then it was over to E-Z's Café for burgers. The day would conclude with a movie, either at Terri's house or at the theater. It didn't matter: they were all about being together. Even when Terri was out walking with friends, Gabriel would tag along. He'd run up ahead, then back, then up ahead again. He seemed to make a workout out of any mundane daily event. And Terri thought his antics cute.

On one of these lazy Sunday afternoons, about two months after they'd been dating, as they were sitting on benches outside of the Central Marketplace, Gabriel revealed his deepest secret. He seemed more nervous than he'd ever been—even more than before a big fight. "Terri," he said, "I'm in this country illegally." She didn't think that much of his big secret. For one, it's not that uncommon in Texas to know undocumented immigrants. Gabriel, however, was acutely aware that this secret could mean his life. His love. His career. Prison taught him the value of keeping his mouth shut. But this new man—the reborn Jesus Gabriel Sandoval Chavez—wanted Terri to know everything.

———————

Good relationships have a defining moment. Birthed in either joy or sorrow, a single act can strengthen any bond and make two people connect on a deeper level. Husbands and wives who've watched and helped each other survive bouts with cancer speak of a sacred understanding that no outsider could begin to comprehend. For Gabriel and Terri, their transforming moment came when the boxer and his girlfriend discovered Terri's roommate had attempted suicide.

The couple was hanging out and watching TV in Terri's Austin house along with Terri's roommate Vanessa and another friend, Devyani. Terri's other roommate, Sherrie, was in her bedroom, pretending to sleep. Sherrie usually hung out with the group, so Terri was concerned that she was so quiet and secluded. She hadn't responded when her name was called, so Terri decided to check on her and make sure everything was all right. Sherrie lay in her bed, neatly tucked under her covers, with a bedside lamp casting a lone light. Terri thought she just looked tired, but her roommate was cutting herself. While the group had all but passed out in the living room in front of the TV, Sherrie emerged from her room—covered in blood—and tried to make it to the front door. Her plan was to get in her car, drive off somewhere, and die. But she'd lost too much blood and collapsed in the kitchen. Devyani found Sherrie splayed out on the floor in a pool of her own blood. She had slit her wrists and her throat and was motionless.

Devyani's scream roused the others, and Terri initially thought her roommate had been murdered. Gabriel tried to calm her down as he searched the house for an intruder. Vanessa called 911, and an ambulance rushed Sherrie to the hospital, where she was saved.

Not surprisingly, Terri suffered posttraumatic stress disorder after the incident, though Gabriel was quick with comforting words when she needed consoling or quiet with an understanding mien when she just wanted to be heard. It was a horrifying period in their lives, though it brought them closer together.

Gabriel's boxing career was in full swing, but his road to international recognition was not smooth. His other self, Jesus Chavez, had a professional record of 4-0 and already other lightweights were starting to walk away from him. For the first four fights, promoters had called Richard Lord to schedule his boxer as a "ringer," a boxer scheduled by managers to beef up their fighters' records. However, Chavez won his first four fights so convincingly and against opponents who were supposedly superior that other trainers were running scared. Ironically, his career was hurt even more after his first career loss in January 1995.

El Matador had bested four tough opponents, including Lewis Wood and San Antonio hometown favorite Rudy Hernandez. Lord scheduled an eight-round bout against Puerto Rican Olympic Silver Medalist Carlos Gerena (8-0) in San Antonio, Gerena's adoptive city. The fight was a defining one for both young fighters. Chavez, however, was the obvious winner. He displayed ring generalship throughout the match, controlled the momentum, and dazed Gerena several times with shots to the head. But boxing is a sporting institution awash in controversy, and that January night was no different. Two of the

judges were Puerto Rican, and they gave the fight to their fellow countryman. The third judge was from San Antonio, and he called Chavez
the winner. After the fight, Gerena reportedly walked over to Chavez's
corner and told El Matador that he did not deserve to win.

Chavez now had a scarlet *L* on his professional record. To an up-
and-comer, that demerit can stifle a career and knock a boxer down a
rung to a lower purse range. Contrarily, that loss demonstrated to
would-be opponents that this Chavez was no patsy. He officially lost to
Carlos Gerena, but pundits knew that Chavez got the best of the
Puerto Rican that night. He wasn't scheduled as a true contender but
as a stepping-stone for Gerena, as in the four previous fights. After that
loss, other trainers realized that fighting Chavez did not guarantee a
win. At best, it taught them that without hometown referees, although
their boxers might have better records, they would be the unofficial
underdog.

With his new professional reputation came local popularity. Terri
learned to adjust to her boyfriend's newfound celebrity status, and she
was a spectator for his tenth professional fight at the Austin Music Hall,
a match that pitted El Matador against Hector Vicencio (14-3) of
Reynosa, Mexico. That evening was a first on several levels. For
starters, it was Chavez's first professional fight in Austin. It was also
Richard Lord's debut as a fight maker, a notion that would give rise to
his Brawl in the Hall series of fights intended to showcase his number
one pupil. It was the first big-time boxing match staged in Austin in
over a decade. It was also Terri's first professional fight as a spectator,
and it was the first time she saw her boyfriend Gabriel in action as Jesus
"El Matador" Chavez.

Terri sat in the front row as the screams of 2,200 local fight fans
echoed in her ears. She was impressed with the way he dutifully obeyed
Lord's instructions, and how he capitalized on Lord's words of wisdom. Chavez spent the first three rounds measuring his opponent.
Come round four, the throng of fans began to chant his last name, and
Lord told his boxer to start working the body. The ten-round fight was
a war of attrition. His vicious left hooks to the body chopped at Vicencio like an ax through wood. With each subsequent round, Vicencio's

punches lost strength. Chavez obliged the cheering fans with a tenth-round knockout.

After the fight, El Matador received a thunderous ovation. Some gym goers stormed the ring, including Richard Garriott. The jubilant Jesus Chavez momentarily morphed into the shy Gabriel Sandoval when he found Terri's eyes down in the gallery. He winked and smiled, and she responded in kind.

From then on, Terri accompanied her boyfriend to his fights. It was an exhilarating time for the young couple. She was excelling with the camera in and out of the classroom. She was also developing an eye for action shots, and she'd be either on the first row or shooting from the canvas for his subsequent bouts. The photographs gave Terri practical experience, but the lens also created a false distance between the college student and the man she cared for deeply. He was a different man, the one who stood in the middle of a roped-off enclosure, both giving and receiving punishment. Sometimes, just those few inches of plastic, metal, and glass were all Terri needed to suspend the violent reality of it all.

By the time he captured the WBC Continental America's Featherweight title in March 1996, Chavez had amassed his own entourage. Richard Garriott and his girlfriend traveled to Brownsville, Texas, to watch a real-life success story unfolding. Terri drove down to the bout with Lord and Gabriel, and scores of boxing fans—Hispanic and white alike—made the long trek down to the border.

Terri graduated from the University of Texas in 1996 and briefly moved back home to Dallas. She and Gabriel stayed in contact via daily phone calls. As Terri was the one who had a car, she made the 215-mile road trip back down to Austin. No matter where it was held, though, she never missed a fight. In March 1997, when Chavez moved up another weight class (130 pounds) and challenged Luis Leija for the North American Boxing Federation Super Featherweight championship, Terri was there. Leija was a bruiser, and Chavez was not used to fighting at a heavier weight.

Prior to the match, El Matador followed his prefight ritual. He shadowboxed in his dressing room as James Brown crowed "Get on the Good Foot" from a boom box. Terri sat on a folding metal chair and watched silently.

Her boyfriend's tension was contagious, and she felt the pressure right along with him. Ten minutes before go time, Texas boxing coordinator Dick Cole entered the dressing room with Count Dracula (ring official Reuben Carrion), an affectionate moniker Chavez reserved for referees. "Ever see *Sesame Street?*" Chavez asked aloud. "They got this little vampire who says, 'One, two, three'. . ."

Chavez stopped dancing and the radio was turned off. Cole and Carrion went over the rules of the fight: Watch the head butts and low blows. Three-knockdown rule in effect. Mandatory standing eight count if a fighter is in trouble. Chavez nodded.

The room cleared out but for the boxer's inner circle of Lord, Garriott, his fourteen-year-old brother, Jimmy, whom he flew down from Chicago to watch the fight, and Terri. He shot her his shy smile, and she responded by walking toward him and taking one of his heavily taped fists in her hands. He laid his cheek on her shoulder.

"I hope nothing bad happens to you in there," she said in a soft whisper. Gabriel kept his cheek on her shoulder as he spoke to her, "I hope nothing bad happens to either of us. I want to win, but I don't want to hurt anybody. I actually worry about my opponent when I'm in there. I pray that we both walk out okay."

This would be the last prefight moment between the couple while both resided in the same state. Terri was preparing to move to New York City and take a crack at professional photography in the media capital of the world. Chavez would continue to climb the boxing ranks toward the super featherweight championship of the world. But not just yet. For that solitary instant—the precious minutes before El Matador would win his first championship belt at 130 pounds—there was the soft-spoken, shy Mexican boxer. And there was Terri.

9

¡Viva México!

Terri and Gabriel, the student and the athlete, were living separate lives in Austin. They shared a common space, however—boxing. But it was just a hobby for Terri. She wanted to start stockpiling photography experiences, and to do that, she had to leave.

Good photographers aren't born in isolation. They live and learn by measuring life's beats and reaping its bounty. There's only so much book learning a photographer can take before theory clouds the mind and distorts the artistic eye. Terri knew this, and she needed to act on her impulses. New York City is the center of the photographic universe, and the old cliché rang true to her: a shutterbug who can make it there can make it anywhere.

The pretty dark-haired lady from Dallas awkwardly hugged her boxer boyfriend, her bags packed. He'd come visit her in the Big Apple, he promised, as soon as he could snag a cheap plane ticket. She'd be waiting, having learned the city by the time he came, and would show him the splendor and bustle that is New York City. She sobbed softly as he struggled not to—for as long as he could. Good-byes are tearful, especially when they keep two people apart indefinitely.

El Matador returned to his room at the back of Lord's Gym and collapsed on his battered mattress. Sadness overwhelmed him. All good things inevitably came to an end in his life. There he was again, alone in his room, facing another period of uncertainty. His parents were in Chicago and his girlfriend on a direct flight to La Guardia Airport. He comforted himself with a reminder that he had a job to do. Promises to keep. He'd made it out of the ghetto and was on a money-lined road to immortality. To become WBC super featherweight champion would mean a space for him in the history books among other great lightweights like Julio Cesar Chavez. Richard Lord kept his mind focused on the task at hand: "Son, you've got the tools and the talent," he said repeatedly. "Stay focused. You'll get your shot. Just make sure you're ready when you do."

He was the reigning North American Boxing Federation Super Featherweight Champion, a belt he won in a gritty bout against Luis Leija in March 1997 with Terri in his corner. It was a national title that catapulted El Matador onto a short list of top-ranked super featherweights. He was ranked number five in the world when Lou Duva and Main Events came knocking. They recognized his talent, and they thought he would be a formidable opponent for Genaro Hernandez (38-0-1), the current WBC super featherweight champion. At the time, though, another boxer was making loud noises in the division, both with his skills and his mouth. Floyd Mayweather Jr. was tearing up the circuit, besting opponent after opponent. Richard Lord and Lou Duva figured by the time Chavez was the number one–ranked challenger for the WBC belt, Floyd Mayweather would be the champion and consequently his opponent.

The plan was to fight a few more tough bouts to defend his NABF championship and cement his stake as a worthy world championship contestant. In three consecutive Brawl in the Hall matches, Chavez defeated Louie Espinoza (52-11-2), John Brown (17-3), and Wilfredo Negron (15-2). El Matador didn't know who his next opponent would be and didn't care. The boxer was in the best physical shape of his life and felt confident that Richard Lord and Main Events would make a good next fight.

He continued to train in the gym with Lord during the day and by himself late at night. He was developing into a true professional—one who rose to peak performance the night of a big fight. Waiting around for that big fight, though, became increasingly hard for Jesus.

Lord gave him the keys to his old Ford pickup truck, and when the boxer needed to get out of the gym and break up the monotony, he'd maneuver the truck onto Lamar Street and cruise down to the University of Texas campus. The cultivated lawns and ancient oak trees always calmed his nerves. They were the ones he saw from his window seat in the airplane that flew him illegally from El Paso to Chicago three years earlier.

He was viewing the landscape illegally again, this time from the driver's seat in Lord's pickup. The trainer had been bugging him lately to get a driver's license. "I don't want you to get put in jail for not having insurance and not having a driver's license and all that stuff," Lord told him. "We don't need that to interfere with your boxing career." The trainer was not aware that "Jesus Chavez" was more than just a ring name; it helped fool the authorities into thinking he was a legal resident.

Jesus was comfortable enough by now to believe that the trail had gone cold. He'd been living and fighting in the United States for more than two years and had stayed out of harm's way. He had made a name for himself in Austin. Plenty of cops trained in the gym daily, and he considered them friends.

Chavez got his hands on another fake social security card around the time Lou Duva got him a match as the undercard of the Andrew Golota versus Lennox Lewis heavyweight title fight on pay-per-view in Atlantic City's Boardwalk Convention Hall on October 4, 1997. He'd fight against former International Boxing Federation champion Troy Dorsey, an aging though still dangerous fighter. Dorsey had the distinction of being the only athlete in the world to hold titles in boxing and kickboxing.

El Matador shifted into overdrive and began training intensely with Lord, then again at night by himself. When Chavez, like any other boxer, readied himself for a fight in proper course, he got increasingly impatient for fight night. The waiting was a confusing period, and a boxer would do anything to occupy his time and his mind in the interim. To kill time, Jesus decided to take that fake social security card and get a Texas driver's license.

He took Lord's pickup truck to a local bureau of the Department of Public Safety (DPS) and presented his bogus social security card to a lady behind the counter. The name associated with that number did not match the face in front of her, and she alerted a policeman working at the bureau.

The cop approached the boxer and asked for a second form of identification. Jesus said he'd forgotten it, that he only had the social security card, which is the standard line law enforcement is used to hearing in cases of identity fraud. The officer wasted no time arresting Jesus and detaining him in a DPS holding cell for false documentation.

Panic seized the boxer as he was escorted into the bowels of the bureau and into a waiting cage. The holding cell is where DPS officials were instructed to keep illegal aliens until the INS could show up and deport them.

Deportation wasn't on the boxer's mind. He was behind bars again, and that grim reality hit him harder than any uppercut. Jesus trembled as he tried to wrap his head around being back in jail. Despite the shock, he remembered he could make a phone call, unlike when he was brought to Cook County Jail six years earlier. The police officer let Jesus make a collect call, and he used it to phone Richard Lord.

"Oh shit!" Richard shouted aloud as the boxer broke the news to him over the phone. "Okay. You hang in there, Jesus. I'll be right down."

The trainer's first instinct was to get on the phone and call the people he knew in law enforcement. They all said the same thing: they couldn't do anything without knowing the particulars of the case. But Lord was unable to reveal the particulars, as he didn't know them. He drove over to the Department of Public Safety bureau and demanded to speak to Jesus Chavez.

At around the same time Lord arrived, a DPS official arrived to transport Chavez and turn him over to the INS. Lord strained his eyes and furrowed his brow to get a look at the guy. He looked familiar. Then it clicked: that guy was a boxing fan. Lord had talked to him in the past at a Brawl in the Hall.

The DPS agent was surprised to see Richard and asked the trainer what he was doing there. Lord explained that the person he was called on to deliver to the INS was none other than El Matador. The DPS agent looked at Lord curiously.

"You mean El Matador's an illegal immigrant?" he asked.

"I suppose so," Lord replied. "To be honest, that's news to me also. What's going to happen to him?"

The agent described the procedure. The INS rounded up a dozen or so undocumented immigrants a day and loaded them on a secured bus for the Mexican border. His job was to make sure Jesus got to the INS and on the bus.

Lord pleaded with the agent to get with his superior and try to work something out. El Matador was a big name in Austin and he wasn't a flight risk: he wasn't about to disappear into the American interior. The boxer, Lord said, was a focused athlete who had a big bout coming up in Atlantic City. The agent listened to Lord but was hard-pressed to find a solution. He had his orders, and to disobey could mean his job. Lord tried to sweeten the pot, promising autographs and boxing tickets to upcoming events—anything he wanted so long as Jesus could return to the gym with him. After much wrangling, the agent did speak with his superior—himself a boxing fan—and Chavez was remanded to Lord's custody. The DPS agent had to report the boxer to the INS, though, as that was policy. An INS agent, Lord was told, would be in touch.

Richard Gonzales, an Immigration and Naturalization Service agent based out of the San Antonio office, was assigned Jesus's case. He too was a boxing fan, but his commitment to the government superseded his sports enthusiasm. He phoned Lord shortly after the driver's license incident and said that the INS had linked Jesus Chavez to an ex-con Chicago tough named Gabriel Sandoval, and that the government would initiate deportation proceedings immediately. That was unless Chavez wanted to agree on a date to leave the United States voluntarily. Lord and Chavez contacted a local immigration lawyer, who after determining there was no other legal recourse, began working with the INS on the details of the voluntary departure.

Lord and Chavez agreed on a date when the boxer would sally forth to Mexico: October 14, 1997, eleven days after the fight with Troy Dorsey in Atlantic City. They figured that was enough time for him to heal so that he wouldn't be returning to Mexico with black eyes and bruised ribs. However, they didn't plan any sort of grandiose going-away party. The boxer wouldn't even make it back up to Chicago to bid farewell to his parents. They would be in New Jersey for the fight, and Terri planned to take the bus down from New York City as well. They'd have a little get-together after the match, along with Richard Garriott, but that was it. Everyone figured the boxer would be back in the country in a few weeks on some sort of a waiver. Main Events assured them of it, as they were willing to sponsor Chavez as an employee.

Chavez, Lord, and Garriott flew to Atlantic City a week before the big fight. He felt strong, ready to make his fourth NABF Super Featherweight title defense. They jogged along the Jersey shore in the preceding days, and Chavez did some media interviews where he announced that he'd be leaving the country voluntarily after the fight.

Richard Lord told the press that El Matador would deport himself while lawyers maneuvered to get him a type O visa, which would recognize him as a specially skilled individual who needed to be in the United States to take advantage of his talent. He said the process should take six weeks to two months, and once approved, Chavez would be able to return to the United States and continue boxing while working toward his citizenship.

El Matador operated under that assumption, so he didn't fight Dorsey as though it would be his last American bout. He did box the former champion hard though, trading shots with him and ultimately wearing down the boxer/martial artist by pounding him inside and smashing his ribs. Referee Earl Morton refused to let Dorsey answer the bell in the eighth round. The fight was a resounding success for Chavez, physically, mentally, and financially. He made $50,000 with the victory, the largest payday of his career thus far. That money would go a long way in Mexico, he thought.

Jesus figured he'd take his cash and take a break from the boxing world while he was in Mexico. He'd been training so rigorously that a vacation seemed well deserved. Delicias was just slow enough for him to relax and enjoy some family time—perhaps even a Tecate or two. Time off. That's what Mexico would mean.

Family and friends congratulated El Matador after his impressive win, one that captured the attention of boxing fans more than the main event did. Lennox Lewis stopped Andrew Golota in ninety-five seconds, eliciting a mixture of cheers and boos from the sold-out audience. But fans talked passionately about the Chavez versus Dorsey fight, as both pugilists proved they could dole out punishment as well as take it. Dorsey was overwhelmed by his opponent's presence, while Jesus's inner circle was underwhelmed with the prospect of his departure.

Terri returned to New York the next day, the Sandovals to Chicago, and Richard Lord, Richard Garriott, and Chavez returned to Austin. The boxer bummed around the gym for the next eleven days, letting his bruised face heal. He packed a small suitcase with clothes and some personal items, including his NABF belt to show his grandparents. He didn't empty his room, assuming that this was just a bump on the road. Richard Lord drove his boxer to the airport, and El Matador boarded a plane for El Paso and then took the series of buses—the same buses his father took three years earlier—to his grandparents' humble house in Delicias.

Good-byes are sometimes forever, even when they're not intended to be. The act of leaving a place—a way station that produced memories and recollections—opens a man up to confusion on his return, timely or not. Thomas Wolfe told us we can never go home again. Jesus

Chavez proved that making an attempt at returning just meant you started from scratch.

Jesus arrived in Delicias late at night on October 14, 1997. Hermila Sandoval smothered her grandson with hugs and kisses, happy to have him in her house again. Jesus Sandoval Sr. gave the boxer a firm embrace and patted him on the back. Jesus Chavez was there involuntarily, but Gabriel (as he was still called by his family) was received warmly. He wasted no time getting into a vacation frame of mind. He kicked back on the family couch that night and watched some Mexican television. Gabriel thought the newscasters spoke too fast and their accents were tough for him to follow. Indeed, Gabriel had been out of the country too long to relate.

Meanwhile Lord phoned Richard Garriott and Trevor and Karen Glanger, Terri's parents. They discussed the best course of action, ultimately agreeing that they needed a better lawyer.

Lord and Garriott phoned Main Events and explained the situation to Lou Duva, who hired an attorney. They retained a team of lawyers with the firm Baker Hostetler in Washington, D.C., which in turn hired Marc Kadish, a law professor at Chicago Kent University School of Law since Jesus's legal troubles stemmed from his days in Chicago. Baker Hostetler determined that seeking a pardon was the best strategy, and Kadish had been successful in the past with doing just that. So the boxer's lawyers said it would be best for Jesus to agree on a voluntary date to leave the country while Kadish and company began pursuing a pardon from Illinois Governor George H. Ryan.

Kadish said that while he would try to get Chavez back into the country through legal channels, Lord, Garriott, and the Glangers should begin a letter writing campaign to the Illinois Parole Board requesting clemency for the boxer. Richard Garriott also told his sister-in-law, documentary film maker Marcy Garriott, about this case and about the quagmire Jesus was in. Marcy thought this story had the hoof prints of a full-fledged documentary, and she began researching the story shortly thereafter.

The Main Events legal team was grinding its gears, though the promoters were neglecting their matchmaking duties. Main Events did not have a prominent Latin American presence in boxing at the time, instead opting to make fights in the United States, Canada, and Europe, where there were bigger purses. They assigned a man named Lou Mesorana to take care of their investment south of the border.

Mesorana was a journeyman who'd been around boxing forever. He trained fighters when living in New Jersey, but when Main Events relocated him to Corpus Christi, Texas, he became a bag man. Lou rearranged his schedule to be able to make jaunts down to Mexico for Chavez when he was needed.

Right away, a power struggle ensued between him and Richard Lord. Lou thought he was doing his job, keeping El Matador on the humble. Lord viewed the coming of Mesorana as an outsider meddling in a situation that was born out of mutual understanding and hard damn work. The new guy thought Lord was being overprotective, the old guy figured Lou was sabotaging their relationship, not giving Jesus his phone messages and attempting to drive a wedge between them.

As that drama began to unfold, legal wrangling in the United States began spinning out of control. Days turned into weeks, which turned into months. Jesus still hadn't heard a good word from the north about his situation, and his long-overdue vacation was turning into a long bout of inactivity. He began training again, jogging around town and in the outlying mountain ranges. He had inquired of some local residents where a man could box around Delicias, and all advice led Jesus to the *gimnasio municipal*, the town's lone public gym and the place where he shot baskets when he was a boy. Some local teenagers and a few people in their twenties worked out there, hitting one heavy bag that hung underneath the bleachers.

Enough time had passed that Lou Mesorana and Main Events needed to get Jesus a trainer, and he was set up with Nacho Beristain in Mexico City. By this point, Jesus was becoming antsy if not downright discouraged. He was in constant contact with Richard Garriott and his sister-in-law, Marcy Garriott, who was now producing a documentary based on the boxer's life.

Marcy served as the go-between. She explained that the lawyers were doing everything they could, and that some Austin residents were leading a letter writing campaign to the Illinois Parole Board and the governor's office. A pardon hearing was scheduled for March 8, 1998, and everyone hoped he'd be back shortly thereafter.

It had been five months since Chavez voluntarily left the United States. "That doesn't seem right," Chavez thought. "What the hell is taking so long? This isn't looking good." He telephoned Terri constantly, but their conversations ranged from heartfelt and sincerely longing to standoffish and noncommittal. Terri was loving New York City but hesitated to tell her boyfriend about Big Apple exploits. It would only bring him down, she thought, and he was in a sad enough place that hearing about the bustle of an American city would add insult to injury.

Lou set up a few fights for El Matador in Mexico City and Chihuahua, which he won handily. He was gaining a local fan base, but the more Mexican publicity he received, the more the country seemed to resent him. To them, El Matador was a northerner. An imposter. He admitted to himself that they were right.

The March 8 pardon hearing in Chicago was attended by Lou Duva, along with Chavez's friends and family members. It received local television coverage, and seemingly went well, although it was hard to tell since the prisoner review board does not release findings publicly. Instead, it makes private recommendations to the governor.

Months later, in January 1999, Governor Ryan rejected the request for clemency. Possibly the prisoner review board saw Duva's presence as a sign that the pardon request was more about making money than it was about a rehabilitated boxer's desire to rejoin his family and resume his career in the United States.

———————

Delicias felt like a holding cell. It was quaint and pretty, unlike any prison Chavez had known, but it was devoid of opportunity. His

Spanish was coming along, though not as fast as he'd hoped. And the blow from the Illinois parole board weighed on the boxer's confidence.

Not long after Chavez's clemency appeal was rejected, Floyd Mayweather Jr. won the WBC super featherweight championship from Genaro Hernandez in Las Vegas. And not long after that, Main Events informed Chavez that he'd been named the number one contender in the world for Mayweather's belt.

His emotions were all over the place. It was a tremendous honor to receive such a notable nod from the WBC ranking committee, as a number one ranking meant that Mayweather would have to fight Chavez. But Top Rank, Mayweather's promoter, could exercise its right to have Mayweather fight in the United States or not at all. For the first time, Jesus felt truly victimized by his predicament. The championship was right there for the taking, but there was not even a sliver of hope that promoters would agree to stage the fight in Mexico.

With no solution in sight, it was time for some drastic action. Chavez was confined to a Mexican life, so he better make the best of it. In the United States, the media often portrays pugilists as professional thugs or meatheads. In Mexico, the boxer brings great hope and recognition to his country. Chavez set out to win the hearts and minds of the Mexican people and especially the respect of his fellow Chihuahuans. There was one fight available for him in Mexico that would propel him to the highest status of athletic prowess in his adoptive country, though on paper, the match was a serious risk not necessarily worth taking.

Julio Alvarez, the Mexican national super featherweight champion, had a record of 20-4, which was less impressive than Chavez's 25-1. For a super featherweight, though, he was taller, broader, and arguably stronger. He came from a fighting bloodline.

Jesus moved through the professional ranks by taking tough fights against skilled and renowned fighters, but both Nacho Beristain and Lou Mesorana advised him against fighting Alvarez, especially because Alvarez wanted to fight in Mexico City, his hometown. The conditions set by the Alvarez camp were that Chavez would have to put his NABF title on the line, and consequently his number one WBC ranking.

The boxer's parents, Jesus Sandoval Jr. and Rosario Sandoval, Austin, 2003.

Grandparents Jesus Sandoval Sr. and Hermila Sandoval, Delicias, Mexico, 1996.

Jesus (center) after winning the 1988 Chicago Golden Gloves.

Tom O'Shea playfully punching Sean Curtin, Chicago, 1971. O'Shea and Curtin trained young Gabriel Sandoval before he was known as Jesus Chavez.

Gabriel Sandoval, a.k.a. Jesus Chavez, and sister Lidia, Chicago, 1984.

The exterior of the F-Housing unit at Stateville prison in Joliet, Illinois.

The B-housing unit at Stateville prison, one of the wings that Jesus called home while he was incarcerated.

Interior of B-house.

Chavez works out at Lord's Gym in Austin, 1997.

The U.S.-Mexico border, where both Jesus Jr. and his son illegally crossed.

Jesus, Terri Glanger, Adam Pitluk, and a local boxing fan hanging out in Rosales, Mexico, 2000.

Local youths and amateur fighters watch Chavez train in the gimnasio municipal *in Delicias, Mexico. The gym consisted of two heavy bags and a double end bag, and was located underneath the bleachers.*

Richard Lord gives the boxer advice between rounds, Las Vegas, 2004.

Richard Garriott attends a prefight press conference in Austin, 2003. In the background are Sirimongkol Singmanassuk (left) and Chavez.

Barbara Hines is an Austin-based lawyer who heads the immigration clinic at the University of Texas School of Law. She was responsible for getting Jesus admitted to the United States legally.

Chavez (right) hammers away at Julio Alvarez (left), the Mexican national champion, in Mexico City, 1999.

A victorious Chavez mugs for the camera, Mexico City, 1999.

Chavez (left) and Leavander Johnson trade punches during the third round of the IBF lightweight world title fight at the MGM Grand Garden Arena in Las Vegas on September 17, 2005.

After winning the IBF lightweight title, El Matador is hoisted into the air by his corner, including his brother Jimmy (left with finger extended).

Alvarez, however, did not put his Mexican national championship on the line.

The judges' scorecards were sure to favor the hometown fighter. Unless he could best Julio by knockout, the fight would more than likely go to the Mexican national champion. Indeed, as the sports pages indicated, El Matador had everything to lose by taking this fight.

But what Chavez and Lord understood—something that eluded the rest of his camp—was that to beat Alvarez in his hometown was to win over the Mexican public. To the masses, El Matador was still a *pocho*, a Texas gringo who did not appreciate his surroundings and couldn't relate on a personal level. Chavez was linked by heritage to Mexico, and he was going to do everything possible to become the people's champion. He realized, though, that a loss would mean the end of his career. This was the toughest fight available in Mexico, and there weren't any American fights with American dollars on the horizon. It was a do-or-die situation for Jesus Gabriel Sandoval Chavez. "If I lose this fight," he told Marcy Garriott, "It'll be the end of the Matador."

The fight was scheduled for April 19, 1999, in Mexico City. Beristain brought Jesus to Distrito Federal to train in February, two months before the fight. Delicias was a valley town, and the trainer wanted his boxer's lungs to acclimate to Mexico City's altitude. He also wanted the boxer to become accustomed to the pollution so that his nervous system wouldn't go into shock.

Chavez caught a flight to the capital and checked into a hotel. He was alone again, a stranger in a strange town. He tried to avoid loneliness by focusing hard on the upcoming fight. The boxer took his meals in the same hotel café three times a day, as he still had the stomach of a *norteamericano*. His two-year residence in Mexico helped his Spanish come around, but his stomach was slow to follow.

Beristain had Jesus do some roadwork in the mountains. He followed behind the boxer in a small leaded-fuel burning car as El Matador snaked his way up mountain switchbacks and into thin air. Day after day, his lungs seemed to weaken rather than adjust. He wheezed increasingly and moved sluggishly. Jesus started his training running up the mountain, though he continued to break down halfway up.

In the gym, Beristain had him spar some boxers with Alvarez's height and build, and each one continued to rock Chavez with combination punches. He was usually a fast fighter, quicker with the jab than his opponents, but Jesus was getting beaten to the punch every time.

Beristain figured the pollution was getting to him. Each breath of air Chavez took while working out seemed like work in itself. Jesus had no motivation to condition. All he wanted to do was sleep.

With two weeks until fight time, Chavez was worried about his predicament. He usually peaked in the red zone before a match, especially a big one like this. But he wasn't getting any better. His poor physical condition, coupled with his overwhelmed mental state, crippled his enthusiasm.

Jesus was lounging in his hotel room when he received a phone call from a member of his legal team in Washington, D.C. They were processing his case, the lawyer assured him, but in the meantime, they wanted him to apply for a visa. At the very least, he would be allowed to train and compete in the United States on a visa. The stipulation was that he'd have to return to Mexico when he wasn't doing a work-related activity. The government needed a drug test to even consider him for such a visa. The test was for illegal narcotics that were prevalent in Mexico: marijuana, methamphetamines, cocaine.

The boxer and Nacho Beristain went to a clinic in Mexico City where a lab technician drew three vials of blood. Beristain's nephew, a certified medical technician, analyzed the specimen.

Chavez returned to his hotel and received a second call, this one from Beristain. The trainer sounded strange, like he was probing his boxer to see if he'd been lying to him throughout their relationship. "Jesus, have you been having trouble sleeping at night?" Beristain asked in a curious and firm voice.

"No," the boxer replied.

"Have you been taking sleeping pills?"

"I'm not taking anything."

Beristain was satisfied with that answer, which as far as he was concerned, only made matters worse. "That blood test you took earlier, you tested positive for an extremely high concentration of barbiturates," the trainer said.

"Barbiturates?" Chavez replied, struggling with the pronunciation. "I don't know what is barbiturates. What does that mean?"

Nacho explained that someone had been slipping a sedative to the boxer, a performance-decreasing drug. Jesus ate all his meals in the hotel café, and apparently someone with access to his food—most likely an Alvarez supporter—was trying to ensure a victory for his opponent. No one was ever arrested, nor was an investigation ever launched, but Beristain appealed to the Mexico City Boxing Commission and requested a postponement. Two weeks was hardly enough time for El Matador to get all the dope out of his system let alone undergo a full detox and prepare for such a big fight. The commission had one of their own doctors examine Chavez, and to no one's surprise, they found a stomach infection.

The fight was put on hold until May 23, 1999, just over one month. Julio Alvarez, who more than likely had no idea about the drugging incident, took the postponement to be a sign of fear from the Chavez camp. *"Tiene miedo,"* Alvarez told a reporter. He's scared. And the majority of the Mexican media followed suit. An editorial cartoon in a Mexico City newspaper depicted Chavez with a cowering expression, sweat pouring from his face and standing on shaking legs. An impressive-looking Alvarez stood above the wimpy boxer, with a chiseled face to accompany his chiseled physique. "Poor Jesus," the caption said. "He doesn't feel good."

The poison quickly worked its way out of El Matador's system. Beristain did not let up on him in the mountains or in the gym, and the hurried pace seemed to have a decontaminating effect. But like drug addicts who become physically addicted to a narcotic, the boxer's body began to fail him. His energy was back, though his immune system was weak, and the persistent sweat along with the elevation left him susceptible to colds. It was a surreal feeling for Chavez. He felt strong, but his internal temperature fluctuated violently while his external body temperature changed from hot to cold instantaneously.

Jesus called Richard Lord in Austin and told him what was happening down there. Richard seemed concerned, though he was standoffish. The tense situation among him, Jesus, and Lou Mesorana exacted a personal toll and strained the professional relationship on Lord's end.

The friction hurt Chavez. This was turning into the sort of situation that consistently marred the sport of boxing. But his pride kept him from being humble before Lord. He talked like a cad on the phone, and Lord did not sugarcoat his own tone. The conversation was like a couple in a fight. They wanted to make up, but neither was willing to concede anything. By the time they hung up—each irritated with the other—Lord had agreed to fly down to Mexico City and help with the last weeks of training. He also agreed to be in El Matador's corner. The boxer had never fought a professional fight without him there.

With Lord's arrival, Chavez managed to focus on his sparring and running and put the pressure and social significance of the fight—and the fact that he'd been drugged—on a back burner. Lord told his charge three nights before the fight that he was impressed with his stamina and his punching power. The trainer was pleased to see that the long bouts of inactivity in Delicias hadn't cobwebbed Chavez's pugilistic attributes.

The prefight press began spinning. Alvarez was followed by a throng of fans everywhere he went: press conferences, the weigh-in, and even his training camp. They wore white T-shirts with his name stenciled across the back, and they draped themselves in Mexican flags.

Chavez's entourage consisted of Lord, Beristain, and Lou Mesorana. His parents couldn't make the trip because it was too expensive. His grandparents also couldn't afford the flight and couldn't tolerate the 880-mile bus trip. And even if they did, his grandmother did not like to watch him fight live. She got too nervous. Hermila was content with catching glimpses of her grandson on television between Tecates and cigarettes.

Alvarez tried to portray Chavez as a lonely coward. In a press conference, he said, "I have all my people behind me. I have more than three hundred people backing me up. I'm fighting in my hometown, and *I* don't feel lonely *here.*" One reporter asked Jesus who was backing him up. "I have my mother's blessing," Chavez replied. "That's more than enough for me."

Jesus and Lord concocted a strategy when fight night was only two nights away. Seeking to win over a hostile crowd, his theatrics were as important as his ring work. This wasn't the dual citizenship crowd he was accustomed to and Alvarez was no Lewis Wood. If Chavez was going to impress them—to make them believe that he was as Mexican as they were—he needed to embrace elements of their culture. He was, after all, El Matador. Why not give them a matador's show?

He and Lord ventured out into the Mexico City streets looking for a matador's *torero.* By dressing like the fabled bullfighter, he would don a mask of sorts. A bullfighter was what he billed himself as, and a bullfighter is what he would be.

He bought a black jacket, broad in the shoulders and tapered at the waist, which accented his muscular physique well. He also bought a sword and a red cape. El Matador was now authentic. No longer was he a bullfighting imposter. Indeed, his bon mot had come a long way from Tom O'Shea and his inner-city matadors. Lord sensed his fighter's confidence growing. That, Lord thought, was all we need. The kid's got the tools and the talent. Now that he had his health and confidence, El Matador was ready to put forth a champion's performance.

A boxer who holds a sanctioned championship belt has the option of making his approach to the ring first or second. With the belt comes the choice. Julio Alvarez was pressing the Chavez camp to let the Mexican national champion make his way to the ring second, even though his title was not on the line. Richard Lord didn't give Jesus the chance to think about it. He automatically refused and said that El Matador would exercise his right to enter the ring last, as the champion.

On fight night, Alvarez began his descent to the ring and the crowd exploded into thunderous rage. Chants of "Al-var-ez! Al-var-ez!" resonated off the steel rafters as the Mexican national champion looked supremely confident with his white satin robe, angular facial features, and light sweat covering his unblemished light brown body. Alvarez was tall at 5 feet 9, and his thick black hair and pointy nose and chin made him look like a Latino rock star. His limbs were long and wiry, solid muscle through and through. He mugged for the thousands of fans in his shiny white satin robe, giving the people what they wanted. He was a showman and an athlete: a double threat.

Back in the dressing room, Chavez tried to tune out the fans. He had become accustomed to the jeers of audiences. However, he had the ability to transform hostile fans into cheering ones by virtue of his ring generalship.

Lord and Chavez were alone in the dressing room preparing to make a champion's entrance. The rest of Chavez's entourage—Beristain, Mesorana, and a local cut man—waited in the hallway for El Matador to emerge.

The boxer had a layer of sweat covering his body. He bounced around and threw measuring jabs into the air. Lord leaned against the concrete wall, arms folded in front of him as he watched Jesus move. He was unusually quiet, likely because he had no words of encouragement to offer. The trainer knew that Chavez would need to win convincingly if he were to budge the local judges. He was still somewhat put off by their tiff, and he privately fumed.

The boxer jogged in place. He paused suddenly to stretch his legs before he resumed his jog. "This is my day," Chavez said aloud.

"Yep," Lord replied, matter-of-factly.

"This is my day," Chavez repeated. "My day."

"This is your title," Lord offered.

"My title," the boxer said.

"It's time," the trainer said as he grabbed the black and gold matador's jacket from a chair and held it out for Chavez to snake his arms through. "Remember that you need to put the pressure on him," Lord instructed as his charge donned the elaborate costume. "You know what you've got to do. Now get out there and do it, boy."

Two ushers pulled the heavy steel doors open for El Matador, which tipped off a wave of boos. The majority of the arena couldn't see him as he walked toward the ring and the waiting Mexican national champion, and they booed instinctively. But when Chavez entered the ring wearing the authentic *torero* and holding a red cape, some of the hostile audience cheered.

He held the red cape out in front of Alvarez and shook it up and down a little, yelling "Toro!" in his direction. The jam-packed auditorium came to life and briefly cheered for El Matador. He was putting on a great show, and the fight hadn't even started.

The bell signaled the start of the fight, and the two boxers rushed each other immediately. Chavez began his body assault, landing hard hooks to Alvarez's ribcage and diaphragm. The Mexican national champion responded with two measured hooks to Chavez's head. They swapped leather at a furious pace for the whole round, and both fighters returned to their corners after round one thinking he had set the fight's tone.

Alvarez answered the bell for round two like a raging bull. He charged to the center of the ring and started chopping away at Chavez. A barrage of combination punches fell all over El Matador's body. Chavez countered as best he could, slipping jabs when Alvarez relented a little bit. One straight right caught Julio on the jaw and dazed him. The Mexican national champion responded with a sophomoric antic that most pros only used in dire frustration. Alvarez, an accurate puncher, dropped his shoulder, bent his knees, and unloaded a hard left hook—with all his might—to Chavez's crotch. The punch surprised Jesus not only for its placement but the sheer power behind it. He quickly doubled over and backed out of the fray. The referee was in perfect position to see the punch. He stepped in the middle of the boxers and cautioned Alvarez to keep his punches up.

Vicious cheap shots like that, especially early in a fight, can take a lot of intensity out of a boxer. With that low blow, Chavez had one of his legs cut out from under him. He took a few minutes to regroup, going to a neutral corner, grabbing the third ring rope with both gloves and kneeling low. He took deep breaths before springing to his feet.

Alvarez stood glaring at Chavez from the other neutral corner. His red, white, and green mouth guard—the colors of the Mexican flag—forced his upper lip into a smiling position. El Matador finished out the round and sluggishly walked through the next two until he finally recovered from the low blow and essentially woke up.

He told Lord during the one minute between rounds that he was back. Awake and ready. Chavez answered the bell in the fifth round and in all the following rounds like a stalking predator. He pushed Alvarez around the ring, quick-stepping forward and making Alvarez walk in reverse until the Mexican national champion's back was against the ring ropes. When Chavez had his opponent contained in a corner of the ring, he went to work. El Matador let his hands go, peppering Alvarez with power shots to his face and torso. The crowd fed off Chavez's energy, and for the first time, the chants were not "Al-var-ez" but "Cha-vez!"

Both fighters began to tire in rounds six and seven, but that didn't stop them from swinging. Lord told Chavez round after round that he needed to turn up the intensity. He wasn't trying to be encouraging inasmuch as he truly felt that barring a knockout, there was no way for Jesus to win that fight in that city against that opponent. Chavez dutifully responded, charging to the center of the ring, planting his feet, and snapping out punches. Alvarez was catching his second wind, and he thought he could out-power El Matador should they trade shots in the middle of the squared circle. The flurry turned the crowd on its tail and pandemonium engulfed the arena. Both boxers swung so hard and fast that their arms occasionally tangled and the referee had to physically separate them. The ref came out of those situations significantly wetter than he had gone in, as both boxers were sweating profusely and panting and frothing like overrun horses.

Julio landed his best punch of the night in the tenth round. Chavez was chasing him around the ring when the Mexican national champion took one step forward to meet his opponent's momentum and landed a hard straight right to the chin. El Matador's legs wobbled and he came dangerously close to putting his gloves down on the canvas, which would have been considered a knockdown for Alvarez. But Chavez dug down deep and pulled together his remaining stamina to make it out of the round.

Richard Lord gave his boxer an order before the eleventh: "Up and down, Jesus," he said. "Up and down. If you hurt the body, you'll find the head." Chavez nodded in agreement and blinked violently through swollen eyes. The boxer followed instructions and hammered away at the body in the eleventh before striking the face of his opponent.

But Alvarez wasn't ready to stop. He answered with countershots up and down El Matador's body. In the twelfth and final round, the audience stood and watched two combatants fight as though the match was even and that the winner of the twelfth would prevail. That's exactly how the fighters felt. Both met each other yet again in the center of the ring, and both taunted the other with body language and funny faces. Each was trying to goad the other into making a mistake, but neither took the bait. They finished the match the way they started it: two tough brawlers throwing leather in the center of the ring. Chavez slipped in two hard rights before the final bell. The referee stepped in to separate the two.

Chavez had his back to Alvarez's corner, and the Mexican national champion had to walk past his opponent to get to his trainers. El Matador ran interference, standing in Alvarez's way and raising both hands victoriously above his head. The hometown favorite looked befuddled by that action and didn't know how to respond. The crowd was cheering aggressively, apparently in support of the gringo.

The boxers stood in their corners awaiting the decision. The ring girl, who tantalized the men in attendance with sultry moves between rounds, delivered the judges' decision to the referee. Both boxers walked to the center of the ring and took their spots on either side of the official. The ring announcer entered and the crowd fell silent. "Ladies and gentlemen, the winner of this fight, by unanimous decision, is . . . Jesus 'El Matador' Chavez!"

Applause and whistles rang out from the audience, and Jesus jumped up and down, raising his hands in the air. Richard Lord, jubilant that his fighter managed to win over the judges, put Chavez on his shoulders and carried him around the ring. When he set El Matador down, the boxer stood in the center and bowed to all four sides of the auditorium, choking back sobs as he did. Jesus rarely cried, though he was very emotional. Occasionally his feelings got the best of him.

Two judges had scored the bout 115-113, and the other 115-114. They were honest, confounding expectations.

The ring announcer approached the boxer and conducted an interview for all to hear. "Congratulations," the announcer said over the microphone to the now silent auditorium. "You showed that you are number one in the world, and you showed that you're a Mexican."

El Matador, breathing heavily from the emotion and the exhaustion, spoke fluent and eloquent Spanish into the microphone. "It means a lot for me to have beaten Julio here in Mexico City," he said, the crowd hanging on his words. "Now I have accomplished . . ." Chavez continued, openly sobbing and choking on the words as he spoke, ". . . one of my biggest wishes."

The entire auditorium stood and applauded. This was a proud fighter they were observing in the ring, one who put himself on the line for their entertainment and their respect. Some of the women in the crowd sobbed along with El Matador, while some of the men desperately tried not to. Chavez raised his left hand above his head and held out his index finger. He managed to shout through the tears. "¡*Viva México!*" he cried. And so did the people.

10

We're up Here, and They Just Don't Know

Jesus Gabriel Sandoval Chavez stood atop a mountain on the outskirts of Delicias, Mexico, and took a deep breath of clean, dry air. For once, his eyes weren't watering and his lungs felt clear. He gazed down at the dusty towns of Delicias, Rosales, and Saucillo, central Mexican desert villages with roadside taco stands, numerous auto and appliance repair shops, pothole-riddled asphalt roads, and scores of poor Mexicans going about their daily routine.

In the spring the sun rose early and by midday was scorching. It cooked central Mexico's parched brown earth to a hard crust, which in turn renewed the dust. The heat-soaked terrain readily absorbed the sun's brilliance and then cast a pervasive glare that illuminated and warmed the thousands of people, animals, and rickety vehicles in the valley with a brilliant corona, all of which unknowingly collaborated with the wind to stir up an eddy of dust that caked everything. It was unavoidable and ubiquitous. The swirling earth formed lines of dirt in the folds of people's clothing, on their exposed arms, and in the corners of their eyes, the result of hours of blinking away dirty tears.

It was 6:00 A.M., and Chavez sighed in gratification. He turned to his friend, Martin Vasquez, and the two stood like statues. All was well in the morning calm. No horns were beeping, no one was yelling at a rude neighbor—at least not within earshot—and their senses honed in on the sights, sounds, and smells of the desert as the mountain began to awaken.

They were breathing normally after running six miles up a loose gravel trail in less than ninety minutes. The trail snaked its way up the mountain, strategically built by the state of Chihuahua to avoid saguaro cactuses while allowing government officials to climb to the top and spot brushfires. The mountain was too steep for the trail to lead straight up, and tacking was the only way to summit without hundreds of yards of top rope. But laymen weren't supposed to climb that mountain anyway. It was exclusively for official use.

The two adjusted to the elevation as they watched the sun rise east of the pueblos, making the terra-cotta structures in the valley glow. "Look at them down there, man," said twenty-seven-year-old Jesus as he squinted into the dust. Martin, a twenty-three-year-old kung fu black belt and Chavez's best friend and training partner, nodded and mopped wet grime off his forehead with a soiled white polo shirt. "They're all running around, working and moving about, while we're up here and they just don't know."

Even though it was a cool seventy degrees in the early-morning air, both men were overheated. They wore heavy denim pants to avoid cutting their legs on the overgrown Palo Verde trees and shin stickers as they climbed. Chavez and Vasquez stood at the far edge of a granite bluff lined with desert shrubbery for nearly an hour as the sunlight intensified. They talked about their brutal training regimens and what sort of conditioning they'd do later on. It was focus mitt day at the *gimnasio municipal*, and Martin would wear the mitts while Chavez unleashed a barrage of powerful jabs and uppercuts. Then they'd switch roles, and Chavez would wear the mitts while Vasquez put together combinations of straight punches and high kicks.

They talked about Chavez's persona non grata status with the U.S. government—a popular subject among friends—before they headed down the mountain to the boxer's aging Dodge Charger, which was parked illegally on government land. No one bothered him about small indiscretions because he was a local hero, which was a rarity around Delicias. Anyone else would be kicked off the land immediately or, worse, shaken down by the authorities. After all, numerous signs warned trespassers of their fate should they decide to hike the trail. Chavez used to mind them, but when he became a name around town, he began to disobey local laws. The cops wanted to see him succeed and bring a successful sporting name to their tight-knit community, so they willingly obliged his training needs. For Chavez, a boxer in a town not equipped for any sort of athletic training, climbing the mountain was a necessity. The authorities agreed.

These were two Mexican athletes at the height of their prowess. Chavez climbed that mountain five times a week, usually alone, both to condition his lungs and to escape the grinding poverty six miles below. Many Mexican nationals in Delicias were proud people. They made do with the resources at their disposal, like fertile soil on the town's outskirts that produced lush pecan trees and orange groves, and they benefited from cheaper prices on goods than were offered fifty miles away in Chihuahua City. Nevertheless, for as hard as they worked, they barely eked out a living.

Lately the boxer had been feeling lonely, and the kung fu black belt readily accepted the invitation to run up the mountain with him. When he wanted alone time, Jesus would climb the mountain and reminisce about how well he had it just two years ago. He would retrace the steps of his peculiar life up on that crag and question whether he was just unlucky or whether there was some grandiose reason for his plight. He would think about Stateville maximum security prison in Joliet, Illinois, and about the pervasive fear the institution instilled in its residents. And he would think about his rise to power in Austin, Texas, from no-name boxer living in the back of Richard Lord's boxing gym to top contender in the world for Floyd Mayweather's WBC super featherweight championship boxing belt.

Many days, he would think about Terri, his girlfriend from Austin who was trying to cut her teeth in the photography world of New York

City. Then of course there were his parents, brother, and sister in Chicago. He wondered how they were doing—what they were up to. Jimmy was growing up fast and was following in his brother's footsteps at the Matador Gym in Eckhart Park. Lidia was married now with her first child. Gabriel longed for the day he'd meet his nephew as he gazed down on the valley of his adoptive country. He used to think it was only a matter of time and red tape before the Sandoval family would all be sitting around the kitchen table at his father's West Rice Street house on Chicago's West Side. But life went on, with or without him, like it or not. As the seasons changed in the north, the weather went from temperate to sizzling hot in Chihuahua. Time continued to pass and fold over onto itself. Jesus Gabriel Sandoval Chavez began to lose the only feeling that kept him from going insane in prison: hope.

When the dread overwhelmed him; when the boxer could no longer face that he had been living the American dream and had ruined it by becoming too comfortable in his surroundings; when he forgot the one cardinal rule he learned in prison, to always, no matter what, be on high alert, Jesus would slip into melancholy. His environment became oppressive and he in turn became claustrophobic, ironically, since he had a huge country to maneuver in. His grandparents' love and kindness felt different from that of his parents. And he felt alone, utterly alone, since his pleas for a green card and his longing to go home were falling on deaf ears. When those feelings closed in on him, Jesus yearned for companionship. As he learned over time, only a run up the mountain and a good friend could cure what ailed him.

After an hour, the thin air on the mountaintop became so hot from the omnipresent sun that it emanated its own dry smell. From the valley, Chavez looked like an impressive statue rising from the summit. His 5 foot 6 body was perfectly chiseled and cast a shadow twice as large. His shoulders were wide at their apex and flawlessly tapered to a *V* at his waist. His black hair was short and unkempt, and the strain from the cardiovascular workout he had just completed caused two blue veins to protrude from the side of his neck. His wide brown eyes were watering but clear and he blinked hard into the air: the nervous tic was still present.

He inhaled through his nose and the breath escaped between his gapped front teeth and pursed lips. As the minutes passed, it was the heat and no longer the morning run that began to roast Chavez. He was breathing regularly and his heart was no longer pounding against his breastbone, but he was still sweating profusely despite the gentle breeze that should have chilled his wet skin and cooled him off. So the boxer and the black belt headed down the mountain.

The descent into the valley was steep at first. Thick, prickly shrubs snagged their pant legs with every step along the mountain path. Blood began to appear as a few thorns pierced their denim trousers. They jogged down the trail, keeping their weight back against the mountain slope and their hands at the ready.

Once the men maneuvered halfway down the loose gravel trail, they became playful. They started racing each other down the mountain, grinning as they kicked up dust and rocks. Vasquez, the tall one at 5 feet 7, high-stepped some bushes and tried to grab Chavez's shoulder and wrestle him to the ground. But as he reached for the boxer, Chavez broke out in a Speedy Gonzales run, laughing as he yelled ¡Inmigración! at Vasquez. The two were engaged in a little game: Vasquez played the role of an INS officer chasing the boxer. Jesus played himself.

The two had several near wipeouts as they battled to be the first one down the mountain, back into the dust bowl. The mountain symbolized escape; the valley captivity. Back at sea level, Chavez continued his daily training regime for an as yet unscheduled championship bout under the bleachers of the poorly equipped, miserably hot *gimnasio municipal*. He would end this day—as he did almost every day—at his grandparents' humble flat outside of Delicias rather than in a plush apartment in Las Vegas, his father's small house in Chicago, or even a cramped room at Lord's Gym in Austin. He would fight some bouts in Mexico against opponents with half his talent, and he'd earn between $10,000 and $30,000 a year while a bunch of boxers he'd beaten in the United States made ten times that. And since he bested Julio Alvarez, the Mexican national champion, fellow Mexican boxers were hesitant to take a fight against El Matador. Alvarez was considered the best at that weight. But here was this guy who showed up out of nowhere—formerly an

American as far as the people were concerned—who defeated their hero despite being poisoned and despite Alvarez's home-ring advantage. Even with all those problems, that was still a pleasant memory. This, on the other hand, was frustration to the nth degree.

Jesus continued to train on the off chance that he would one day return to America and fight Floyd Mayweather Jr. for the World Boxing Council super featherweight championship. He was, after all, the number one contender. He would not succumb to the grim reality that his preparation might be in vain. He was more disciplined and regimented in exile than he had ever been in the United States. Jesus had a one-track mind while cooling his heels in Mexico. He had two names there, two identities and two countries he considered home, a testament to his bifurcated world.

Coming off the mountain and returning to life in Delicias meant returning to a life sentence imposed by the U.S. government two years earlier. The only perk Chavez enjoyed was his status as sole celebrity for hundreds of miles. The entire country recognized him after he beat Julio Alvarez a year earlier. Nevertheless, stardom did not console him. Other than an occasional run through town, the boxer seldom left the house at night. He worried that a band of boozers with beer muscles would test their manhood by jumping him. Potential trouble lurked on every corner in that rough-and-tumble town. People drank to curb boredom, and they drank a lot—all day long at the lead, zinc, silver, and copper mines in neighboring Naica, into the dusk along the banks of the Conchos River, and all night long at Alamo Tecate, locally known as the drive-in.

Hordes of people piled into pickup trucks and dilapidated Chevys and Buicks, drove along winding back-country roads, and descended on Alamo Tecate for a night of hard drinking. Cars and pickup trucks maneuvered through the rows of tables and parked within arm's reach of picnic table–like stands. Waitresses brought them bucket after bucket of Tecate. Everyone drank, and neither the waitresses, management, nor police seemed to mind that the drivers became as intoxicated as their passengers. At 2:00 A.M., when the waitresses stopped serving, the cars pulled back onto those winding roads and drove off into the desert night. The roads weren't that easy to follow in the daylight let alone at night, when the moon was the only light source for miles. The vehicles seem to toboggan down the roads, swerving and veering as they went.

Sometimes there were accidents. The Tarahumara Indians, Chihuahua's only remaining indigenous people, were known for wandering the deserts with nothing but flimsy sandals on their feet. Occasionally they came out of their mountain cave dwellings and headed to town at night to buy food and alcohol for the tribe. The desert was unbearably hot during the day, but nights got bitterly cold. The Tarahumara would drink away the chill, but from time to time, a tribesman would fatally cross paths with an Alamo Tecate patron after last call. The town would express outrage momentarily, then look the other way and ignore the problem.

Bravado in men was measured by how well they handled themselves with their fists, as well as how much alcohol they could consume. It was not uncommon for an exchange of words to escalate into unbridled rage. These were the people Chavez feared the most. In a one-on-one fight, he would prevail. But men do not always fight fair.

Then there were Chavez's social problems. Even with his prison tattoos from the Stateville days, El Matador was an attractive man. He had deep brown eyes and was built like a Marine. His skin was tanned dark brown and flawless, save for his prison tats.

His looks, coupled with his celebrity status, made him popular with the *señoritas* in Delicias. While many twenty-seven-year-old professional athletes in the United States would have made good use of those attributes, Chavez did not even date a girl in Mexico. Instead, he pined away for Terri.

Back in Austin, Jesus and Terri would walk hand in hand along Sixth Street, a thoroughfare brimming with pubs, barbecue joints, and University of Texas students. They'd listen to music streaming from the various venues along Sixth Street and Congress Avenue during the cool Texas nights, and Jesus would hug Terri from behind as they'd stand among the wandering pub crawlers and college students while the different sounds meshed at the confluence of Sixth and Congress.

Two years later, with Terri in New York and Jesus cast away in Mexico, he occasionally wandered around Avenida Agricultura, Delicias's town circle, late at night—when he worked up the courage to leave his humble flat—and flagged down the mariachis for hire that cruised around the square. The wages Jesus made from boxing in Mexico were considered scandalous by U.S. standards, but in Mexico that money propelled him into the upper echelon of Delicias high society and enabled him to spend a little, which was still not saying much. Even though some residents had creature comforts like cars and refrigerators, many were impoverished and had no money to spare. Jesus could afford to pay all five musicians $10 apiece to perform for an audience of one, but $50 in one night was still an expense for him. The boxer saved his money for his biggest expenditure, a $500 monthly phone bill that he incurred because of lengthy international calls to his parents in Chicago, Richard Lord and Richard Garriott in Austin, and Terri in New York City.

Chavez instructed the troubadours to play only sad ballads—ones that reminded him of his lady-in-waiting. After a couple of songs, a crowd usually gathered in the square as the horns melodically trilled and the tenor and baritone harmonized. El Matador let the people listen without making them chip in. It wasn't very often that townies got to hear a free concert.

On a couple of occasions, Jesus and Martin headed off to 1888 in the center of town, more so to be around people their own age than anything else. Named for the year it was built, 1888 was the local brothel. Neither athlete indulged himself with the ladies but found cold comfort in its dimly lit entryway and old-world charm. 1888 was built of solid wood and brick. A gigantic beer barrel—some twenty feet tall—marked the entryway. It arrived in Delicias from Germany full of beer in the late nineteenth century. The actual bar was over one hundred years old, and in lieu of stools, 1888 had hundred-year-old barbershop chairs for patrons to lounge in. The beams were original, with the cottonwood curing over time in the hot desert sun. The bar's owner, Andres Bunsow, was third-generation Delicias stock. He spent some time in California before returning to the town and taking over

1888 when his father died. Bunsow took pains to keep the bar as a pristine throwback to a different era. And indeed it was.

José, the head bartender, recognized Jesus and Martin, as he was a big boxing and all-around sports fan. He slipped them Carta Blancas under the table as well as shots of 100 Años tequila—top shelf stuff— all the while urging them to return and regale him with tales of hand-to-hand combat. The prostitutes lounging in the bar were some of the only women in town who didn't solicit the boxer and the black belt for "companionship."

Pati, a fresh-faced courtesan with a firm build and a silver-capped front tooth, never bothered the athletes but got the skinny on their activities from José. It meant losing money, as sitting around shooting the shit with José did not pay the bills: Flirting with the drunken *hombres* and convincing them to rent a room for a couple of hours did. But the boxer and the black belt did not come in frequently enough for her to pass up an opportunity for good gossip about the town celebrity.

Pati believed that she could relate to Jesus even though they never spoke. They were living a life that they did not necessarily choose for themselves. Theirs was an existence born out of circumstance. Pati needed to make a living, and her body was her trade. Like many of the other prostitutes, she had little education though she once had big dreams. She would leave that town—she'd make it to Chihuahua City if not the United States. But those dreams came and went like all the others.

The boxer understood what it was like to be stuck in a situation, and so did Martin for that matter. Martin wanted a life like the one Jesus had in the United States. The kickboxer from Delicias would do anything to have a little adventure in his mundane day to day. Martin thought Jesus made the West Side seem intriguing, despite its hardships.

Life in Mexico was mostly joyless for El Matador, even after he established himself as a countryman. When he arrived in his land of exile for the second time in 1997, after spending three years in America as an illegal immigrant, Jesus spoke terrible Spanish. He had an American accent and seasoned his words with Chicago street slang.

During his first year south of the border, Chavez was recognized only as the guy who went running through town with his deaf Dalmatian, Chula (Pretty). He often ran around Avenida Agricultura in the heart of town and tied his dog up at a parking meter while he ate tacos at Del Borrego De Oro, or the Golden Calf, on Calle 2 Poniente. It was the local eatery for people his age, and although he didn't know many of the patrons, Jesus liked the twenty-something atmosphere. And he loved the tacos. The Golden Calf was decorated like a 1950s diner with vinyl-covered booths, polished-chrome napkin dispensers, ramekins of salsa, and salt and pepper shakers always on the vintage tables. Two cooks worked behind the bar stool–lined counter—which was always packed—and cooked the heaping piles of raw meat. Tacos were served in soft, fresh corn tortillas by the fours with wedges of lime. Jesus would eat two orders and chase them with a Fresca.

He was acutely aware that patrons at the Golden Calf, as well as many townies, called him gringo behind his back. His grandfather jokingly called him "nothing but a dirty *pocho*," meaning "traitor."

Despite the urge, Jesus never pummeled his townie tormentors. He knew that it wouldn't make him feel any better. He was a professional boxer, but his violent days were behind him. He respected the sport and his own talent too much to engage in a street brawl: He had his share of fights in prison and realized in hindsight that they accomplished nothing.

It wasn't until he bested the Mexican national champion in 1999 that he earned any respect in his native country. At around the same time, his Spanish finally improved and he sounded like a Mexican national. And after a unanimous decision victory over Alvarez, nobody called him names other than Matador or *campeón* (champion). That too always weighed on Chavez in Mexico. They called him El Matador, but he'd never even been to a bullfight. "Even if I had, I'd probably cheer for the bull." El Matador related to the underdog only too well.

In Delicias, Jesus resided in a tiny room in his grandparents' modest but comfortable flat, sharing space with his retired grandmother and grandfather and sometimes his uncle, Julio. His room was at the rear of the ranch. It combined American luxury items with a distinctly Mexican flair. The stucco walls were decorated with posters of Mike Tyson and David Bowie, autographed from the rock star's time training with Richard Lord in Austin. And there was a poster of the most famous Mexican boxer of all time, Julio Cesar Chavez. Trophies that Jesus won on the amateur boxing circuit in the Midwest before his imprisonment lined the bookshelves, while awards and accolades from the Mexican Boxing Commission cluttered his nightstand. Even though the American boxing world had cast him into exile, refusing to schedule championship bouts for him in Mexico because of the weak peso, the Mexican boxing community finally accepted and later heralded him as a native son. It made no difference in Delicias, neighboring Rosales, nor 880 miles away in Mexico City that Chavez was a twice-deported ex-con Texas gringo who was in the country by force. The people grew to love him, and he them.

El Matador had one big-ticket item in his tiny room: a twenty-inch Sony TV that he used to watch his own video footage—not out of vanity but for training. His real trainer, Nacho Beristain, was a two-hour flight away in Mexico City, and his other trainer, Fernando Castrejon, was an hour and a half away in Tijuana. Chavez flew to the Mexican capital or to Baja California Norte for training every two or three weeks, depending on whether he could snag a cheap ticket.

Mexico City was the epicenter for professional boxing, and the country's best fighters trained there, giving Chavez some expert sparring partners, including number two–ranked featherweight Guty Espadas and WBC straw weight champion Ricardo Lopez. He toyed with the notion of moving to Distrito Federal permanently, but he couldn't leave his grandparents. Jesus had lost too many years in the joint to willingly live without family around him. Also, he abhorred Ciudad de Mexico's industrial fumes and violent streets. When Chavez trained in Mexico City, his lungs burned for the first few days because of the pollution. The smog made Delicias's dust bowl seem like fresh country air. Chavez journeyed to higher altitudes for his cardiovascular regimen because training in Mexico City, he said, was like smoking while you ran.

He passed the time by working out on the mountain and under the bleachers of the city's lone municipal gym. Still, his training routine in the gym came with inherent problems. The old municipal gym, with its chipping green and yellow paint and rusty warehouse-style door, housed the city's only indoor basketball court. Bleachers stretched from the splintering wooden floor to the asbestos-coated ceiling on either side. The wooden bleachers, bare walls, and high ceilings turned the municipal gym into an echo chamber, and the smallest sound resonated throughout.

Underneath the home team's bleachers was the boxing gym. A single lightbulb burned dimly against the lime-green walls. Three tattered heavy bags hung from the ceiling, as well as a speed bag and a double-end bag. The double-end was more like a slingshot than a piece of boxing equipment. It was anchored to the floor and a low-hanging bleacher by recycled hunks of rubber and reinforced with rope, making the action much quicker than usual.

The most depressing part was the sparring ring. There were no ropes. No turnbuckles. Not even a mat. Fighters battled each other like gladiators on the bare cement floor. There was a square of concrete between the bleachers and the side door, and pugilists impro-vised by using that as their ring. They figured it was square—why not use the walls as ring ropes? On several occasions, a fighter was knocked out twice by one punch—first by the other boxer and then by landing on the cement. El Matador couldn't spar at full force for fear of fatally injuring someone with a knockout blow.

As many as thirty people at a time worked out in the Delicias gym under the guidance of two flabby, underskilled volunteers who supplied them water from an old laundry detergent bottle. When the bottle developed leaks from being thrown around, the trainers simply covered them with duct tape. One of the old trainers sparred with fighters who were half his age and one third his girth. After each session, he appeared to have barely cheated death, sweating profusely and breathing abnormally hard. There was no phone in the gym and no way to call for help if an accident occurred.

It took a tough, extraordinarily dedicated fighter to train in such conditions. Or absolute boredom. Whatever the case, youths flocked to the gym. The moment El Matador walked in the door, the room cleared out and the boxers crowded the one bench or they stood around to hang on his every word and move. El Matador obliged them, offering advice, even one-on-one instruction. He was their hero, the only proof of a bigger world outside Delicias, even though he was stuck there just as they were.

El Matador trained rigorously for an invisible opponent. He was the number one contender for a world championship title shot for more than two years, but in Mexico there was nothing to contend for. Fortunately his friends in the United States hadn't forgotten about him. Richard Garriott, Richard Lord, Terri Glanger and her family, and Lou Duva and Main Events promotions were diligently working with a lawyer to bring him back to the States legally.

In the meantime, though, there was Delicias. Over the next year, the boxer continued to rise at 4:30 A.M. five days a week and run up the mountain, leaving his problems behind to swelter in the diesel and dust.

11

Just a Camera

Back in the United States, the boxer's promoter, Main Events, continued leading the legal charge. After Governor Ryan rejected Chavez's pardon request, however, a sense of uncertainty set in.

Marcy Garriott interviewed a New York University law professor known for work on immigration rights issues for her 1998 documentary on Chavez. The lawyer asked Marcy why she traveled to New York when one of the country's foremost immigration attorneys lived right there in Austin.

Barbara Hines spent twenty-five years in private practice before becoming director of the immigration clinic at the University of Texas School of Law. She spent the first seven years of her career doing pro bono work for Legal Aid, the nation's oldest and largest provider of legal services for the indigent.

Hines was something of a firebrand while cutting her legal teeth. Back in the 1960s, she protested the war in Vietnam and campaigned for women's rights. Hines marched against the war and readily admits to having a hundred-page long FBI file from that time period. She decided that a legal career would be the only way for her to champion justice and effect change for the exploited and downtrodden.

Hines majored in Latin American studies at the University of Texas and then went on to get her law degree from Northeastern University in 1975. She says she stumbled onto immigration law. Hines got a job at Legal Aid of Austin and because she spoke Spanish, twenty cases were dumped on her desk. She's been in the field ever since.

Marcy initially approached Hines in the summer of 1998 for a comment on her documentary. The lawyer looked professional in her business suit and shoulder-length curly black hair. Her face was pretty and round, with sharp, piercing eyes. She offered some interesting facts about immigration law for Marcy's film, none of which made the original work but did make the DVD supplement in later years.

Marcy did not ask her to work on Jesus's case when they first met. The Main Events legal team was already grinding away, and Barbara's own work load was massive. Her immigration law seminar had a towering caseload. The University of Texas School of Law is one of the premiere graduate schools in the country, and Hines's seminar students benefited from her years of experience. They also had an opportunity to handle real-life immigration cases. She created the project after successfully taking on the government in a lawsuit that involved students from Bowie High School in El Paso.

Bowie students were predominantly Mexican American, and a significant number were offspring of undocumented immigrants. The school sits on the Texas–Mexico border, and for years students reported being harassed by the border patrol. Agents would linger on Bowie High School's campus and hassle the kids when school let out in the afternoon. Her two main plaintiffs were a blind student who was detained by agents on the way home from a graduation practice and the football coach. They verbally harassed the handicapped senior and then threw him against a wall, injuring his arm and head.

The school's football coach was driving a couple of his players to an away game. Border patrol agents apprehended him and accused him of being a smuggler. When he tried to explain himself to the arresting officers, one put a gun to his head.

A jury found in favor of Hines and placed a five-year injunction on the border patrol, whereby they could not violate the constitutional rights of the students or staff by stopping or arresting them anywhere in the school district. The patrol commander was forced to resign.

Hines became a legal celebrity after the case, or "legal legend" according to *Texas Lawyer* magazine. Hines, ever the educator, wanted to mentor students to litigate and become advocates for immigrants, and she did so by creating the legal seminar in Austin. She assumed correctly that law students would benefit from a practicum that brokered in people's actual immigration issues rather than focusing narrowly on theory and case law.

Word spread throughout Texas about her success helping those who couldn't afford to help themselves, as well as those who were scared to square off with the government. Marcy Garriott showed up at Hines's office right at a time when the lawyer's caseload was as big as it had ever been.

Garriott explained who Jesus Chavez was, how he was the reformed incarnation of Gabriel Sandoval of West Chicago, how he was the number one contender in the world for the super featherweight championship, how he had a throng of Austin locals supporting him, and how his legal case had run into persistent obstacles at every turn. Long after Marcy left the office, Jesus Chavez and his case stayed on Hines's mind. In early 2000, Marcy brought Hines a finished copy of the documentary and updated her on the legal hassles the boxer had encountered in the interim. Barbara doubted that all possible avenues had been pursued and offered to take a look at the case herself. Marcy gave her the boxer's Delicias phone number, and the lawyer called one afternoon.

She was surprised at how polite he was over the phone, given his profession. Antiwar radicals and feminists are not immune from forming their own preconceived notions about boxers from time to time. Jesus explained his predicament. He was open about his feelings—how much he missed his family. Yes, he wanted to return to the United States and box, but he desperately wanted to be within arm's reach of his parents. He wanted to watch his brother grow up, and he wanted to meet his nephew for the first time.

Hines appreciated his sincerity. The boxer was genuine. Unfortunately for him, though, her caseload with the seminar didn't permit her to take the case pro bono, as the students already had their assignments for the semester. Hines relayed that sentiment to Marcy Garriott, who relayed it to Richard Garriott.

Richard immediately offered to bankroll the effort. He knew it would cost tens of thousands of dollars, but money was not the issue. He believed in this case: he believed in El Matador. By February 2000, Hines was on the beat.

She scoured the hundreds of pages in Gabriel Sandoval's personal file. She read the arrest report from that day in 1990 as well as his parents' petitions for amnesty. She read about the outcome of the Illinois prisoner review board and the subsequent rejection for clemency by Governor George H. Ryan. Hines became an expert on the Sandoval family, about how their application for amnesty in 1986 resulted in temporary resident status in 1987 and green cards in 1991. While Barbara investigated the long-term strategy for Gabriel's return, she worked quickly to get him a special short-term visa for humanitarian purposes. His mother was hospitalized in Chicago with liver failure. She rallied as a result of his short visit.

Marcy's documentary, *Split Decision*, premiered at film festivals in Chicago and Austin in the same time frame, resulting in sold-out screenings and standing ovations for Chavez at the two screenings he was able to attend. This was a burst of support that Jesus needed. The enthusiastic audiences meant that he hadn't been forgotten. It was at the Austin premiere that Hines met her client in person.

Hines discovered in one month of research the applicability of a provision of the law that had evaded Chavez's former legal team: If

Jesus had never been legally admitted to the country, the strict aggravated felony provisions of the new law did not apply to him in his effort
to come back to the country. Although Congress had passed stricter
immigration laws to deport people with aggravated felony convictions,
because of either oversight or omission, Congress did not extend these
provisions to persons who had never been permanent residents. Ironically, the law was harsher for those who were in the United States
legally than those like Jesus who were not. The language was confusing, and law enforcement officials and attorneys were also confused.
Many thought that the strict prohibitions against those with criminal
convictions applied to everyone.

In 1997, the Main Events legal team was operating under the
assumption that Chavez was at the mercy of the year-old 1996
revisions. Hines, though, recognized that because Jesus had never
been admitted to the United States legally as a permanent resident,
these strict new laws did not apply to him.

Hines says this could be the reason why the boxer's first legal team
spent four years working on a gubernatorial pardon. No one realized
that there was another potential way to resolve the case. What he in
fact needed, if it could be obtained, was INS permission for reentry
after being deported in order to proceed with the application his father
had filed for him.

Jesus Sandoval was a full-fledged U.S. citizen, and he sponsored his
son. Then Hines petitioned the INS for permission to reapply after
deportation, documenting Jesus's admirable rehabilitation and support
from other Americans. Much to her relief and the Sandoval family's
joy, the INS granted both permission to reapply and a green card
within a year.

When Jesus received the long-awaited phone call from Hines saying
that she'd meet him at the U.S. consulate in Juarez in February to pick
up his papers, the news was bittersweet. All the waiting forced him to
acknowledge his surroundings. He realized when the lawyer broke the
long-anticipated good news that he was a Mexican now, inasmuch as
he always thought he was American. He would leave his grandparents'
house in Delicias and return to Austin, though he knew his departure

from Mexico would not be permanent. With his visa, no departures would ever be permanent for Jesus Gabriel Sandoval Chavez again.

———————

Hines met Gabriel at the U.S. consulate in Juarez in February 2001. Also along for the long ride home were Marcy Garriott and her husband, Robert. The boxer was all smiles as he waited in line at the consulate and then approached the bullet-proof glass separating him and an agent. Hines was at his side.

The lady behind the glass was polite and she couldn't help smiling back at the twenty-nine-year-old. She handed him his papers through the hole in the glass. He took them and offered his hand through the narrow opening: an opening about the same size as the one in Stateville that he'd offer his hands through before a corrections officer slapped handcuffs on him. "Gracias," he said through a toothy grin. The agent graciously accepted his hand. "De nada," she replied, still smiling.

Gabriel turned on his heels and faced Barbara Hines. He thanked her, speaking with his eyes as well as his mouth. She hugged him. "Congratulations," she said. "I can't believe it."

They got into Hines's car with Gabriel behind the wheel and waited in line to drive across the border and back to Austin. It was the same border stop he crossed illegally a decade earlier with his father. Only this time, he had papers. He would drive across the border a legal U.S. resident.

The immigration agent working the tollbooth seemed abrasive at first as Gabriel maneuvered the car to his booth and produced his documents. "Hi!" Gabriel exclaimed to the agent. The agent did not return the greeting. He just took the papers and looked them over.

"You American?" Chavez did not reply.

"What are you bringing back from Mexico today?" the agent asked at long last. Gabriel hesitated. There were a million ways to answer this question: my life, my career, my newfound bifurcated identity. Instead, he answered the agent simply and literally. "Uh," he started, "just a camera."

Another moment of silence. The agent continued to study Gabriel's visa, and he perked up when he read the "occupation" box on his papers.

"You're a boxer?" he asked.

"Yeah," Gabriel said.

"Yeah? Professional?"

"Uh-huh." He felt a little nervous being questioned. The border patrol agent was genuinely interested, but for Gabriel, old habits die hard.

"What weight class?" the agent queried.

"Super feather."

"Super featherweight? Are you the champion?"

The boxer grinned now, as though he'd been waiting to be asked that question for four years. "I'm gonna be soon."

"Oh yeah?"

"Yeah. This year."

"Okay then. Good luck! Have a safe trip home."

"Thank-you. I will."

12

Homecoming

His return to Austin was sweeter than the boxer anticipated. Jesus figured he'd slip back into the country—legally—crash at Richard Garriott's mansion until he found an apartment, then return to Lord's Gym and the daily grind. Richard Lord, Richard Garriott and his sister-in-law, Marcy Garriott, and Barbara Hines celebrated with dinner at Britannia Manor, hopeful conversation, and all-around warmth.

Austin had changed in the four years Jesus was gone. The University of Texas was expanding and sprawling into downtown, and housing was becoming scarce. The dot-com boom treated Austin well, bringing prosperity and soaring rents and mortgages with it. Students began living farther off campus in favor of cheaper accommodations. Jesus moved into a predominantly student-occupied apartment complex about ten miles north of downtown, just off of Interstate 35.

It was a modest structure, a two-room apartment with two bathrooms, a living room and a kitchen. The walls were institutional beige, and the neighbors were seven to eleven years his junior, with a few older residents spread around. Sometimes tenants had parties and blasted their music, which Jesus heard through the paper-thin walls. But he didn't care. In fact, he welcomed the sounds of Austin, of America, and even the muffled white noise. For most of his adult life, the boxer had spent his evenings in solitude—in the dank backroom of Lord's Gym, in the backroom of his grandparents' Delicias home, in Cook County Jail, Illinois River Correctional Center, and Stateville.

Mostly he was excited to get down to business. The boxer had a renewed confidence that his legal woes were behind him for good. He was still the number one contender in the world for Floyd Mayweather's WBC super featherweight championship belt, and Top Rank, his new promoter, wasted no time getting him in the ring for some warm-up bouts.

Two weeks after El Matador received his green card, a fight was scheduled in Austin. The Frank Erwin Center on the University of Texas campus had never hosted a professional boxing match in its twenty-four-year history. The complex primarily hosted Longhorn basketball games and gymnastic meets. He was scheduled to fight Tommy "Boom Boom" Johnson (50-8-2), a former IBF featherweight world champion whose long and impressive career was winding down. Nevertheless, boxing pundits expected a good match, as both fighters were known for their constant action. When it was advertised in the local media and on ESPN2 as the upcoming Friday Night Fight, residents snatched up 6,500 tickets to see the return of their adopted son.

Richard Lord and the rest of the gym goers were overwhelmed to have Chavez back in the gym where he was once a fixture. The newer guys couldn't believe they were meeting El Matador, the source of local locker room lore over the past four years. They marveled at his footwork and hand speed, at how well he worked the heavy bag and sparring partners. It was a homecoming. Jesus regaled his gym friends with stories of Mexico, with accounts of the Julio Alvarez fight and of being accepted as a Mexican national. He identified with two countries now, both of which embraced him. Moreover, he related to the Mexicans living in the United States—hardworking people like his father—in a way he did not four years earlier.

The trainer was just happy to have his friend and favorite fighter back in the ring. Jesus showed his work ethic by driving to the gym—legally—twice and sometimes three times a day. He ran the steps at the football stadium faster than he had before leaving the country, a testament to those long, hard runs up the mountain in Delicias.

As the February 23, 2001 fight neared, El Matador was in top physical form. Bob Arum, CEO of Top Rank Boxing, knew even before the introductions that Chavez would win the fight. They wanted a warm-up bout to see how their employee had conditioned himself in Mexico, and whether his name as a headliner on national television could carry an audience and generate enthusiasm.

Boom Boom was too seasoned to be foolishly optimistic. The thirty-six-year-old pugilist hoped that Chavez had a weaker chin than publicized; or maybe he could sneak in that uppercut of his that used to send opponents down for a canvas nap. Mostly, though, he hoped he could get through ten rounds and have enough gas left in the tank to catch a promoter's eye and set him up as a banner warm-up fight for bigger names. The bigger the name, the more money he'd make, and the easier retirement would be.

The packed Frank Erwin Center was loud and raucous by the time the main event commenced. Richard Garriott paid for and helped pass out red capes and three-pointed matador hats to fans sitting ringside. Giant posters read, "Welcome Home, Matador," and "Austin, Texas: Home of Jesus Chavez."

Boom Boom made his way to the ring amid boos, though the jeering fans did not rock the arena. Most in attendance were seasoned boxing aficionados and thus respected the long and storied career of Tom Johnson. Johnson felt welcome enough to do a little mugging for the crowd. But when the mariachi music blared from the overhead speakers, the crowd erupted into thundering applause. This was indeed a hero's welcome. A homecoming. Austin had been without its lone boxing champion for four years, and the local media covered the return of the warrior enough to generate quite the buzz. Chavez did his best to keep the explosive gathering at a distance. He wanted to impress them, to give them a great show, and to win.

Lord did his trainer duties prior to the fight and got the boxer locked in and focused. He emphasized the magnitude of this fight. Chavez was about to put on a show for national television as a headliner and in front of his hometown audience with scores of boxing pundits tuning in around the country. Just as Boom Boom wanted to show he still had the juice, Chavez wanted to show that he was the premiere 130-pound threat—that he hadn't gone soft in exile. To maintain that coveted number one ranking and earn a shot at Floyd Mayweather Jr., he needed to beat Boom Boom convincingly.

Both Lord and Chavez approached the ring wearing stoic expressions, looking straight ahead at their opponent and not glancing at the excited fans as they made their way to the ring. Even during the introductions, as the ring announcer broadcasted the name "Jesus 'El Matador' Chavez" in Austin for the first time in four years, El Matador simply raised his gloves and bounced around. The screaming fans could not penetrate his concentration. In fact, the only person who was smiling in Chavez's entourage was Barbara Hines, his lawyer. She was tapped with carrying the NABF championship belt to the ring.

The bell signaled the start of the fight, and Chavez raced to meet Boom Boom in enemy territory. El Matador moved so quickly that his opponent didn't have enough time to meet him in the center of the ring and barely had enough time to put his guard up. Close to Johnson's corner, Chavez began to batter the older fighter with a salvo of body shots. Johnson lowered his arms to deflect some of the blows and Chavez responded by raising his punches to his opponent's head. Boom Boom tried to battle back, slipping feeble jabs when Chavez paused to inhale, but then El Matador once again let his fists go and continued to overwhelm his opponent with flurries of combinations. The same happened in rounds two and three, and the fans responded with fevered screams while they waived their red capes.

Their collective energy melted Jesus's frosty exterior. By round four, he started toying with Boom Boom. Chavez opened his eyes and mouth wide, dropped his arms to his side, and goaded the veteran to try and hit him. Johnson was tired and hurt, struggling to raise his arms and lunging wildly at a tireless Chavez. He swung and missed and swung and missed. El Matador then started back in and boxed Boom Boom into a neutral corner. The opponent struggled to hang in by hugging Chavez and tying up the boxer's arms. His plan worked for the moment, until the referee had a chance to separate the two. Chavez looked down at the reporters sitting ringside and winked at them. That action, coupled with his ring generalship, was what the journalists would write about. Boom Boom refused to answer the bell in the eighth round. El Matador was back.

Johnson proved that he still had a rock for a head. He endured punishment at the hands of El Matador that he hadn't felt since "Prince" Naseem Hamed stopped him in the eighth round two years before.

At the postfight press conference, Jesus addressed an adoring media consisting of Mexican and American reporters, as well as his trainers, promoters, parents, and brother. "I love being back," he said with Top Rank president Bob Arum at his side. "I feel like this is my home."

Conspicuously absent from that press conference and from the ringside seats was Terri. Jesus Chavez made it out of Mexico and back to a high-octane career in the United States, but Gabriel Sandoval, the shy young man Terri knew from his days of obscurity, did not return. He was still grounded in his roots and maintained his overall deference as the prisoner-turned-gentleman, though the naïveté was gone. Their relationship could not handle the time and distance and they parted amicably, or as amicably as two people could who had shared so many years and knew each other's lives so intimately. They agreed to stay friends and to keep in touch, but that proved too hard. Their approach to curing the headache was to cut off the head. Or cut out the heart, as it were.

Jesus was once again living to train, only this time, there seemed to be an endgame. No longer was he willing his way up a mountain in Mexico on the off chance of one day being granted clemency or a green card. His presence in Austin, Texas, coupled with a decisive victory over Boom Boom Johnson, meant a looming title shot and tens if not hundreds of thousands of American dollars. The American Dream was no longer out of reach.

The future now seemed limitless. He struggled to wrap his head around that simple truth. Only twenty-nine, his impoverished childhood, jail time, and two deportations were still fresh in his mind. And the memories were much more tangible than his promising future. A seminal fight with WBC super featherweight champion of the world Floyd Mayweather Jr., one of boxing's preeminent champions, was one last hurdle Chavez needed to clear.

Mayweather became an obsession for Chavez while in Mexico. He watched the champion's fights when they were rebroadcast on Mexican television, and he scoured the pages of Mexican newspapers for news of the undefeated 130 pounder. Without Lord's commentary and advice at arm's reach, Chavez assumed the responsibility of both trainer and coach. He'd sit in his cramped room in the back of his grandparents' house in Delicias and replay Mayweather footage as well as footage from his own fights.

Chavez made mental notes and calculations about what shots the champ threw and in what circumstances. After rolling tape, he'd return to the spartan municipal gym and practice his offense and defense with the two heavy bags. Sometimes, when he wanted a faster opponent, he'd use the lone lightbulb burning dimly against the lime green paint to produce a larger-than-life opponent on the wall. Shadowboxing remained an old friend; it was how he honed his skills in prison during the hardest time in his life.

He went to Lord's Gym and to the University of Texas stadium daily as he awaited word of his next fight. Lou Mesorana served the boxer well in Mexico, so El Matador kept the manager on his payroll. All fight contracts and negotiations for future fights now went through Lou. Top Rank and Bob Arum came calling with a fight plan in April 2001. They were impressed with Chavez's showing in the Boom Boom fight, and they particularly liked how solid his fan base seemed.

Arum, a master promoter, knew one more warm-up fight would help for a bigger buildup to Chavez versus Mayweather. He decided to have the boxer fight on the undercard of an upcoming Mayweather fight in the champion's hometown of Grand Rapids, Michigan.

"Pretty Boy" Floyd (25-0), as he liked to call himself, was scheduled to fight Carlos Hernandez (33-2-1), a relentless El Salvadorian fighting out of West Covina, California, about nineteen miles east of Los Angeles. Hernandez's style was similar to El Matador's; both threw up to a thousand punches each time they fought.

Chavez was to fight Juan Arias (33-1), a Mexican living and training in Napa, California. The bout was made just a month before fight night, so Jesus and Richard Lord did not have much time to scout Arias. Instead, they trained for a fighter like Mayweather, a boxing technician with seemingly no flaws, except for maybe himself.

Mayweather had weak hands and often injured his fists and his wrists on his opponents. The pain affected his punching output in the later rounds, though when he did connect, his shots were explosive. And that's exactly what happened in the Hernandez fight.

Both fighters were well conditioned and both wanted to make a statement. Hernandez gave Mayweather the fight of his life, but the champion nearly knocked himself out. He landed a solid right to Hernandez's head in the sixth, winced in pain as he let out a scream, and put his gloves on the canvas. Although Hernandez didn't land a punch, the referee ruled it a knockdown since the champ touched his hands to the mat. That was the first and only time Mayweather was knocked down since turning pro in 1996. Indeed, Pretty Boy did break his hand on Hernandez's head; despite being injured, he racked up the score on the judges' cards earlier in the fight so he could afford to play defense for the last six rounds—stealing a few with hard left jabs in the final seconds—to win a unanimous decision over the challenger. Arias, it turned out, was not prone to injury like Mayweather, but he didn't have the champion's talent, either.

As he had in the undercard of the Lennox Lewis versus Andrew Golota fight in New Jersey before he left for Mexico, El Matador provided a significantly more exciting and action-packed fight against Juan Arias. Just as Hernandez pressured Mayweather to become the only boxer in a year to go the distance with the champion, so too did

Chavez put the screws to Arias, forcing him to box defensively for most of the fight. Arias got few chances to string punches together, though when he did, the exchanges were heated and electrifying. Chavez controlled the tempo from the opening bell. Mayweather's hometown crowd gave the boxer a thunderous ovation as referee Monte Oswald raised El Matador's hand in victory. He won a twelve-round unanimous decision and, more importantly, proved again that he was the number one challenger in the world for Mayweather's belt.

Bob Arum sat at ringside and grinned the entire night as both Chavez and Mayweather, Top Rank fighters, demonstrated that they were worthy opponents for each other. He grinned because in the boxing world, where it is often tough to schedule title shots with fighters signed to different promotional companies because of contract and money disputes, Arum would be able to set up Chavez versus Mayweather without hang-ups. And he'd be able to keep a lid on the profits. The fighters would get theirs, Mayweather twice as much as Chavez. But he would get his too. And what was more, Lou Duva and Don King wouldn't be around to share the profits.

Chavez returned to Austin after his fight and rested. The moment the doctors cleared him to train, he was back at Lord's. Top Rank was ironing out the logistics with Mayweather's people and with Lou Mesorana while Chavez tried to remain focused on the upcoming challenge and not the dollars.

Top Rank and Pretty Boy Floyd had consistently butted heads over Floyd's money and billing. Mayweather had always been outspoken, and he'd never been afraid to call out those he felt were short-changing him. Bob Arum usually skirted Mayweather's insults, choosing to play the diplomatic public role and assure Floyd—and his fans—that bigger fights and paydays lay ahead. Privately, though, he fumed about the mouthy fighter.

Mayweather was an exceptional talent and a good earner for Top Rank, but he was also a cocky kid who rubbed most people the wrong way, including his own father. Floyd Mayweather Sr. raised his son in a Grand Rapids gym. Senior coached junior through a successful amateur career and to the international stage. But Pretty Boy fired his father shortly after the Carlos Hernandez fight, citing a "difference of opinion."

At the same time, Chavez became embroiled in something of a trainer conundrum himself. Top Rank respected Richard Lord. He was a true patron of the boxing craft, fundamentally sound and knowledgeable about the sport. But he was not a company man. Lord had always been a lone wolf, and Top Rank wanted to have its investment trained by the best, or at least people they considered the best.

Ronnie Shields made enough of a name in the sport that he didn't have to bother training neophyte fighters. And he didn't have to pound the pavement scouting prospects. Rather, once a fighter established himself as a contender (or once he was already a champion), Shields came on the scene. He had an impressive résumé, with fighters like welterweights Vernon Forrest and Pernell Whitaker and heavyweights David Tua and Evander Holyfield.

Top Rank lobbied El Matador to train with Shields for the Mayweather fight. Bob Arum, with his silver-tongued spiel, convinced the boxer to go with a name for his title shot. And Jesus agreed. Lord would continue to be a corner man, but Shields would call the shots.

Chavez drove to Houston and trained at Shields's regular gym. That was a disheartening move for Richard Lord. He had a hard time with the thought of another trainer molding his boxer in another gym and knowing there was nothing he could do about it. But Top Rank and Jesus had made their decision. Lord had to wait in the wings and work as an assistant.

Shields began to draft a fighting plan for El Matador. He would attack the body early and pressure the champion throughout. The goal was to throw as many punches as possible, never letting up throughout the fight. Don't let Pretty Boy catch his breath. Pressure. Pressure. Pressure. That, Shields said, is how you beat an undefeated fighter. You overwhelm him . . . and in Cocky Boy Floyd's case, you hope that he's looking past you to his next fight.

———————

Arum scheduled the fight for October 6, 2001, at the Paris Hotel and Casino in Las Vegas. It was the break Jesus used to envision at lights out in prison. And here it was, so close: he couldn't believe that a prison dream was coming true.

Las Vegas is boxing's Mecca. A boxer who headlines a card in Sin City has hit prime time. He is world renowned. Chavez versus Mayweather would be televised on HBO's *Boxing After Dark,* and El Matador would have a chance to finally show the entire world on international television what a gritty guy he was.

October 6 was two months away and Mayweather began having chronic headaches and jaw pain. He claimed his hands were 100 percent, but his teeth were affecting his game. A dentist determined that impacted wisdom teeth were causing his discomfort and needed to be removed. Mayweather said he wouldn't be ready to defend his title against a puncher like Chavez until the swelling went down. Arum had no choice but to postpone the fight. No date was scheduled at the outset.

And then the events of September 11, 2001, occurred. The worst terrorist attack in U.S. history produced damaging economic repercussions from coast to coast. The Las Vegas tourism industry was hit particularly hard. Flight-panicked Americans hesitated to board airplanes, and the Vegas thrill seekers and fun goers stayed home. Only the serious gamblers were coming.

The Paris Hotel and Casino had agreed to pay $750,000 for the privilege of hosting the October 6 fight. On October 5, the day before Mayweather and Chavez were supposed to face each other, Arum announced the fight would be rescheduled for November 10. Paris didn't even submit a bid at the next go-around. They knew the box office, even with the HBO deal, wouldn't recoup the hosting fee. Not surprisingly, Las Vegas hotels laid off over 20,000 employees and were operating with a skeleton staff for the remainder of 2001. Chavez would have to wait to fight in the world's grandest fighting city.

Arum went looking for a tourist and boxing-friendly town for the November 10 date. His main criteria was to pack the house. Period. San Francisco had also taken a hit after 9/11, but not to the extent of

Las Vegas or Atlantic City or even Los Angeles. The city by the bay also boasted a large boxing fan base and a large Hispanic population to boot. Arum inked a deal to have the fight hosted at the Bill Graham Civic Auditorium in the heart of downtown. Best of all, the venue was owned by the city and county of San Francisco. The local economy and not a casino would be the beneficiary of Chavez versus Mayweather.

Shortly after the announcement, trash talking between the two fighters began. Chavez in the past was usually reserved when asked about an opponent. Mayweather rarely was. So Chavez tried to gain leverage by getting in Pretty Boy's head. "He is overrated," Chavez told reporters. "He is considered one of the best fighters, pound for pound, in the world, but I don't consider him like that."

Mayweather responded. In spades. "I'm the best athlete in the world, hands down," the champion rebutted. "You got athletes like Kobe Bryant; he can have an off night and still be the great Kobe Bryant. Tiger Woods can lose ten golf tournaments and still be the great Tiger Woods. In boxing, if you have an off night, they'll eat you up and destroy you. Your payday drops, you lose your contract.

"But right now, I am dominating everyone they put in front of me and doing it with ease. I'm not bragging or boasting; it's the truth. [Chavez] said I was overrated. On November 10, I am going to give him a chance to show I am overrated.

"Jesus can pick which way he wants to go out: on his face or on his back."

————————

Lord, Chavez, and Shields arrived in San Francisco four days before the fight. The boxer felt strong and conditioned, though the pressure of fighting on such a huge card, coupled with the age disparity between the fighters (Chavez was two days shy of thirty to Mayweather's youthful twenty-four) and Pretty Boy's stellar track record began to psychologically work on El Matador.

He tried to take it easy in the days leading up to the fight. Martin Vasquez, his buddy from Delicias, flew in for moral support, as did his parents and brother. Mayweather flew in from his home in Vegas two days before the weigh-in.

The scheduled twelve-round bout packed Bill Graham Civic Auditorium in the boxing-starved city. More than 7,000 fans crowded the stands to see a great live fight—a good-size crowd for lightweights—and to help make San Francisco a future stage for big-time prize-fighting.

El Matador went through his preboxing routine in the dressing room. He jumped up and down and threw punches into the air. Ronnie Shields softly spoke throughout the boxer's warm-up: "Keep the pressure on him. Work the body and don't let those fists stop flying." Richard Lord, who was also in the dressing room, was conspicuously quiet.

Ring announcer Michael Buffer crooned through the sound system and El Matador, the challenger for the first time in four years, jogged to the ring. Richard Lord was just behind, holding Chavez's NABF super featherweight championship belt.

Jesus was unsure what kind of reception California fans would give him. He'd never boxed in that state before. Actually, he'd never been west of Texas in the United States. But San Franciscans were as enthusiastic about the boxer as fans in Austin. Mexican Americans support their own. A majority of the audience did not know about Gabriel Sandoval, nor were they aware of Gabriel's upbringing in Chicago or of the trials and tribulations he endured as he clawed his way to the top of the super featherweight division. All they knew of him was that he listed Delicias and Austin as his hometowns. He, like so many, was a Mexican transplant trying to carve out a life for himself in Los Estados Unidos. And there was the Mexican flag, carried to the ring by one of Shields's assistants, being displayed as prominently as the Texas state flag, carried to the ring by another assistant.

El Matador was shocked that his fan base cheered louder than the incumbent champion's. Pretty Boy Floyd descended to the ring with an entourage twice the size of Jesus's. But San Franciscans didn't sound nearly as enthusiastic. Jesus honed in on this lack of applause. It was a twelfth-hour confidence boost. For that one night, San Francisco was his hometown.

Chavez looked fit, but Mayweather looked like he should have been fighting in a higher weight class. Prior to the fight, Floyd announced that this would be his last bout at 130. He wanted to step up in weight and face stiffer competition. Also, the more a boxer weighs, the more money he stands to make. Fans and promoters operate under the unwritten rule that big guys are more entertaining. Boxing pundits, however, know better: the lightweight divisions are more competitive and chock-full of better talent.

Floyd looked pretty. His hairless body glistened with a thin layer of sweat. His muscles were taut and defined and his skin was smooth and unblemished. His hair was cropped close to his head with a stylish fade, and his face looked like it had never been hit. Deep brown eyes stood out, along with his handsome round facial structure. But his brilliant smile and ivory white teeth commanded the most attention.

When the two fighters approached each other in the center of the ring for instructions from referee Jon Schorle, the 5-foot-9 Mayweather seemed to dwarf his 5-foot-6 opponent. They both weighed in a day earlier at 129.5 pounds, but Mayweather looked like he put on twelve pounds overnight. And he carried the weight well.

They received their instructions and returned to their corners. Ronnie Shields once again reiterated his all-out pressure strategy and reminded El Matador—as if he needed reminding—that this was the moment he'd been waiting for all his life. Ironically, Shields wasn't intimate with the boxer's life details. Richard Lord was, though he stood there and said nothing.

At the opening bell, El Matador charged forward and started pounding away at the champ. He worked the body per instructions and occasionally went upstairs to Pretty Boy's head. Chavez needed to stay inside with Mayweather because of Floyd's longer reach and lightning-fast jab. He managed to keep the pressure on throughout the first round, suffering from only one big punch landed by the champion in the waning seconds of round one.

Chavez returned to his corner barely out of breath. Mayweather returned to his baffled. The champion spent half the round backpedaling and the other half with his back to the ropes. He used his impenetrable defense, taught to and preached by his now unemployed father, to keep El Matador's damage to a minimum. His defense was unconventional but effective: Mayweather kept one arm erect and close to his body, with the glove close to his face, and the other arm horizontal across his stomach. As Jesus delivered his punches, Floyd rocked his shoulders back and forth, dodging most of the shots by positioning his arms in between El Matador's incoming leather and his own tender organs.

The following rounds consisted of more of the same. Chavez unloaded everything in his arsenal on the champion. Floyd's wind and his chin had hardly been tested in previous fights, as he knocked most opponents on their backs in the early or middle rounds, a testament to the fact that some little guys do in fact have knockout power.

Mayweather's offense through the first four rounds was mostly defense. He slipped in hard counterpunches, though he was unable to mount a charge. Meanwhile, Jesus chopped away at the body and occasionally the head. He stayed downstairs because Mayweather found Chavez's motionless head when the challenger attempted to go upstairs. The shorter Chavez essentially opened himself up for a counterstrike. And like other Mexican boxers before him, El Matador didn't move his head in the ring. He left it out there like a sweaty target. Mayweather's heat-seeking missile jab scored a direct hit each time it launched.

As the rounds progressed, though, Chavez began to tire. His barrage of combinations were taking their toll: he was punching himself out. Shields's instructions in the corner were to keep on doing what he was doing, that the strategy was working. As the trainer spoke, Chavez looked across the ring at Mayweather. He sat motionless in his corner. The champ wasn't breathing nearly as hard as he was. And despite all those punches, Pretty Boy remained blemishless. Shields told him not to worry about Mayweather.

"Fight your fight, not his," the veteran trainer said. Lord, for the first time on the long journey with El Matador, was not inside the ring ropes. He was standing on the ring apron while Shields gave instructions. Lord manned the water bottle and the spit bucket. He said nothing.

By round six, Chavez's tank was emptying. The punches continued to come, but they were losing their zing. Mayweather was overwhelmed with the sheer number of blows his opponent threw. Carlos Hernandez had let the leather go when he faced Mayweather, but Jesus Chavez was even more intense and pressing. The challenger brought the fight to the champion and crammed Pretty Boy's arms tight to his body, where they could do the least amount of damage. Mayweather, however, noticed that despite their persistence, Chavez's punches were softening. Floyd developed a sixth sense early in his boxing career whereby he sniffed out a tiring boxer and strategized on the fly. Mayweather decided to weather the sixth and turn up the heat in the seventh.

But the bullfighter had plans of his own. He'd been coming out strong to the body in each round. Jesus assumed Mayweather was expecting the same attack in round seven, so instead, Chavez sprinted to the center of the ring and unleashed an overhand right that landed flush against Mayweather's face, catching him completely by surprise. El Matador knew that he was running out of time. If he was going to test out the champ's chin, he'd have to make his move before his own gas gauge hit empty.

Mayweather staggered backward against the ropes and Jesus started measuring him up with straight shots. Jesus thought he saw an opening to the head and he pulled his right back like an archer preparing to snap his compound bow. He shifted his weight to his back leg and squared his shoulders.

But Mayweather, a crafty ring veteran even at the young age of twenty-four, noticed El Matador's tell, and he slyly slipped in an uppercut. Chavez's neck snapped backward as Mayweather unleashed a torrent of devastating punches.

Jesus was dazed. His knees buckled and he violently jerked forward, though he did not go down. A trainer worth his salt will start taking mental inventory of how many times a fighter's head snaps back from an uppercut, as that can be potentially dangerous. And his head seemed to be snapping back an awful lot.

El Matador instinctively started flailing away at Mayweather, hoping that his numerous punches would cause the champion to go on the defensive. Chavez's fists of fury forced Mayweather to back off and a war-weary Chavez made it out of the round.

Back in his corner, Chavez panted as his team went to work on the swelling around his eyes. Ronnie Shields had a more concerned catch in his voice as he spoke. He asked the boxer if he wanted to continue, a question that Chavez had not been asked before. Richard Lord shot Shields a puzzled glance, as if to say, "What are you, nuts?" But he said nothing.

"Yeah, I want to go on," Chavez said through deep breaths. "I'm ahead of this guy."

"Okay. Then keep punching," Shields replied. "And watch out for that uppercut. Don't leave your head out there. Don't give him a chance. Keep the fight inside, but careful where you put your head."

The ding of the bell in round nine triggered an alarm inside Pretty Boy Floyd's head. He set the tone of the round by allowing Jesus to get inside, then rocking the challenger back on his feet with a vicious uppercut. He threw more straight shots, then fired that uppercut again.

Chavez continued to press forward, taking each punch as it came, but his offense was waffling. And as the seconds ticked by, Chavez's neck snapped back more frequently. Mayweather was fighting with a renewed confidence and on a reserve of energy. However, El Matador had fight left in him. Toward the end of the round, Chavez managed to mount a comeback and started throwing punches again, confusing and mystifying Mayweather.

No other fighter before Chavez—a man who leaves his head wide open—had been able to withstand such ferocious punishment by Mayweather. But there was Chavez, surging forward. He dug down deep and used the high-octane fumes still in his tank to lunge at the champion with all his remaining power. He landed two devastating punches to both sides of Mayweather's face. It took nine rounds, but Chavez cut Pretty Boy's pretty face twice: one cut over one eye, one under the other.

He returned to his corner after the ninth round on an emotional high, believing, as did Lord, that he could win the fight if he won one of the last three rounds. But Ronnie Shields had other plans.

The trainer didn't ask Jesus whether he wanted to continue. Instead, he kneeled in front of the sitting boxer, looked him in the eyes, and said, "I'm sorry, kid. That's it."

Chavez was breathing heavily and thought that maybe he heard the trainer wrong. "Huh?" he quipped in between gasps.

"That's just the way it's gonna come down. Don't fight it. You did a hell of a job."

And with that, Shields took the towel he had slung over his shoulder throughout the fight, turned to referee Jon Schorle and threw it in his direction.

"We're done," he said to Schorle in a matter-of-fact tone.

Richard Lord, who'd been biting his tongue for the first time during a Chavez fight, could no longer contain himself. He erupted with a rage that'd been suppressed for years. "Shields! You sorry son of a bitch!" he bellowed from the apron like a man possessed. "What the fuck do you think you're doing?"

Lord began to cuss out the trainer-for-hire. Ronnie Shields looked stunned by Lord's sudden wrath. Richard was carrying on so loudly and with so much animation that Ronnie became concerned for his safety. He walked over to the security guards who were now in the ring. Shields stood next to the behemoths in uniform while the ring slowly cleared.

Richard was beyond angry. The usually reserved trainer's squinty eyes widened to the size of saucers and his neck and forehead veins seemed to expand the size of his head. He stomped around the ring, turning his gaze from Shields, who pretended not to notice him, to Jesus, who was standing in his corner bewildered. "God dammit," Lord swore under his breath. He spit on the canvas and he shouted at Shields from across the ring. "How the hell are you gonna stop this fight with three rounds left? The kid never even went down! He was ahead on the cards! Do you hear me, Shields? He was ahead on the cards!"

HBO ringside commentator Larry Merchant entered the ring to interview the defending champion and the gutsy challenger, now minus his NABF super featherweight belt for the first time in four years.

Merchant asked Chavez about the abrupt fight stoppage and why his corner decided to throw in the towel. "I feel like a winner tonight," Chavez said, very diplomatically. "I gave the greatest fighter in the world the best fight he ever had. Ronnie Shields stopped the fight because he knows there are many more nights for me to come . . . He's my trainer. I listen to him."

Shields answered the same question moments later. Lord faded into the background to avoid making a scene in front of the camera. "Beginning in the seventh round, Jesus was getting hit badly by uppercuts," Shields said. "That's when I knew this was coming to an end. Floyd's a great fighter and a great champion. I'm not allowing my fighter to go out on his back."

When the cameras were turned off, Lord started in on Shields again. "He was winning the fight, Ronnie," he said in a stern and cutting growl, his eyes deep in his head and unblinking. "You fucked up. You stole the kid's victory."

Lord was half right. Officially, all three ringside judges had Mayweather narrowly ahead on the scorecards. Chavez had thrown twice as many punches (925 to 456) while landing slightly fewer clean shots (185 to 197). In a fight that close, judges tended to favor the champion. But those cuts El Matador gave Pretty Boy at the end of the ninth could have leveled the playing field at the start of the tenth.

HBO scorekeeper Harold Lederman, known throughout the world as a fair and balanced boxing judge, had Chavez ahead on the cards. And so did ringside commentator and boxing legend George Foreman.

It was a tough loss all around. The boxer's inner circle—those who had patiently waited for Chavez to receive his green card and return to the United States—celebrated the effort but were divided as to whether Shields did the right thing. Richard Garriott was noticeably saddened and his face seemed to pucker. He had watched Chavez train for this fight, even making the trip to Houston when he sparred in Shields's gym. Marcy Garriott, on the other hand, gave Shields the benefit of the doubt. Jesus's safety was rightly his trainer's paramount concern.

El Matador fought like a warrior, and he gave an undefeated champion all he could handle, but even a gallant loss at the end of the day is still just a loss. The more time passed, the more the boxer felt he'd been cheated by his cornerman. Jesus fired Ronnie Shields in January 2002 and returned to Lord's Gym. He and Richard Lord were a team again, though the Mayweather loss knocked Chavez back a few notches in the world's eye and in the world rankings. Once more, Jesus and Lord had some heavy lifting to do if he were to be a contender for the championship again. Now he was in a race against his own biological clock. Not many lightweights capture a world championship at thirty.

He slipped to number three. No longer was he the number one contender for the WBC super featherweight championship. What's more, the title was going up for grabs, as Mayweather stepped up to the lightweight division and vacated the championship. Top Rank continued to have confidence in El Matador but wanted him to fight against various fighting styles before taking a second title shot.

So it was back to the Texas farm system for Jesus. His first fight after coming off the loss in San Francisco was in March 2003 against Gerardo Zayas (22-4) at the Frank Erwin Center in Austin, the same venue where Jesus destroyed Boom Boom Johnson.

The bout didn't draw many fans: only 2,800 tickets were sold. Chavez did his part to court the meager crowd. He made his ring entrance wearing a University of Texas Longhorns jersey with the numeral 1 on the back. The fight was somewhat boring as El Matador knocked out his opponent in three rounds.

Three months later, he boxed another Julio Cesar Chavez facsimile: Julio Cesar Sanchez-Leon (20-11-1), at the Freeman Coliseum in San Antonio. The fight drew a paltry 1,600 fans, and Chavez dealt handily with Sanchez-Leon, winning by a technical knockout in the seventh.

Come November 2002, a year after the Mayweather loss, he manhandled Johnny "Live Wire" Walker in front of a healthy crowd of 5,000 in Laredo, Texas. To no one's surprise, one year after his second

career loss, Chavez was tied with Carlos Gerena as the number one
contender in the WBC.

Jesus usually stayed out of boxing politics. He had a promoter in Top
Rank and a manager in Lou Mesorana. But when the WBC rankings
touted him as being tied with Gerena for number one, the boxer said
to Lou, "Do whatever it takes, but make the fight happen." Gerena was
one of the two blemishes on Chavez's record, Mayweather being the
other one. He lost a controversial split decision to Carlos in his fifth
professional fight in 1995, attributable to hometown judging, and El
Matador wanted payback.

As he awaited word from Top Rank and Lou Mesorana, Chavez became reacquainted with Austin life. The boxer became a fixture around
town: at the gym, at local eateries, and even at a Barnes and Noble
bookstore. He occasionally thought of Terri, like when he passed by
the Kerbey Lane Café, where they had their first date, or whenever he
went running on campus past her old digs. But as the adage goes, out
of sight, out of mind.

Chavez hadn't put much effort into finding another girlfriend since
Terri. He remained focused on regaining his number one ranking, and
Lord was fond of reminding him that girls make a boxers' legs weak.

He was in an Austin Barnes and Noble one day participating in a
panel discussion with local author and gym buddy Jan Reid. When the
discussion was over, a tall, curvy brunette approached him. At first he
thought she had him confused with someone else because this woman
was, as he described her, absolutely beautiful. Her black hair hung
straight against her honey brown skin. Her eyes were wide and clear
brown and she held her head high. Her shoulders were broad, though
they looked perfectly proportioned on her athletic body. Her full lips
and pearly whites were alluring and her beaming smile was contagious.

She introduced herself as Aunisa Stroklund, to which he responded
by saying how pretty her name was. Then she handed him a book of
Thomas Kinkade paintings that she'd just purchased and told him it was
a present. Aunisa made sure to point out before they parted company
that her name and number were written under the front cover. Jesus
thanked her and offered his own gap-toothed smile. He followed her

body with his eyes as she walked out of the bookstore. Too excited to subscribe to the unwritten rule of two—waiting two days to call a girl after she gives out her number—Jesus called her later that night.

They made plans to get Mexican food the next day. Over lunch, Aunisa admitted that she knew who he was, although she wasn't a big boxing fan. She told him about herself, that she had recently graduated from the University of Montana and moved to Austin to live with her mother. Shortly after establishing herself in the Lone Star State, she enlisted in the Texas Army National Guard and rose through the ranks to become an officer.

The lunch date went well by first-date standards. For Jesus, though, it was perfect. It was comfortable and the conversation moved smoothly; it was just what he needed in his life. He connected with Aunisa on a higher level. She spun his head and stimulated his mind in one afternoon. He wanted to know her, to understand how this beautiful woman who seemed so cultured could be an officer in the army. She fascinated him. He intrigued her.

Lou Mesorana told his boxer that scheduling a fight against Carlos Gerena was difficult. Top Rank was offering a fight against Jorge Paez, another veteran boxer, as the headliner of "Latin Fury" night at the Mandalay Bay in Las Vegas on March 22, 2003. Chavez jumped at the chance. Vegas was still very much on his mind.

A week before the fight, Paez pulled out. An MRI scan revealed that he had suffered brain damage after twenty years of fighting profes-sionally. Jesus once again prepared to have his hopes dashed. Vegas would have to wait. Again.

Lou Mesorana frantically worked the phones and came up with a wild card before the night was postponed. Carlos Gerena apparently didn't like the scuttlebutt that Chavez was gunning for him. The years put enough distance between his last fight with Chavez to give the Puerto Rican a false sense of accomplishment. So Gerena stepped up and volunteered to take the place of Paez.

Jesus and Aunisa flew out to Las Vegas together on March 19, three days before the fight. The boxer had been spending a significant amount of time with his new girlfriend. The war in Iraq was surging, and Aunisa was put on alert by her commanding officer. Her Texas National Guard unit was going to be activated and called to duty in Iraq. The orders could come down at a moment's notice, so the couple tried to spend as much time together as his training would allow.

The mostly Hispanic audience of over 8,000 for the Gerena fight was the sort of stage Jesus craved. The bright Las Vegas lights seemed like a Hollywood movie set, and the auditorium of the Mandalay Bay was like the ones Hollywood depicted in big blockbuster prizefights.

He came to the ring wearing camouflage trunks as a tribute to his soldier girlfriend. Jesus recognized the duality of his action: the United States was like a yin to his yang. Uncle Sam had locked him up, kicked him out, and brought him love. While the government kept the boxer's antennas raised, the people, however, had always been his best friends. The camouflage trunks were El Matador's salute to the men and women fighting bravely in Iraq. And to his girlfriend, who would join their ranks within the year.

Las Vegas was everything Jesus had thought it would be, but Carlos Gerena was nothing like he remembered. The Puerto Rican who fought so gallantly when they met in 1995 put up little fight. Chavez fed off the fans' energy and put the same pressure on Gerena that he had put on Mayweather. It was a rout. Chavez assaulted the body and took the air right out of the Puerto Rican's lungs. In the sixth round, Jesus caught Carlos with the same hard overhand right that stunned Mayweather, and referee Kenny Bayless called the fight.

Richard Lord bolted into the ring and lifted Chavez high above his head. The boxer closed his eyes and allowed the bright white Mandalay Bay lights to wash all over him. The roaring crowd sounded muffled, though, as his mind wandered back to his cramped cell in solitary confinement at Stateville.

Jesus had often dreamed of this moment: standing in the middle of a Las Vegas boxing ring and slugging it out toe to toe with the best the world had to offer. He was bruised and battered, bloodied and spent as expected. He was a mature thirty-year-old man and a boxing veteran. And for the second time, he was the number one contender in the world for the WBC super featherweight championship belt. His lights-out prison prognostication was dead-on accurate. Gabriel Sandoval, now world-renowned as Jesus Chavez—hoisted high in the middle of a Las Vegas boxing ring—was victorious.

The name Sirimongkol Singmanassuk doesn't exactly inspire fear in those who hear it; most people can't even read it let alone pronounce it. A boxer from Thailand (39-1), Singmanassuk became the WBC super featherweight champion when Mayweather abandoned the division. Singmanassuk had fought 95 percent of his matches in his native land, so almost nothing was known about him. As a rule, though, Thai boxers are fierce, relentless warriors.

Chavez was the number one contender, so he was guaranteed a fight against the man with two last names. Bob Arum and Top Rank had to work overtime to iron out scheduling kinks. Singmanassuk wanted the fight to be in Thailand, but Arum and Chavez refused. Thailand has notoriously corrupt boxing judges. "You can't win there," Chavez said. "Even if you knock the guy out, I'm told they'll find a reason to disqualify you."

Arum's insistence that the fight be held in the United States paid off, and the challenger chose the location for the fight. Chavez chose Texas and Arum chose the Austin Convention Center. The building known for hosting business conventions and auto shows was going to host the city's first-ever major world title bout on August 15, 2003.

Training for that fight was like hunting by moonlight. There was very little film on Singmanassuk, so Lord prepared Chavez for a stereo-typical Thai fighter's style. They keep their guard high and extended from their face, like a shoot fighter. That sort of stance favored Chavez. It was a virtual telegraph that the fighter was avoiding head shots. It was also a clue that the opponent's ribs would be unprotected.

Lord planted a strategy in Chavez's head whereby he'd work the body to find the head. The theory was that if he hammered Singmanassuk's body hard and often enough, the foreign boxer would get befuddled and drop his guard to protect his kidneys. Either that or he'd start swinging carelessly at Chavez's head to stop the attack. When that happened, Chavez would crouch down low and let the blows glance off the top of his dome. Then he'd spring up and, using his legs as thrusters, sock Singmanassuk in the chin.

The convention center sold out and nearly 5,000 fans congregated to see their hometown hero make hometown history. Singmanassuk and his camp arrived a week early and went into seclusion. They did not hold a press conference, nor did they even make their presence known. But come fight night, Singmanassuk appeared as a menacing fighter who looked like an Asian Ivan Drago. The twenty-six-year-old's body was flawless, like Chavez's at the same age. His angular face, square jaw, and vacant eyes were expressionless, though his hair was hard to miss: thick and black and spiked.

Chavez made his way to the ring first, as he was the challenger. This wasn't the largest crowd he'd fought in front of, though it was by far the noisiest. He waited in the ring and let the cheers engulf him. Singmanassuk entered moments later to an equally loud but surly auditorium. If he didn't know what it meant to fight in Texas before, he did when he got to the ring.

––––––––––

The two fighters sized each other up for the first four rounds by fighting at a distance and throwing mostly measuring jabs. There was action, though the pace did not initially favor Chavez. He liked to explode onto the scene and wear his opponent down in the first few minutes. The lanky Thai boxer did a superb job of keeping Chavez at bay with his praying mantis–like stance and reach.

Lord tried hard to keep his cool in between rounds. He was mentally sweating out there with his fighter and he was physically sweating in the corner. Before the sixth round, Lord was getting antsy. "You falling in love with this guy or what?" he asked El Matador sarcastically. "Go after him! Two to the body, one to the head. Slug it out!"

The sixth round was fought flat-footed, as were the remaining six. Chavez traded with the champion for three solid minutes on end, throwing shots to the body, then going upstairs. Like Mayweather, Singmanassuk was overwhelmed by this attack. Unlike Mayweather, he was unable to put together an effectual defense. Singmanassuk had been knocking his previous opponents out cold, but none of them came at him like El Matador, surging forward with a charge in the later rounds that would have made General George Pickett envious. Chavez cut Singmanassuk in the eighth, proving that the Asian Drago was not a machine. He's a man.

Right before the twelfth and final round, referee Laurence Cole summoned the two opponents to the center of the ring to touch gloves. Jesus wanted to make a deferential gesture to the Singmanassuk camp. He felt the Thai fighter was a worthy adversary. A true champion. He conducted himself with class in the ring, and Chavez appreciated the camp traveling halfway around the word for a Texas-style fight in the state capital.

Chavez tapped gloves with Singmanassuk, looked him square in the eye, and lowered his head. Then he turned to Singmanassuk's corner, put his arms down to his sides, and bowed.

The crowd cheered wildly. Texans are passionate fans, but they pride themselves on being sportsmen. Gentlemen. They applauded the visiting fighter. Unfortunately for Singmanassuk, the confidence vote came too little and too late.

The final bell sounded, and the fighters hugged. Richard Lord entered the ring smiling. He tried to suppress his emotions, but he knew the outcome of the fight even before the judges' scorecards were tallied. So did the rest of the convention center. Had the fight been close, the judges would have really had to show their stripes, for even though they were in the challenger's hometown, a tie usually favors the champion.

Luckily, the judges' honesty wasn't put to the test. The fight had been one-sided.

The announcer took center stage and the auditorium fell silent. "Ladies and gentlemen, after twelve rounds of boxing, we have a unanimous decision. And new WBC super featherweight champion: Jesus 'El Matador' Chavez!"

Jesus closed his eyes and raised both arms above his head. His face tightened up and he sobbed deeply. This time, the boxer could hear the crowd. They were screaming at a pitch he'd never heard a boxing audience scream at before. They were proud of him, of this tremendous accomplishment. Jesus's brother, Jimmy, who was part of the ring entourage, took the WBC championship belt and wrapped it around his big brother's waist.

Richard Lord came up from behind his boxer and grabbed the nape of Chavez's neck with his right hand. The civic center was in pandemonium, so Lord leaned in close and put his mouth to El Matador's ear. "You did it, son," the cagey trainer whispered. The boxer continued to sob as he nodded his head gently in agreement. It was a defining moment between trainer and trainee. The gruff man with the disheveled hair rarely showed tenderness, though in the center of the ring, with El Matador wearing the championship belt of the entire world, Lord couldn't hide his heart. "You did it. I just want you to know how . . . just want to tell you how . . . how proud of you I am, Jesus. I'm so proud of you. You fought like a champion tonight."

———————

Deep in the bowels of the Austin Civic Center, in the damp basement where the water pipes tangle and the air-conditioning units drone in their cavernous surroundings, a dozen reporters crammed into the designated media center for the postfight press conference. Bob Arum sat in front of the microphone and fielded questions, stalling the reporters while Jesus showered and changed. He tried to keep the buzz going, congratulating El Matador in his absence and saying how Austin is a great fighting town. And he extolled the virtues of Sirimongkol.

"You have to realize the Thai fighter made his mark being a great offensive fighter," Arum said. "He really is a tremendous offensive fighter. You didn't see it tonight because Jesus put so much pressure on him that he couldn't get off."

Finally Jesus entered the room wearing a plaid short-sleeve button-down shirt, his new green and gold chattel slung over his shoulder. Reporters don't usually cheer before a press conference, but this group did.

The boxer's face was black and blue and swollen. His eyes looked like slits peeking through a round, doughy face. He smiled as they cheered. Then he embraced Arum, sat down, and made his statement. The room became silent and reporters scribbled hurriedly.

"This was a tough fight," he announced into the microphone, "and I knew that Sirimongkol wasn't going to quit. I take my hat off to Sirimongkol because he came to my house. But I don't think there's fighters out there that fight the style that I fight. I'm the type of fighter that comes, and comes, and comes, and keeps on coming."

Jesus paused and breathed deeply, trying to keep his emotions in check. "I'm the happiest man right now," he said in a cracking voice. Redness showed in his cheeks—through the bruises—as he struggled even harder now to keep it together. "I can't wait to soak this down and I know that there are harder things to come after this. I'm going to prepare myself for every single defense that I do. I'm going to be the best champion I can be for all the people that came and supported me today, and for all the people that supported me in the past. I love y'all."

In that moment, El Matador stopped dreaming. He had not only kept the promise he made to himself and to his father in prison, but he saw the dream through to fruition. Indeed America was the land of opportunity. Jesus Sandoval Jr.'s face trembled and his eyes watered as he watched his son address the American media as the champion of the world.

13

El Terrible

With the World Boxing Council super featherweight championship belt safely in his Austin home, Jesus Chavez breathed a little better. He slept a little easier, kicked his boots up a little higher.

Chasing a dream is exhausting, especially when it has been the foremost thought in your mind for thirty-one years. It becomes an obsession. With every minute of every day concentrated on achieving one goal, other life pursuits seem mundane. Chavez had envisioned being the WBC super featherweight champion since his *cholo* days in Chicago, his four years in the Illinois prison system, his years living underground in Austin, and his four-year exile in Mexico. He wanted to be a great champion, yes, but the possibility of having another title shot, especially after he lost his title challenge in 2001 to Floyd Mayweather Jr., was a daunting prospect. So when he managed to string together successful wins against top lightweights Gerardo Zayas (22-3), Julio Cesar Sanchez-Leon (20-10-1), Johnny "Live Wire" Walker (18-4), and Carlos Gerena (38-3), and after he bested the tough Thai fighter Sirimongkol Singmanassuk (43-1), Jesus could honestly say that he accomplished every dream he ever had. And with each subsequent win, Richard Lord's office became more of a shrine to Austin's favorite championship boxer. Every inch of wall space that wasn't already covered with boxing posters from yesteryear—and even some of the spaces that had been—were papered over with Jesus Chavez promotional banners, posters, and newspaper clippings.

After that tremendous and unthinkable victory—the jubilant awareness that all his dreams were reality—Chavez was confronted with being someone else's dream. Somewhere in the world, in another dusty Delicias-esque town or in a maximum security prison or urban ghetto, a hungry boxer was feverishly training and fighting with all the spit and vinegar he could muster, and with the express objective of dethroning Chavez. The hunter had become the hunted. And Top Rank president Bob Arum had plans for his new champion.

Chavez made $80,000 for his victory over Singmanassuk. With every subsequent title defense, Chavez was guaranteed more money. In addition to fortifying his legacy as a great champion, every time he successfully bested challengers meant he'd climb the purse pyramid. Arum announced at a postfight press conference in Austin that he'd have Chavez fight two or three times in Austin, as champions get to choose their preferred fight venue, before he'd reinsert Chavez into the fray of big-name opponents. But this was a hollow promise, and Chavez and his inner circle knew it. There was one fight scheduled against Justin Juuko (39-7-1) of Uganda, but Chavez tore his right shoulder in a preparatory sparring session in Austin. Juuko would have been anything but a "warm-up bout," as Juuko had fought some of the best boxers in the sport, including Miguel Cotto, Diego Corrales, and Floyd Mayweather Jr. When Chavez learned he could not fight Juuko, his promoter ran out of patience and wanted to get him in the ring immediately against the best in the world.

Top Rank had invested heavily in another Mexican boxer and was grooming him for the 130-pound championship. El Matador, the perennial ringer, was now being used as a seat warmer for El Terrible.

Erik "El Terrible" Morales was a *guapo:* a good-looking young man. His pronounced, angular features made him look older and more mature than he was. His cheekbones were high and his nose pointed.

Traditionally these attributes are detrimental to a fighter. Chiseled bone structure makes a boxer prone to cuts. But Morales's skin was thick and stayed together, even after the hardest uppercut. He was tough, known as much for how well he took a punch as for how hard he landed them. He was the man to beat, the pound-for-pound best boxer in the world according to many boxing pundits. Top Rank Promotions staked its future in the lighter divisions on El Terrible. He was their rising star. Since the departure of Oscar De La Hoya, Morales was being groomed to be the next Julio Cesar Chavez—the next fighter to be a champion at three different weight classes. Although Arum promoted both Erik and El Matador, he referred to Morales as the "next [Julio Cesar] Chavez."

El Terrible was already the champion in the 122- and 126-pound divisions. Moving up a third weight class to the aggressive 130-pound group would be a boxing feat often attempted but seldom achieved. Top Rank and indeed the rest of the boxing world wanted to see that from Morales. Besides being a tremendous boxer, Morales was promoted vigorously by his camp, which made El Terrible the marquee name of the lightweights. The Tijuana-born fighter had an enormous Mexican and U.S. fan base, drawing capacity crowds every time he fought in Las Vegas or Los Angeles.

Bob Arum had been in Chavez's corner during the Singmanassuk fight. Without a doubt, he was pulling for Chavez, and not just because El Matador was a Top Rank boxer. The winner would inevitably take on Morales, and fight fans would pay top dollar to watch two tough Mexicans battle it out at the MGM Grand, the boxing capital of the world. Arum thought that a Chavez versus Morales bout with Morales trying for his third championship in his third weight class would be a good, strong fight, and would ensure a Morales victory. Chavez was being set up.

El Matador and El Terrible had history. They knew each other from past encounters in Tijuana and had once shared the same trainer. When Arum announced to the world that WBC super featherweight champion Jesus Chavez, coming off an impressive victory over Thailand's Sirimongkol Singmanassuk, would fight two-time world champion Erik Morales on February 28, 2004, at Las Vegas's MGM

Grand, Chavez wasn't surprised. There would be no warm-up fight in Austin but Chavez didn't care. He always knew in the back of his mind that this fight would happen sooner or later. El Matador was as sure of that inevitability as he was that he'd win the WBC belt if only he had a second chance. No one questioned Chavez's heart. What they questioned was whether the fighter, who was four years his opponent's senior, still had the juice to outlast the younger, harder puncher.

Morales, backed by Top Rank and by boxing analysts, was looking past Chavez to the distinction of three belts. Chavez, now the hunted, was looking squarely at Morales. To beat El Terrible meant the boxing world would finally respect Chavez as a true champion and not just someone's ringer.

———————

Jesus had known the name "Morales" since his days in exile, just as Morales had known the name "Chavez." They were countrymen, more so after Chavez beat Mexican national champion Julio Alvarez in Mexico City in May 1999. Alvarez was supposed to be the next big-name Mexican boxer. He employed the most famous manager south of the border, Fernando Beltran. Beltran managed his boxers out of Tijuana, and right about the time Alvarez was preparing to fight El Matador, Erik Morales was starting to emerge as a serious prospect at 122 pounds.

Chavez was the man at 130 pounds—the most worthy challenger for Floyd Mayweather Jr.'s super featherweight championship. But the boxing world knew that such a fight was unlikely as long as Chavez's legal woes continued.

Morales was training and living in Tijuana, his place of birth, while Chavez was in dusty Delicias. Chavez was living out his life sentence in Mexico—imposed by the INS—while hopefully gazing north to Las Vegas and Floyd Mayweather. But only Chavez, Barbara Hines, Richard Garriott, and Marcy Garriott believed the INS would ever let him return to the United States. Lou Duva and Main Events Promotions had essentially written the boxer off. But Chavez still had hope, so he decided to find Fernando Beltran, someone to manage him while he started seriously training for Mayweather. Meanwhile, Beltran, although well aware of Chavez's potential since he beat Alvarez, was being courted by Morales.

Chavez bankrolled his own travel expenses to Tijuana and went seeking Beltran. He stayed in a cheap motel in Baja, California and took a cab to Beltran's gym. Much like Lord's in Austin, it included some bags and a practice ring. What struck Chavez, though, was Fernando's office. Whereas as Richard Lord's office was a shrine to Chavez, Beltran's office was a shrine to Morales. Pictures of El Terrible were taped to the cinderblock walls, and promotional banners hung from the rafters.

The Mexican promoter was surprised when he saw Chavez standing at his office threshold, as Beltran had not only promoted Alvarez but was now promoting Morales. Beltran's master plan was to make Morales a star, and in so doing, he would have to take El Terrible to the super featherweight division and Floyd Mayweather, or whoever was the reigning champion at the time. Beltran respected Chavez and he was touched that the fighter came to Tijuana to request his services.

Beltran welcomed Chavez and introduced him to trainer Romulo Quirarte. Quirarte was training lightweights Manuel Medina and Jose Luis Castillo, junior middleweight Yory Boy Campas, and Mexico's lone heavyweight prospect, Ernesto Quirarte. Medina in particular would become Chavez's workout buddy. When Jesus could snag a cheap plane ticket to Tijuana, Medina would pick him up at the airport and take him running. He held the heavy bag for Jesus and sparred with him.

What impressed El Matador the most about Romulo Quirarte was that the old man was one of his hero's first trainers. Julio Cesar Chavez and Romulo Quirarte also had history. For Jesus, training with Quirarte was an honor.

As El Matador became a fixture around the Tijuana boxing scene, Quirarte introduced him to Erik Morales in 1999, who trained at the same gym in Zona Norte. When they first met, Chavez said they were cordial and engaged in small talk. How's your training going? Who are you fighting in the future? Morales was going to move up in weight, and even if Chavez was still in exile when that time came and Morales would have to fight a different 130 pounder in the United States, El Terrible knew he'd have to defeat Chavez in Mexico if he wanted to win the hearts and minds of the people.

Chavez continued training in Beltran's gym, and both Beltran and Quirarte were impressed with the way he worked the heavy bags, speed bags, and double-end bags. They also had confidence in his ability after they saw his ring work. But Beltran did not adopt Chavez as a realistic prospect just because Chavez was ranked number one by the World Boxing Council. He kept his focus on Morales, and he continued to add items to the growing Morales gym shrine. Beltran was a crafty manager/promoter. He was studying Chavez's style and taking mental notes of the shots he threw and when. In essence, Beltran was both testing and chumming the waters for Morales. He'd occasionally joke with Jesus about a fight with El Terrible.

"Matador, you and El Terrible should fight one day," he'd say.

"Hey *compañero*, whenever he's ready, he knows where to find me," Chavez replied lightheartedly. "I'm ready for him, but is he ready for me?"

This was a good time for El Matador, despite his unfortunate situation. He felt honored to receive Quirarte's expert tutelage and be around the best Mexican boxers, which doubled as being around the world's best boxers. Still, Chavez couldn't get his head around the fact that here these guys were, training hard and preparing for prize fights in a country he was prohibited from entering. They'd have some bouts in Mexico, but they were primarily concerned with attracting the attention of American promoters. With American promoters came American fights and American dollars. Manuel Medina, Yory Boy Campas, Jose Luis Castillo, and Erik Morales would all go off to various hotels and casinos to fight. El Matador would be left behind to keep the bench warm.

He was frustrated. At times, he was contemptuous. Jesus tried to transform that angst into muscle, and he trained even harder. Meanwhile, El Terrible was being promoted to the extreme. The irony was tremendous. Both Chavez and Morales trained out of the same gym in Mexico, yet the roads they traveled to get to Las Vegas and their February 2004 championship bout at the MGM Grand were decidedly different.

———————

Tijuana, Mexico bills itself as the "world's most visited border town." Indeed, the local population of over a million seems larger because of the steady influx of tourists, day and night. Since it is only fifteen miles from San Diego, souvenir hounds and day-trippers who want the dubious distinction of saying they've "been to Mexico" stream over the border each day, where vendors of mass-produced trinkets line the major thoroughfares and side streets. Vendors call to passersby, harassing them to visit their stores. "Okay. It's my turn," a vendor says as a family of four strolls down Avenida Revolución, the main shopping drag. "I got best deals," another vendor says in broken English. Or, "Come see my junk."

After dark, hordes of thrill-seekers, underage San Diego youths, and Marines from nearby Camp Pendleton descend on Tijuana for the notoriously *loco* nightlife. And with intoxicated Americans come local pickpockets and other criminals.

But for someone who wanders from the major drag—halfheartedly patrolled by the Mexican police—Tijuana's sleazy veneer gives way to an even seedier underbelly, populated by violent criminals. Possessing anything of the slightest perceived value could mean your life. Out of this grinding poverty comes great boxing but also human desperation, leading otherwise God-fearing men to become lawless.

This is Tijuana's infamous North Zone, or Baja California Norte, or just Zona Norte. Dilapidated storefronts, with their lead paint flecked and their windowpanes distorted from years of accumulated grime, line the narrow streets while automobiles running on leaded gasoline putter by in a plume of dirty exhaust. The area is extremely rough and its people are extremely poor. Many residents are petty merchants or work for them. Their wages are barely subsistence level, and a tourist who makes a wrong turn with his $500 Nikon can mean dinner for the next two months.

If an American is mugged and battered, U.S. authorities can come down hard on Mexican authorities and perhaps threaten a nationwide travel warning, threatening a loss of American dollars. If a Tijuanian batters—or murders—a fellow Tijuanian, authorities may file a report but usually reserve their services to opportunities for profit. It takes money to make local authorities work; money these people don't have.

There was one local, however, who traveled in and around town un-afraid and undisturbed. He drove down the threatening avenues and menacing boulevards in his new Chevrolet Silverado, shiny and silver. He parked it anywhere it would fit and left it unlocked. On occasion, he left the windows down at the intersection of Coahuila and 5 de Mayo, the core of Tijuana's free-fire zone.

No one dared touch El Terrible's car, much as the authorities in Delicias did not touch El Matador's. They were local heroes, and local heroes were scarce around those two towns.

It was on the second floor of a building on Coahuila and 5 de Mayo—a small generic storefront with a sign that read *Comestibles* (groceries)—where Morales became the boxing powerhouse who would reign over the lightweights. On the first floor of that same run-down building was where he'd been born.

———

Jose Morales Damian, Erik's father, had been a decent flyweight in the 1970s. He was a native Tijuanian who became known around the neighborhood as much for his boxing as for his skill in repairing air conditioners. Damian owned the building that housed his boxing gym, if it could even be called that. There was a ring in the corner of a room with one side flush against a windowpane. If a sparring boxer hit too hard while his opponent's butt was to the window, that boxer could seriously injure himself by breaking the window out with his neck and back, or, worse, by flying right though the ropes and then down two stories.

Morales was born into the family business in 1976 with boxing in his blood. Named after Eric the Viking, a sea-faring warrior, Damian assumed that his boy would box as he did.

Erik's childhood consisted of school and boxing. Damian, a strict disciplinarian, made sure his son had a full education. Erik was a quick study—a visual person—so when he returned home from school one day at the age of six and asked his father to teach him how to box, Damian took the smallest pair of gloves he could find and laced them on his son. Damian's hawk-faced boy loved to be in the ring the way most children his age loved to be in the sandbox. Watching his father spar from toddlerhood, Erik convinced himself that getting hit wasn't bad. It was just part of the sport, which to him meant it was just part of life.

By age twelve, Erik was a sparring partner for flyweight professionals. He was talented inside the ring but, as his father put it, "nothing special." Not immediately, anyway.

He fought as an amateur until he was sixteen, when he decided to turn pro. Despite his stellar amateur record of 118-6, Jose Morales Damian had other plans for his son, who was excelling in school. He consistently brought home good grades and was even considered one of his school's smartest in math and science. That's when something unheard of in boxing happened: Jose Morales Damian did everything he could to discourage his son from becoming a professional boxer, while the boy's mother, Isabelle, insisted he go pro. Finally Damian came around and admitted that his boy had promise, though he continued to maintain that a boxer's life was not good enough for bookish Erik. But the elder Morales was not one to stifle his son's ambitions, so he agreed to help his son's professional career. Sort of.

Damian found the toughest opponent he could for Erik's "coming out" fight in March 1993. Jose Orejel was a Tijuanian thug who also was about to make his professional debut. He was known for his ferocious punching power, the result of a tough Tijuanian life. Damian trained his son for six months in his one-room gym to prepare for his professional debut. He didn't want his son to get hurt, but he hoped several rounds on the receiving end of Orejel's blinding jabs and combinations would convince the aspiring pugilist that academia was a more practical—and certainly more benign—pursuit. In essence, Damian hoped his son's first professional bout would make him a college man. But the opposite happened.

Erik charged to the center of the ring in the first round and unloaded a torrent of combination punches on his slower opponent. Midway through the second round, Morales further stepped up the action, brutalizing his opponent and scoring a technical knockout. His father was elated, though he remained determined that his son was destined for a better life than boxing could offer. So for his second fight, Damian scheduled another bruiser, Jaime Rodriguez, an up-and-comer who was touted as a hopeful Tijuanian prospect.

Second fight, same result. Morales stopped Rodriguez in the second. It wasn't until young Erik knocked out Oscar Maldonado in the third round of his third fight that Damian admitted his son had a future as a professional boxer. "My son's got something in his hands," he told a local television station in 1993.

Those hands destroyed challenger after challenger. He stopped six of his first seven opponents, earning the nickname "El Terrible," a bon mot that followed him into the United States.

The lightweight division and the super bantamweight division (122 pounds) were obscure in the world of international boxing, especially in the 1990s when heavyweights Evander Holyfield, Lennox Lewis, Michael Moorer, Riddick Bowe, and Mike Tyson (upon his prison release) dominated boxing news. Morales remained a local legend until he knocked out Daniel Zaragoza (55-8-3) in September 1997 for Zaragoza's WBC super bantamweight title, a fight that ended Zaragoza's career.

That victory meant winning his first world championship and attracting the attention of Bob Arum and Top Rank. Arum corralled Morales into his growing stable of Mexican fighters after El Terrible won the super bantamweight title, but it wasn't until the subsequent year when Morales defended his championship belt against Junior Jones (44-3) in Tijuana's sold-out El Toreo (Bull Ring) that Arum started touting his boxer as the "next Chavez."

Young Erik was unstoppable. He continued to destroy opponents either by knockout or by TKO. He was Tijuana's rock star throughout the 1990s, steering an undefeated record into the new millennium. While he was busting up those he faced, he was winning the hearts and minds of Baja California Norte. In 1999, Arum extended Morales's contract for three years and $10 million. Rather than take the money and bolt for Las Vegas or San Diego or LA, El Terrible bought himself a home in Tijuana and his parents a new home a few miles away from his: Morales refused to leave his roots. He took the $10,000 signing bonus and used every cent to furnish Tijuanian schools with computers, a luxury that would otherwise have been unimaginable. Each Christmas, the 127-pound boxer assumed the role of jolly Saint Nicholas. He bought five hundred dinners for the people in his old neighborhood, followed by a slew of toys for children who would otherwise have received lumps of coal.

Back in the ring, Morales wowed Mexican boxing fans when he moved up in weight and defeated Kevin Kelly (51-4-2) for the interim WBC featherweight championship and then Mexico City warrior Guty Espadas Jr., a match that quashed any doubts about Morales being a contender at a higher weight.

Bob Arum sparked a desire in Erik and Jose Morales that was as grand as Tijuana's Otay Mountains. The desire was unthinkable, especially in Mexico, where the name Julio Cesar Chavez commands respect like no other. To aspire to be a world champion at three different weight classes, something that only Julio Cesar Chavez was able to do, seemed almost blasphemous. When Morales questioned whether he had the resolve to be mentioned in the same breath as JCC, there was Arum, quick with a compliment and his perfunctory affirmations.

By the time Morales fought his second of three matches against Marco Antonio Barrera (54-3), another of Mexico City's native sons, in June 2002, Morales was 35-0 with 28 knockouts. El Terrible lost a tough unanimous decision to Barrera the second time around in front of a packed house at the Las Vegas MGM Grand. Morales had won their first meeting in 2000 by split decision, a fight in which pundits thought Barrera had the edge. Those same pundits thought Morales had the edge when he lost by unanimous decision two years later. Nevertheless, Morales dealt with his lone defeat like a true champion. He went back to Tijuana and got in the gym even before his injuries healed. Jose Morales Damian, once the nay-sayer in the Morales camp, trained his son like a robot with only one programmed objective. Five months later in November 2002, El Terrible was back in the ring against another top-ranked fighter, Paulie Ayala (34-1). Morales won a lopsided unanimous decision, then did something few featherweights had done before him: he fought two big-name fights within six months of each other (defeating Eddie Croft 23-6-1 and Fernando Velardez 24-4-1), and he moved up to super featherweight (130) and beat Guty Espadas again. The Espadas victory at what was Morales's third weight class drummed up the "legend" chatter. El Terrible was fighting with a vengeance and Arum wasted no time setting Morales on a crash course with destiny. The title shot at 130 would be Morales's biggest payday. It was a fight that Arum could schedule easily and internally.

Standing in the way was a fighter that Arum and the rest of the boxing world decided to look past. Arum was marketing Morales as the next Julio Cesar Chavez, thereby neglecting another Chavez: another champion. Jesus Chavez wasn't about to roll over for Arum, Morales, or a boxing world eager to see a living legend in the making.

———————

In December 2003, Jesus Chavez received a call from Corpus Christi, Texas. It was Lou Mesorana, his manager, who was brimming with news. Arum was going to schedule a fight between Chavez and Morales, an HBO Boxing After Dark event, broadcast live from the MGM Grand in Las Vegas. For Chavez, this was an exciting call. He'd known since his Mexican exile days that Morales was in his future. Chavez initially felt honored that he would meet Morales as the 130-pound champion—the fight would be on his terms.

What El Matador didn't realize at the outset was that Arum was not taking "his terms" into account. Morales wanted this fight because he thought he could beat Chavez easily, thereby collecting a historic third world championship. Morales would be the odds-on favorite, and the MGM Grand was as close to home-field advantage as Morales could get. He had fought two bouts there already, packed from floor to ceiling with Tijuana fans who made the 360-mile trek to the Strip.

Chavez arrived in Vegas four days before his Saturday matchup. He crossed the threshold into the MGM Grand and was immediately struck by the fifteen-foot hangings of the two fighters. One flag hung lengthwise on one pillar, the other on an adjacent pillar. The boxers were in traditional fighter poses, each one holding his guard just under his face. The photos were black and white and intentionally grainy. As these were pugilists from the purist's school—fighters who did not dance around the ring but met their opponents in the center of the squared circle—Top Rank Boxing decided to bill the clash as just that. Suspended between the two flags was a scrawling banner: Chavez vs. Morales—Brave Warriors Collide.

Jesus was taken aback when he saw his poster. There he was, a co-poster boy of the MGM Grand, in good company with a boxer many pundits touted as the best in the mythical pound-for-pound weight class. The posters were a thunderbolt to the already prepared boxer. Morales looked tough, and he was there in Vegas to take the WBC super featherweight championship belt from Jesus. But Mexican boxers come to throw leather. Brave warriors would indeed collide.

———————

The night of the fight, as the 8:30 P.M. witching hour drew near, Jesus was in his dressing room warming up. Richard Lord was there as always, and so was trainer Fernando Castrejon. Jesus danced around and shadowboxed the way he always did before a fight, though he kept getting interrupted by HBO producers looking for a live prefight shot.

Richard Lord was concerned about his boxer. El Matador had the talent and heart to shock the world, but something about this fight worried him. Perhaps it was because Jesus was coming off a shoulder injury and six months of inactivity. He also was uneasy about the way Arum went about scheduling the fight. Chavez needed shoulder surgery, but Arum wanted the fight in February. Top Rank didn't openly say that if Chavez refused to fight Morales soon he'd be stripped of the belt, but they didn't exactly cater to his safety needs. Lord had been around this business long enough to know that Chavez was to be Arum's seat warmer at 130 pounds.

As he laced Jesus's gloves, Lord searched for an expression on the boxer's face—something that would indicate whether or not El Matador was truly ready for Morales. Chavez had that soldier's stare, which Lord thought was encouraging. If Jesus thought he was ready—if he convinced himself that the shoulder was strong and that he could handle El Terrible—then surely he could. Because both men could fight.

Moments later, the sound of "Son de la negra" came trilling through the MGM Grand Garden Arena. El Terrible favored that upbeat Mexican ballad because it inspired his faithful fans who made the journey from Tijuana. The fans were even louder and crazier than usual, though, because Morales was being escorted to the ring by Julio Cesar Chavez.

Meanwhile, Jesus Chavez bounced up and down in his dressing room as he listened to his opponent's music; his own entourage prepared to escort him to the ring. He was the champion, and traditionally champions enter the ring second. Top Rank asked Chavez if he'd enter first and let the challenger enter second—an admission of Arum's favoritism. But Chavez, a proud fighter and deserving champion, refused.

El Matador had come a long way since Lewis Wood in Houston almost a decade before, though there was Lord's consistent scowl—face tight and hair unkempt as ever—and there was his brother, Jimmy, now holding Jesus's WBC super featherweight belt in his hands. Even more familiar to the boxer was that prefight moment: that realization that Jesus Chavez, the reigning champion, would enter the ring as the underdog.

———

El Matador liked to smile at his fans as he made his way to the ring, but on that night, he was stony faced. He wore a baseball jersey and camouflage trunks, a tribute to his girlfriend, Aunisa, who had recently been upgraded to active duty and assigned a tour in war-torn

Iraq. Chavez threw punches into the air while the crowd of white and Hispanic fans screamed its approval. El Terrible awaited his ring entrance, standing still like a watchful animal. El Matador parted the ring ropes, and the two Mexican brawlers gave each other a hard stare. Before ring announcer Michael Buffer had a chance to do the formal introductions, chants of "Chavez" and "Morales" resounded and overlapped each other. The anticipation and excitement were palpable. Neither fighter mugged for the crowd; instead they stared down each other.

They walked to the center of the ring, and no one danced around. They stood face-to-face, tapped gloves, and returned to their corners. The superheated atmosphere kept Chavez and Morales tense. Two countrymen, both at the top of their game and in top physical shape, prepared to do battle in front of a capacity crowd of citizens and immigrants. The MGM Grand was more than a forum that night; it was a grand leveler.

The bell dinged to signal round one, and El Matador and El Terrible charged each other with fists flying. Early in the first two minutes, Chavez caught Morales—and the fans—off guard with a blistering right/left combination. Morales was knocked back into the ring ropes, and the Chavez faithful roared their approval. Chavez tried to finish him off, but El Terrible, although stunned, was a two-time world champion and was not about to go out so easily. He fought off the ropes and survived the first round.

Chavez retreated to his corner confident. Lord and Castrejon instructed El Matador to continue throwing that right upstairs and downstairs. "That right is your key," Lord said. Chavez answered the bell in round two with the same resilience he showcased a round earlier, while Morales looked a little sluggish. Jesus was swinging away, jabbing with his left and unloading the right, when he telegraphed the right too much and Morales caught him with a blistering uppercut. The punch found its target: the fleshy bulb of El Matador's nose. Chavez staggered backward like a cartoon character after an anvil is dropped on his head. His feet struggled to maintain his weight while his arms flailed and his body crumbled to the canvas.

The Tijuana fanatics leaped to their feet and screamed their delight. Chavez was only down for a three count. He ordered himself to get up and get back in the fight while the referee proceeded with a standing eight count. His mind wandered from that vicious blow. A misconception about boxing is that when a fighter receives a solid headshot, he hears bells and whistles. For Chavez, the arena all of a sudden seemed silent. He sprang off the canvas and shook his head, clearing the cobwebs, as the sounds of Morales's fans and the reality of it all crept back.

Chavez needed to make a statement in the remaining minutes of round two. The fight was still in its infancy, and Jesus didn't want Erik returning to his corner thinking he owned the round. To compensate for his bewilderment, Chavez started flailing carelessly at a now confident Morales. They exchanged shots in the center for another thirty seconds when Chavez decided to take a chance. He threw a haymaker, a roundabout right that missed the challenger; searing pain shot through his right shoulder and seized up his body. Chavez had thrown that haymaker with such vehemence that he ripped his already injured shoulder out of socket and severed his rotator cuff. Morales made a move to his right, countered with an uppercut, and Chavez went down a second time. The knockdown came at the end of the bell. Chavez made it to his feet but was completely dazed, not even realizing he'd been knocked down a second time.

Jesus went back to his corner where his cut man went to work. His eyes were swollen with blood trickling out of his tear ducts. "Keep using that right," Lord instructed. "Set it up with your left and then deliver that hard right!"

Chavez didn't say anything. He nodded and returned to the center of ring for round three, throwing almost all lefts. The left hooks to the body continued to wear down Morales, as El Terrible did not compensate for the flurry of lefts that were mostly absent in the first two rounds. After the third round, Chavez returned to Lord and Castrejon, both of who started laying into the champion. "What are you doing?" they badgered. "Throw that right! That's your whole game plan."

"I tore the shoulder," Chavez replied through labored breaths. "My right is gone."

"But you *need* to throw the right hand," Castrejon said.

The trainers told him to try to get in one or two rights anyway. From that point on, El Matador answered the bell with his right fist hanging slightly below his face, in sharp contrast to his traditionalist's stance, where he kept both gloves raised above his head. He threw a hundred lefts for every one right. As the rounds ticked by, the fight doctor and a Nevada boxing commissioner climbed the canvas and questioned Chavez while his corner worked on him. They wanted to know why he was only throwing lefts. "I'm setting him up," El Matador replied. "Don't stop this fight. No matter what, don't stop this fight."

Every ensuing round became tougher to watch than the previous. Chavez continued to charge to the center of the ring and throw a barrage of left-handed punches, each time gritting his teeth as his weary levator scapulae and rhomboid muscles strained and burned from exhaustion. Many of these punches found their target, even though more of Morales's punches found him. El Matador did not run from the healthier Morales but strained himself trying to make his left hand—his weaker hand—find its mark. No one in Morales's camp caught on to Jesus's handicap. Neither did the HBO commentators. It wasn't until the sixth round that they suspected something was wrong with Chavez. Save for Lord and Castrejon, the only other person in the audience who realized what was happening was Mike Tyson. He sat ringside and clapped for Chavez. "That guy is a warrior," he said. "He's fighting on all heart."

But Morales was too strong. He used Chavez's face and body as a human heavy bag. As El Matador was unable to deflect two pumping fists with only one arm, he was forced to sustain vicious blow after vicious blow. The trickling blood gave way to a persistent stream from his eyes and nose, and his face swelled in real time from Morales's unremitting punishment. But Mexican fighters are not trained to quit, and Chavez maintained that he was still in the fight and still had a chance to win.

The doctor wanted to stop the fight each time he inspected the wounded boxer, and in the latter rounds, he all but begged Lord and Castrejon to throw in the towel. But Chavez kept advancing with one arm: despite his handicap, he was the aggressor. El Matador answered each bell and doggedly flailed away with his left. Somehow, this mixture of courage and heart saw him through the twelfth round.

At the end of the bout, pandemonium engulfed the MGM Grand Garden Arena. The fight went to the judges' scorecards, even though everyone who watched knew that El Terrible would win a unanimous decision. The white and Hispanic fans whooped and hollered as they awaited the ring announcer, turning to their neighbor and marveling in the exhibition of guts and grit they had just witnessed. They had acted like demon-possessed fanatics during the fight, barking orders at the fighters and throwing measuring jabs into the air. But after the final bell, they paid homage to the moxie displayed by their country-men. The boxers, however, did not share their sentiments.

Ordinarily, after a bout fought with such spirit, the fighters embrace each other and offer congratulations. But El Terrible and El Matador knew that this score was unsettled. They did not hug: they glowered at each other. Although Morales made history by becoming only the second Mexican fighter in professional boxing to be a champion at three weight classes, the physical injuries told another story.

Chavez threw 873 punches, 856 of which were lefts. Morales threw 957 punches. While remarkable by boxing standards, the number of shots landed was the truly impressive statistic. The right side of Morales's face looked like it had been beaten with a pipe. It was red and fleshy, decidedly rounder than the left, unmolested side, which was still chiseled and angular. His right eye had swollen shut, and his usually pronounced cheekbone disappeared in the swelling that engulfed his right cheek and temple. El Matador landed 233 lefts to the right side of Morales's face, and the fighter looked like it.

For his part, Morales landed 284 punches all over Chavez's head. If El Matador could have defended himself—if he could have somehow used his lame right arm to deflect even a few of those furious blows—that number would have been lower. Chavez took everything Morales had, yet Morales did not escape without severe injuries. El Matador may have separated his right shoulder and torn his rotator cuff, but Morales broke both of his hands on Chavez's head.

"Folks, it doesn't get much better than this," commentator Larry Merchant said at the end of the fight. Morales had the title, but fans hoped that these warriors would battle again. Chavez fans delighted in the fact that their fighter did not quit. Morales made history, but Chavez made the world respect him.

At any other fight, Chavez and Morales would be cheering each other on to victory. They are countrymen who watched each other climb different mountains toward the same heights. But when Morales stepped up in weight, Chavez was not about to hand over his title. Mexican boxers come to throw leather. And as a separated shoulder, a torn rotator cuff, two broken hands, bleeding eyes, and a combined 1,830 punches graphically attest, in the ring, their country is the undisputed champion of the world.

14

"The Fight Could Go Either Way"

While sitting in the emergency room at Valley Hospital in Las Vegas just hours after his epic twelve-round battle against Erik "El Terrible" Morales, Jesus felt searing pains shoot through his shoulder. The rotator cuff was torn and his tenderized body tensed each time the muscles contracted. As the moments ticked by and the pain intensified, the boxer began to experience shooting pains in his knee as well. El Matador staved off one of the world's premiere boxers, though his body paid a taxing price.

Boxers need time to heal. And thirty-two-year-old boxers need more time. Chavez was always a quick healer in the sense that he never hesitated to fight through aches and pains. To pugilistic purists like Lord, fighters don't cry about soreness. They persevere and forge ahead, as long as they have mobility in their arms and legs. Chavez did not have mobility in his right shoulder, and had his situation not been so painful, he would have noticed that his ACL was torn too. But he didn't, not until he sat patiently in Valley Hospital's trauma wing, packed in ice from head to toe.

His girlfriend, Aunisa, was at his side. She'd be leaving for Iraq and a year-long tour with the Texas National Guard in two months, but Iraq was the last thing on her mind at that moment. She was worried about her boyfriend. A well-conditioned soldier, Aunisa knew from eyewitness accounts that the older a body is, the longer the healing time. She congratulated Jesus, sealed with a kiss on his swollen forehead. Despite his hurt, Jesus seemed giddy. He went through the obligatory CAT scans and Aunisa accompanied him to his hospital room.

In the predawn hours, as the boxer lay in his hospital bed, he reached into his gym bag, which had not left his side since he left the dressing room at the MGM Grand, and pulled out a little black box.

"Aunisa," he said through puffy lips. "I'm not very good in these types of situations. You've made my life complete, and I love and respect you with all my heart. Will you marry me?"

Aunisa's eyes widened and she gasped as Jesus opened the box and produced a diamond. She put her hands over her mouth and then over her heart. Her face reddened. Her breath quickened. The lieutenant allowed herself a moment to be just a girl. Jesus helped place the ring on her finger. The two were married in May 2004 in the MGM Grand Chapel in Las Vegas. Aunisa shipped off to Iraq a week later. While she was gone, Jesus underwent shoulder and knee surgeries.

With his wife halfway around the world, El Matador returned to his humble ranch-style home in suburban north Austin. He was longing to get back in the gym, back to Lord's, and back to his ring and footwork. The Morales fight left a bad taste in his mouth, and the inactivity forced him to replay each round in his head. He wanted a rematch, though he did not have a rematch clause in his contract, even though most champions do.

It took Jesus fifteen months to return to fight center stage. And fifteen months to the day of his loss to Morales, Bob Arum and Top Rank scheduled him in a title eliminator against Carlos "El Famoso" Hernandez.

Chavez rejected taking a warm-up fight before taking on Hernandez. The two boxers were both in their thirties, and Chavez did not need a smaller match to prove he was still a contender at 130 pounds. The fight was to be the undercard of a legend. Julio Cesar Chavez decided to come out of retirement to say *adios* to an American audience. His opponent was Ivan Robinson, a mediocre Philadelphia fighter scheduled as a ringer. Jesus and Carlos would each make $300,000, by far the biggest payday for each and a testament to the fact that theirs was to be the more explosive and exciting fight.

Jesus and Carlos had other commonalities besides money. They both fought Floyd Mayweather Jr., and both lost in tough, gritty fashion. And Morales had relieved both of them of their world titles, Chavez of the WBC super featherweight belt and Hernandez of the IBF super featherweight belt. They were also friends, visiting each other's homes and having dinner together. Because they were close, because they were roughly the same age (Chavez was 32 and Hernandez was 33), and because they had watched each other rise in the super featherweight ranks, they knew each other's strengths and weaknesses. Each knew the other would bring the heat in a title elimination bout. Neither boxer was getting any younger, and since they were both promoted by Top Rank, they knew that to the victor came a rematch with Morales. To the loser, though, came middle-aged obscurity and a lesser opponent for fewer dollars in the future. This would be a career-ending fight for one of the fighters, if not in a literal sense, in a figurative boxing one.

The fight was scheduled for twelve rounds at the Staples Center in Los Angeles on May 28, 2005. Chavez was a little apprehensive about fighting Carlos in his backyard. El Famoso lived thirty minutes from the venue, and El Matador did not like the prospect of being a visitor. Once again, his promoter seemed to be setting him up.

On the night of the big match, Staples Center was packed. A majority of the 17,700 in attendance were Mexican or Mexican American. Julio Cesar Chavez was still a huge draw, even at the age of forty-three.

Hernandez entered the ring first for the undercard bout, as he had a worse record (though still an impressive 41-4), to boos. Indeed he was the hometown fighter, but this crowd related on a more personal level with a fellow countryman than a fellow Angelino. They booed the El Salvadorian fighter. Hernandez tried not to let the Mexican crowd get to him as he continued to bounce and throw measuring jabs into the air. His wife, Veronica, looked around the arena with a nervous smile on her face.

By contrast, when Jesus's mariachi music cued up, the crowd leapt to its feet, and green, white, and red Mexican flags waved from all points around the Staples Center. Richard Lord gave Chavez some unique instructions prior to the bout. Lord usually encouraged El Matador to take the fight to his opponent. He told Chavez on numerous occasions to be the aggressor, and Chavez dutifully followed instructions. But Hernandez is a scrapper with more punching power than Chavez. The El Salvadorian would be looking to flail away, as he would have a slight advantage in a street fight. For this match, Lord told Chavez to stay outside and outbox Carlos with his superb technical skills. That's what El Matador did for the first two rounds. He kept his distance and picked Carlos apart with his jabs. Come round three, though, Hernandez began coaxing Chavez into his style of fight, waving El Matador in and telling him to "come on." The technical boxing was working for Chavez, but Carlos wanted a fight. A fight is what he got.

Jesus let his hands go in round three. He strung together the same combination punches that befuddled Sirimongkol Singmanassuk in their title fight two years earlier. Hernandez took the shots and continued to be the aggressor, though one right uppercut managed to buckle his legs halfway through the round.

They continued to hammer away at each other for the next eight rounds, the aggressor versus the combination expert. The fans were on their feet as the boxers made their way to the middle of the ring at the start of round twelve. Referee David Mandoza instructed Jesus and Carlos to touch gloves for the last round. The fight was even on most fans' scorecards, and the boxers eyed each other as Mandoza spoke. They were both bleeding from the nose and mouth. Jesus tried to stare down his old friend, but a small smile pursed his lips. Carlos, trying to out-mug his opponent, also allowed a small smile. The two touched gloves, took a step forward, and hugged each other in the middle of the ring. The Staples Center exploded with deafening applause. Referee Mandoza grinned as the arena crowd continued the ovation during the embrace. He wished both fighters luck and with the flick of his right wrist, signaled for the timekeeper to roll clock and for the action to recommence.

The pugilists shared a moment earlier, but when the referee said fight, they both dropped their guard and began swinging wildly at each other with every ounce of might and moxie in their 130-pound bodies. The cracking of leather on flesh and bone was audible in the second-level seats. For three solid minutes, El Famoso and El Matador tattooed each other with everything they had. Proper form was disregarded as the boxers traded punches until the final bell. Fans screamed at a pitch not heard in the Staples Center since the Los Angeles Lakers won the 2001–2002 NBA championship.

The fight went to the judges' scorecards, and the crowd anxiously awaited the decision. The fight was even going into the twelfth round, which could have gone either way.

Announcer Michael Buffer broadcast that there was a split decision. Judge David Dinkins scored the bout 113-115 and judges Max DeLuca and Lou Filippo scored the bout 117-111 and 115-113 respectively for the winner and new number-one ranked contender: Jesus "El Matador" Chavez.

The boxer's personal promoter, Lou Mesorana, was on the phone with Top Rank two weeks after the Hernandez fight. He pestered Arum and other Top Rank matchmakers to schedule the Morales rematch, as they had an oral guarantee. Chavez felt healthy and had a score to settle. Their February 2004 bout still gnawed at him.

Top Rank, however, was no longer offering Erik Morales as a potential match, instead putting Morales into a long-anticipated explosion with Filipino crowd favorite Manny Pacquiao. Bob Arum was offering a rematch against Carlos Hernandez, this time for $500,000.

Chavez and Mesorana originally agreed, as that sort of payday would go a long way for the boxer and his new wife. As more time passed, however, Jesus liked the idea less. It was a split decision victory, but in boxing, a victory is a victory. On paper, the rematch with Carlos looked good, but in reality it would not serve his career well. For starters, a second victory against Carlos Hernandez would make Chavez the undisputed champion of Carlos Hernandez. A loss, however, would set up a rubber match. At thirty-two, Chavez didn't think his body could withstand two more twelve-round fights with El Famoso. For the first time in his career, El Matador formally recognized that the years were working against him.

Chavez wanted money, yes, but more importantly he wanted another world title. A boxer from the old school, Jesus measured success by whether or not a gold belt was strapped around his waist. He had paid too many dues and taken too many lumps not to have another crack at a championship. But Bob Arum wasn't offering anything. Just El Famoso.

Chavez's contract was on a match-by-match basis with Top Rank. Before he officially inked the deal with Carlos, he fielded a personal call from boxing's favorite American son, Oscar De La Hoya. The Golden Boy had started the aptly named Golden Boy Promotions in 2003. His career was winding down after his second loss to "Sugar" Shane Mosley, and he used his name recognition to entice top name fighters, many of whom departed his former promoter, Bob Arum and Top Rank. Oscar got wind of Chavez's grumbling by way of the boxing grapevine and asked El Matador what it would take for him to join Golden Boy. For Chavez, the answer was simple: a world title shot.

Arum had been hesitant to schedule fights against his former boxer's promotional agency. Apparently some wounds don't heal. So De La Hoya couldn't deliver a match against Erik Morales. Not yet, anyway. What he could offer was a shot at the IBF lightweight world champion Leavander Johnson. It meant Chavez would have to move up a weight to 135 pounds, abandoning the weight he'd fought at for over a decade. It also meant that he'd be fighting a stronger and arguably tougher opponent. He'd make half as much money as he would if he fought Carlos Hernandez, and he'd be the second undercard of dual main events: "Sugar" Shane Mosley versus Jose Luis Cruz and Marco Antonio Barrera versus Robbie Peden. It was a gamble, yes. But it was a world title shot and Jesus couldn't be guaranteed another title shot with Bob Arum and Top Rank. He and Lou Mesorana flew to Los Angeles in June 2005 and signed with Oscar De La Hoya and Golden Boy.

The lobby of the MGM Grand was festooned with boxing paraphernalia on the weekend of September 16, 2005. A regulation boxing ring stood front and center in the magnificent marble-floored lobby of the hotel and casino on the Las Vegas strip. Large-than-life posters of the four boxers on the two main cards flanked the ring with a scrawl across the bottom: Parade of Champions.

Nowhere in the grandiose lobby promotion was there mention of the Jesus Chavez versus Leavander Johnson fight. Richard Lord and Chavez arrived in Las Vegas four days before the September 17 bout. Both were put out by the promoters' disregard. Just a year and a half earlier, El Matador was given a champion's staging when both his and Erik Morales's banners hung from the large Gothic columns and touted their match as "When Brave Warriors Collide."

But there would be no publicity for the Chavez versus Johnson fight. Not unless you count a five-second promo at the end of an hour-long promotional video playing on a loop for guests of the MGM Grand. In the program, Mosley, Cruz, Peden, and Barrera each had a fifteen-minute segment. Before the program started over (as it ran continuously to generate buzz for fight night), photographs of Chavez and Johnson were flashed on the screen while an announcer proclaimed, "Also on the card, Jesus Chavez takes on Leavander Johnson for Johnson's IBF lightweight championship belt." But boxing experts knew that the Chavez/Johnson fight would be at least as electric (if not more so) than the Barrera/Peden main event. They were certain that it would be more interesting than Mosley/Cruz.

HBO ringside announcer Jim Lampley commented before the fight that Jesus and Leavander, two veteran combatants known for their punching output, would most likely be the fight of the night.

"Chavez always puts on a great show, and he's demonstrated time and time again how much heart he fights with," Lampley said. "It took Johnson a lifetime to capture his world title, and he's not about to give it up. His height advantage may give Chavez problems as well. The fight could go either way."

More than 10,000 tickets were sold for the fight, though when Jesus Chavez made his entrance to the ring, less than half that number were in their seats. The IBF lightweight championship of the world contest was the first fight televised on HBO's pay-per-view coverage. Cameras started rolling at 6:00 P.M. Mountain time, and half of the lower level of the arena's west wing sounded their enthusiasm as the challenger descended toward the squared circle. This was the Austin contingent, diehard fans who made the trip from Texas to watch their adopted son. They screamed for El Matador in English as they waved red matador capes.

The other large concentration of fans filled out the upper-level nosebleed seats. They screamed in Spanish and waved Mexican flags as the mariachi music trilled over the speakers. Mexican fans support their own, and while many of those who came to Vegas for the main event were finishing up their blackjack hands and watching the Notre Dame–Michigan State game from the MGM Grand Sports Book, the Mexican faithful in the arena made enough noise from the cheap seats to more than compensate for the lack of bodies at 6:00 P.M.

Chavez looked as determined for this fight as he did for Floyd Mayweather Jr. in 2001. He didn't trot to the ring as was his custom. He solemnly walked, his gloves resting on Richard Lord's shoulders. His eyes were unblinking and even his tic was in check. Chavez opened his mouth wide to stretch his facial muscles. He was readying himself to take a lot of blows to the head. The boxer had a thin layer of sweat over his body, and his black hair was wet and lay flat on his head.

He entered the ring and raised his gloves, which touched off another wave of cheers from the Austin and Mexican fans. Moments later, the cheers turned to boos as the incumbent champion started his slow descent to the ring. Johnson's purple robe engulfed him. His hood was pulled low over his head. A member of his entourage yelled "here comes the champ!" as the fans continued to boo. Leavander had fought twice before in Las Vegas, but he was from Atlantic City, and his fan base was not as large west of the Mississippi River as it was on the East Coast. He had a strong, chiseled body, and he looked ten years younger than his thirty-five years. He too seemed confident and poised as he entered the ring.

The fighters met in the center and received instructions from referee Tony Weeks. They returned to their corners and answered the bell with quick steps right back to the center of the ring. El Matador was the aggressor for the first round. He kept the pressure on the champion and beat him to the punch. Johnson tried to keep the challenger at bay with his powerful jab and longer reach, but Chavez took and seemingly absorbed each punch as it landed on his forehead.

In round two, Johnson went on the attack with hard uppercuts and a flurry of jabs that put Chavez into the ropes. The champion's confidence was coming back and his powerful punches had Chavez noticeably off his game plan. As this was the first time Chavez had fought at a higher weight class, he hadn't yet sampled the sheer punching power that five additional pounds can provide. Johnson's uppercuts were hard, and they were thrown with all the skill and dexterity that only a career 135-pounder can muster.

Richard Lord remained calm between rounds. Jesus wasn't tiring, and he kept putting good pressure on the champion. He was, however, allowing Johnson to fight him from the outside. "You need to cut the distance between you two," he said. "Take the fight to him on the inside. And work the body. We need to start wearing him down. We need to start taking away some of his power."

For the next four rounds, Chavez barely let up. His punches were like a Gatling gun. As soon as he drew back his fists, he threw straight shots to the champ's body. Jesus occasionally went upstairs to the head. Johnson looked bewildered. He was having a hard time stringing combinations together. Chavez's full frontal assault had the champion playing defense most of the fight. Jesus threw so many punches with such speed that Johnson rarely had an opportunity to counterpunch.

Jesus was not tiring in the ring. He sensed his opponent's uncertainty and in round six started throwing more punches to Johnson's head. The champ's neck snapped back from the shots, and each subsequent punch made his head look as if it was touching the middle of his back. Johnson could take a punch, though. On several occasions he looked like he was facing impending doom, but at the end of the middle rounds, he stood in the center of the ring and trash-talked his opponent. Chavez ignored the taunts and returned to his corner while Johnson grimaced in his opponent's direction before returning to his own corner.

"Man, this guy's tough," Lord said to his boxer. "Keep doing what you're doing. You've got him all confused. Keep working the body and you'll find the head. Keep the pressure on him. Let's go to work."

At the start of round eleven, Chavez came out with a barrage of body shots and combination punches to the head that left Johnson propped up against the ring ropes. Chavez did not have the punching power to drop Johnson in the earlier rounds, and in this later round, the ring ropes were the champ's adversary. He was unable to fall.

Referee Tony Weeks stopped the fight thirty-eight seconds into the eleventh round. Leavander's father and trainer, Bill Johnson, entered the ring and hugged his son as Chavez raised his gloves and the fans cheered. Jimmy was on hand to watch his big brother, and he strapped the IBF lightweight championship belt around Jesus's waist. Nevada fight doctors attended to Johnson in his corner. The boxer told ringside physician Margaret Goodman that he felt fine; he wasn't dizzy and he didn't have double vision.

The celebration for Chavez continued in the ring while Johnson made his exit. He shuffled listlessly down the walkway to his dressing room, stumbling a little as if in a trance. Minutes later, he complained to his father that he had a bad headache. He lay down on a bench in the dressing room and shut his eyes. Bill called an ambulance and Leavander was rushed to University Medical Center.

Later that evening, a Golden Boy Promotions spokesman said that Leavander Johnson would not be attending the postfight press conference. The thirty-five-year-old was undergoing emergency surgery to treat a subdural hematoma, or bleeding in the brain.

Jesus Chavez was brought before a packed media room and stood center stage. Rather than boasting of his victory, the new IBF lightweight champion spoke in a somber tone and expressed concern for his opponent. "I just want to say that my thoughts and prayers are with Leavander and his family," Chavez said. Richard Lord looked on, head bowed. "He could use all of our prayers right now."

But no prayers were answered. Johnson remained in a medically induced coma for five days before his family took the fighter off life support. Leavander Johnson was pronounced dead on Thursday, September 22, 2005, at 4:23 P.M. Mountain time.

Jesus Chavez wakes up at 6:00 A.M. and goes running. He logs in four to five miles while the rest of Austin rises and prepared for another day at the grind. Then he returns to his Austin house, hops in his Ford F-150, and makes the ten-minute drive to Lord's Gym on Lamar Street.

The place hasn't changed much over the years. His old room with the battered mattress is still there, as are the scattered free weights, bench presses, and nautilus machines. Richard has added a second boxing ring, and there are significantly more newspaper clippings of the champion on the walls than there were in the days when El Matador called Lord's Gym home.

At thirty-three, the boxer trains and conditions at the same level that he did at twenty-three. His body doesn't heal as quickly after fights, but the ambition and heart are still there.

He struggles to plan for the rest of his life and his imminent retirement. He wants to fight longer, but how much longer? Shortly after Leavander's death, Bill Johnson told Jesus that he wasn't to blame. He told El Matador to continue fighting and to be the best champion he could be. That, Bill said, is what Leavander would have wanted.

When Chavez is home alone, with his wife several oceans away—defending the freedom Jesus enjoys as a permanent resident of the United States—he tries not to dwell on the past, especially because the good old days weren't always good. He has played many roles over the years: gang member, prisoner, border jumper, and, according to some unscrupulous journalists, killer. But above all else, Jesus Gabriel Sandoval Chavez was—and will forever be—a boxer.

Interviews and Bibliography

Prologue

Jesus Chavez, interview by author, November 1, 2000.
Richard Lord, interview by author, January 26, 2005.
Rick Cantu, "Austin's Chavez Ready for Bigger Boxing Ring," *Austin American-Statesman*, May 30, 1997.
Marcy Garriott, *Split Decision*, VHS (La Sonrisa Productions, 2001).
Mickey Herskowitz, "For Featherweight Wood, Boxing Fire Burns On," *Houston Chronicle*, April 18, 2000.
W. H. Stickney Jr., "Foreman Now Pitchman Supreme," *Houston Chronicle*, April 16, 2000.

Chapter 1

Jesus Chavez, interview by author, November 16, 2004.
Sean Curtin, interview by author, February 10, 2005.
Tom O'Shea, interview by author, March 26, 2005.
Jesus Sandoval and Rosario Sandoval, interview by author, April 18, 2005.
Olivia Coolidge, *Mythology: Daedalus, Echo, and Narcissus, the Fortunate King, Atalanta's Lovers* (New Jersey: Silver Burdett, 1989).
Gary Smith, "Bearing the Burden," *Sports Illustrated*, February 1993.

Chapter 2

Jesus Chavez, interview by author, May 5, 2005.
Sean Curtin, interview by author, February 10, 2005.
Tony Godinez, interview by author, April 28, 2005.

Tom O'Shea, interview by author, April 4, 2005.

Frank Lloyd Wright and Prairie School of Architecture, Oak Park, Illinois.

Marcy Garriott, *Split Decision*, VHS (La Sonrisa Productions, 2001).

Langston Hughes, *A Dream Deferred* (New York: Holt, 1951).

Jon D. Hull, "No Way Out: What's More Dangerous Than Staying in a Murderous Street Gang? Trying to Quit," *Time*, August 17, 1992.

Ed Magnuson, "The Curse of Violent Crime," *Time*, March 23, 1981.

N.W.A., "Straight Outta Compton" (Priority Records, 1988).

Jan Reid, "The Contender," *Texas Monthly*, April 1998.

Chapter 3

Tony Godinez, interview by author, April 29, 2005.

Jesus Sandoval and Rosario Sandoval, interview by author, April 18, 2005.

Marcy Garriott, *Split Decision*, VHS (La Sonrisa Productions, 2001).

David Jackson, "Fine Line Between Tough Police Work, Brutality," *Chicago Tribune*, July 14, 1991.

John Kass and William Recktenwald, "More Jails Called Cure to Killings," *Chicago Tribune*, September 1991.

Deborah Nelson, "Automatic 'Adult' Offenses Work Against Kids, Not Crime," *Chicago Sun-Times*, March 27, 1992.

Jan Reid, "The Contender," *Texas Monthly*, April 1998.

Bruce Rushton, "Cruel and Usual," *Riverfront Times*, February 16, 2000.

Terry Wilson, "County Jail Inmate Total Now Tops 8,000," *Chicago Tribune*, September 13, 1991.

www.rainbowpush.org

Chapter 4

Stateville, tour by author, April 18, 2005.

Jesus Chavez, interview by author, April 28, 2005.

Tony Godinez, interview by author, April 29, 2005.

Melinda Beck, "Prisons: Retaking Stateville," *Newsweek*, March 19, 1979.

"Gang-Related Riot Leaves 33 Injured at Prison," Associated Press, August 5, 1982.

David Heinzmann, "Stateville to Assume Joliet Center Role," *Chicago Tribune*, November 29, 2001.

"Three Guards Briefly Taken Hostage in Second Night of Violence at Illinois Prison," Associated Press, July 15, 1991.

Ann Scott Tyson, "Journey of Chicago's Ultimate Street Tough," *Christian Science Monitor*, December 31, 1996.

Michael Witkowski, "The Gang's All Here," *American Society for Industrial Security Management*, May 2004.

Chapter 5

Jesus Chavez, interview by author, May 1, 2005 and May 19, 2005.
Jesus Sandoval, interview by author, April 22, 2005.
"Ciudad and Chihuahua News," *Frontera NorteSur*, September 2001.
Jim Lehrer, *The NewsHour with Jim Lehrer*, January 5, 1998.
Migration Policy Institute, Washington, D.C., www.migrationinformation.org.
Luis Alberto Urrea, *The Devil's Highway* (New York: Little, Brown, 2004).

Chapter 6

Jesus Chavez, interview by author, February 16, 2005.
Richard Lord, interview by author, November 7, 2000, January 12, 2005, January 25, 2005, and January 26, 2005.
Sam Blair, "An Austin Approach to Feminizing Boxing," *Dallas Morning News*, September 29, 1993.
Marcy Garriott, *Split Decision*, VHS (La Sonrisa Productions, 2001).
Lindsey Lane, "Working Out at the Boxing Gym," *Austin American-Statesman*, November 2, 1995.
Leo N. Miletich, *Dan Stuart's Fistic Carnival* (College Station: Texas A&M University Press, 1994).
Jan Reid, "The Contender," *Texas Monthly*, April 1998.
Leonard Shapiro, "Howard Cosell Dies at 77," *Washington Post*, April 1995.
John Spong, "The Shot Not Heard Around the World," *Texas Monthly*, December 2004.
www.boxrec.com
www.eastsideboxing.com/boxing-news/pr1206.php

Chapter 7

Richard Garriott, interview by author, November 7, 2000 and January 12, 2005.
"Gaming Guru Is Building Another Fantasy House," *Austin American-Statesman*, July 2, 2004.
J. C. Herz, "A Designer's Farewell to His Fantasy Realm," *New York Times*, July 15, 1999.
John Markoff, "The Ultimate Obsession," *New York Times*, October 20, 1997.
Renuka Rayasam, "Richard Garriott Betting Big on Private Space Travel," Cox News Service, October 11, 2004.
David Remnick, *King of the World* (New York: Random House, 1998).

World Boxing Council Official Rule Book (World Boxing Council, 2003).
www.electronicarts.com
www.toprank.com

Chapter 8

Jesus Chavez, interview by author, February 1, 2005.
Terri Glanger, interview by author, February 12, 2005.
Handbook of Texas Online, www.tsha.utexas.edu/handbook/online/articles/
view/AA/hda3.html.
Sarah Hornaday, "An Underdog Who Barked Too Loud," *Austin American-Statesman*, August 22, 1995.
Lindsey Lane, "Working Out at the Boxing Gym," *Austin American-Statesman*, November 2, 1995.
Paul Taylor, "Apartheid Foe Hani Slain in S. Africa," *Washington Post Foreign Service*, April 11, 1993.
Mark Wangrin, "Austin's Chavez Wins Technical KO Over Leija in Brawl in Music Hall," *Austin American-Statesman*, March 4, 1997.
www.utexas.edu

Chapter 9

Jesus Chavez, interview by author, February 1, 2005.
Marcy Garriott, interview by author, June 7, 2005.
Richard Lord, interview by author, February 10, 2005.
"Chavez to Deport Himself, Seek Visa to Resume Boxing," *Austin American-Statesman*, October 14, 1997.
"Dorsey's Style Seems Fit for Chavez, Manager Says," *Austin American-Statesman*, October 4, 1997.
Marcy Garriott, *Split Decision*, VHS (La Sonrisa Productions, 2001).
"Lewis Wins in 95 Seconds, Dorsey Loses," *Fort Worth Star-Telegram*, October 5, 1997.
Jan Reid, *The Bullet Meant for Me* (New York: Broadway Books, 2002).
Thomas Wolfe, *You Can't Go Home Again* (New York: HarperCollins, 1973).

Chapter 10

Andres Bunsow, interview by author, April 6, 2005.
Jesus Chavez, interview by author, April 31, 2000, May 2–5, 2000, May 15, 2000, and April 4, 2005.

Hermila Sandoval, interview by author, April 5, 2005.
Jesus Sandoval Sr., interview by author, April 5, 2005.
Julio Sandoval, interview by author, April 5, 2005.
"Pati," interview by author, April 6, 2005.
Adam Pitluk, "Knockdown," *Dallas Observer*, May 18, 2000.

Chapter 11

Jesus Chavez, interview by author, March 27, 2005.
Barbara Hines, interview by author, January 28, 2005.
Marcy Garriott, interview by author, June 7, 2005.
Richard Garriott, interview by author, January 16, 2005.
Laura Barton, "Faces: The People Who Make Austin Special," *The Good Life*,
    February 2002.
Marcy Garriott, *Split Decision*, VHS (La Sonrisa Productions, 2001).
Adam Pitluk, "Top-Ranked Fighter Beats a Real Heavyweight—The INS,"
    Court TV.com, March 14, 2001.
www.legal-aid.org

Chapter 12

Jesus Chavez, interview by author, November 25, 2001.
Carlos Arias, "New Fury: Chavez vs. Gerena," *Orange Country Register*,
    March 20, 2003.
Steve Crowe, "Title a Battle of Nice Guys: Mayweather, Hernandez
    Exchange Compliments," *Detroit Free Press*, May 26, 2001.
Nancy Gay, "Mayweather Stops Chavez in 9th," *San Francisco Chronicle*,
    November 11, 2001.
Cedric Golden, "Chavez–Mayweather Title Fight Postponed," *Austin
    American-Statesman*, August 25, 2001.
Michael Hirsley, "Chavez in Tough Fight to Wipe Out Fateful Night,"
    Chicago Tribune, May 25, 2001.
Robert Morales, "Mayweather Set to Shut Chavez Up," *San Gabriel Valley
    Tribune*, November 8, 2001.
"A 'Pretty' Plan: Cautious Mayweather Stops Chavez in the 9th," *San
    Francisco Chronicle*, November 11, 2001.
John Whisler, "Local Boxer Eager to Meet Champ," *San Antonio Express-
    News*, July 17, 2003.

Chapter 13

Jesus Chavez, interview by author, March 16, 2005.

Richard Lord, interview by author, January 30, 2005.

Erik Morales, press conference, February 28, 2004.

Mike Tyson, interview by author, March 19, 2005.

Cedric Golden, "Big Doors Swing Open for Chavez," *Austin American-Statesman*, August 17, 2003.

Richard Hoffer, "Inside Boxing," *Sports Illustrated*, May 27, 1999.

Alex McGreevy, "A Prince Naseem Rematch Is Top of Wayne's World Title Fight Agenda," *Mirror*, October 20, 1999.

Gary Smith, "Bearing the Burden," *Sports Illustrated*, February 22, 1993.

Steve Springer, "A Born Boxer," *Los Angeles Times*, May 8, 1999.

www.gomexico.about.com

www.news.bbc.co.uk

Chapter 14

Jesus Chavez, interview by author, June 28, 2005.

Jim Lampley, interview by author, June 28, 2005.

Carlos Arias, "De La Hoya Likes the Competition," *Los Angeles Times*, October 15, 2003.

———, "Split Decision for Jesus Chavez," *Orange Country Register*, May 29, 2005.

Carlos Hernandez, postfight press conference, June 28, 2005.

Kevin Iole, "Hernandez, Chavez Fighting over Morales," *Las Vegas Review-Journal*, May 28, 2005.

Adam Pitluk, "Death of a Fighter," *Time*, September 24, 2005.

Acknowledgments

A linear progression of events made this book possible. In order, thank-you to Karen Glanger for coming in to the offices of the *Dallas Observer* in 2000, when I was a cub staff writer, and for pitching the story of Jesus Chavez, her daughter's ex-boyfriend. I pitched the story to my editor, Julie Lyons, at that Monday's staff meeting. A week later, I was on a plane to Mexico—with my photographer, Terri Glanger—to spend a few days with Jesus. The story that ran in the *Observer* in May 2000 is among my favorite works.

Thank-you to Richard Lord for his past and present insight into Jesus and into boxing in general. Lord is a class act and runs a positive and successful operation in Austin. Richard Garriott is one of the more interesting people I've interviewed in my career as a reporter. He speaks openly and freely and is an example of intuition personified. His sister-in-law, Marcy Garriott, was a tremendous help throughout the writing process, assisting with historical fact as well as constructive criticism. Thank-you, Marcy, for your time and dedication to this book. Barbara Hines is a brilliant legal mind who supplied factual information for the book. She is easy to work with, despite her crazy schedule. I have known Barbara since I wrote about Jesus for CourtTv.com in March 2001. And thank-you to Terri Glanger for her exceptional photographs from Mexico, including the book cover, and for being a tried and true friend over the years.

This book would never have happened were it not for Sam Freedman and his book writing seminar at Columbia University's Graduate School of Journalism. I appreciate your encouragement and your hard-nosed instructional style. Sam is one of the best coaches—athletic or otherwise—I've ever had.

Adrian Nicole LeBlanc did a huge favor for me when she read over my book proposal. Your input and suggestions, coupled with your faith in the project, were both needed and stimulating. And "Random Family" is still the finest piece of narrative nonfiction I've ever read. I'm lucky to have had your help.

My cousin, Dr. Ron Wish, was a huge motivational element while I was penning the manuscript, as well as extremely hospitable, opening his home to me when I was a homeless graduate student in New York.

Thank-you to my agent, Robert Guinsler, and to Sterling Lord Literistic for sound advice and for finding a home for this book, and a special thank-you to Kevin Hanover and Da Capo Press. Kevin: You were a tremendous editor. I'd be honored to work with you again in the future, in spite of the fact that you cheer for the bad guys: the Boston Red Sox. We're all Indians fans around here.

Jared Hamilton and Rocky Loessin were excellent travel companions in Mexico. We need to get back down to Delicias and spend more time. Thanks also to Griss Corrales, my guide in Delicias.

The entire Sandoval family, including Jesus Jr., Jesus Sr., Rosario, and Hermila and Jimmy were hospitable in Chicago and in Delicias. Thanks for opening your doors and your hearts to me.

Chicago boxing coaches Sean Curtin and Tom O'Shea were a tremendous help and extremely pleasant to talk to, thus proving that "gruff" is not a prerequisite to being a successful boxing trainer.

Thank-you to Jessica Ramirez, daughter of Mexican immigrants, for help with researching the Mexican diaspora, and to the University of Texas–Arlington Department of Communications.

Thank-you to Cathy Booth Thomas, Greg Fulton, and Howard Chua-Eoan at *Time* magazine, for being great bosses and editors.

Jesus Gabriel Sandoval Chavez has been an interesting story, yes, but a good friend foremost. Thank-you for letting me into your life all those years ago in Mexico and for telling me your entire story unabashedly. It's hard to keep in close contact with people as the years tick by, but you've always been there, even when you weren't in the United States. I enjoyed working with you on this project, and I wish all the best to you, your parents and grandparents, and your wife.

Finally, thank-you to my wife, Kimberly, who was a driving force behind this book. You're still the best (and sexiest) editor ever. I love you.

About the Author

Adam Pitluk is an award-winning journalist and contributor to *Time* magazine. Originally from Cleveland, Ohio, he now lives in Dallas, Texas.

Index